CIS WHITE GAY

Advance Praise for *Cis White Gay*

"A fascinating and horrifying look at how the social justice sausage is made."

—Konstantin Kisin

"This excellent book provides one of the clearest arguments to date as to how we must view gender ideology as a cult. Ben Appel writes with humor, compassion, and, refreshingly, a little righteous anger."

—Julie Bindel

"In this courageous memoir, Ben Appel recounts his journey from a fundamentalist Christian cult to a queer Ivy League subculture, highlighting the unsettling parallels between these two seemingly contrasting worlds. Challenged to reevaluate his deeply rooted beliefs, he grows increasingly alarmed about the psychological and physical harm radical gender ideology is inflicting on young gay people. Having broken free from two forms of mental captivity, Appel underscores the vital importance of something all too rare: thinking for oneself."

—James Kirchick, Author of *Secret City: The Hidden History of Gay Washington*

BEN APPEL

CIS WHITE GAY

The Making of a Gender Heretic

Published by Bombardier Books
An Imprint of Post Hill Press
ISBN: 978-1-63758-628-0
ISBN (eBook): 978-1-63758-629-7

Cis White Gay:
The Making of a Gender Heretic

Cover Design by Conroy Accord

All people, locations, events, and situations are portrayed to the best of the author's memory. While all of the events described are true, many names and identifying details have been changed to protect the privacy of the people involved.

Post Hill Press
New York • Nashville
posthillpress.com

Published in the United States of America
1 2 3 4 5 6 7 8 9 10

To freethinkers everywhere.
Especially the gay ones.

CONTENTS

AUTHOR'S NOTE

Besides my own memory, personal journals, and class notes, this book is based on archival and online research as well as firsthand interviews with former Lamb of God members, current and former Columbia students, gender clinicians, Iranian refugees, detransitioned gay men, and others. Some names and identifying details have been changed. Much of the dialogue is verbatim; the rest is to the best of my recollection. Parts of this book have appeared in different form in essays I wrote for Quillette, Queer Majority, Quarto, Washington Examiner, and Spiked.

PROLOGUE

"Queer is by definition whatever is at odds with the normal, the legitimate, the dominant. There is nothing in particular to which it necessarily refers. It is an identity without an essence."
—David Halperin, queer theorist and author of *Saint Foucault: Towards a Gay Hagiography*

"Queer ideology was the creation of French paedophile Michel Foucault."
—Fred Sargeant, French American gay rights activist and cofounder of the first New York City Pride March in 1970

Americans have been dealt a lot of surprises in recent years.

American women have been surprised to find men in their restrooms, athletic competitions, and prison cells.

American parents have been surprised to hear doctors prescribe double mastectomies for their depressed teenaged daughters.

American lesbians have been surprised to be smeared as "genital fetishists" for refusing the sexual advances of people with penises.

And pretty much everyone has been surprised to see a group that calls itself "Queers for Palestine" protesting in support of an Islamic regime that executes homosexuals in the name of Allah.

Perhaps America's biggest surprise came in November 2024, when the country reelected a twice-impeached president whose first term had culminated in an insurrection at the heart of our nation's capital.

I was not surprised by any of these things.

Horrified? Yes.

Fascinated? At times.

But not surprised.

I was not surprised because in the late spring of 2020, at the late age of thirty-seven, I graduated from Columbia University, where I had spent the previous three-and-a-half years as an undergraduate. In January 2017, I had begun my first semester as a self-described progressive, eager to study nonfiction writing and LGBT rights, and to #RESIST the incoming Trump Administration.

Ironically, I found the "liberationist" pedagogy on offer at Columbia to be anything but liberating. To the contrary, it was a remarkably familiar reprise of the close-minded, intolerant orthodoxy of the Christian cult from which I had escaped at age twelve.

For three-and-a-half years, I watched my fellow students—most of whom were barely half my age—become indoctrinated with a regressive, pseudoscientific, and profoundly anti-Western dogma advertised as liberating, progressive, and just. I also found my own hard-won identity as a gay man challenged by a theory of "queerness" that carried with it mandatory positions about sexual identity and politics.

At Columbia, I read the literature and studied the critical theories that birthed this new dogma. I saw with my own eyes how these theories had persuaded bright but impressionable young minds to see colorblindness as racism and racial essentialism as "antiracist," to see the reality of dimorphism as an oppressive colonial construct and transgenderism as part of a radical political project, and to see Western nations—America and Israel, particularly—as Goliaths to be slain and Islamic jihadists as the heroes to slay them.

I watched authoritarian ideologues turn liberalism—equality of opportunity, universal human rights, and individualism—entirely inside out.

I watched progressivism morph into the most regressive, illiberal, neoracist, antigay, antiwoman, anti*human* political ideology imaginable.

I watched as a new army of zealots—call them Social Justice Warriors, the Woke, the New Red Guard, or the Cult of Queer—assembled to enforce strict adherence to its religion...or else.

And I watched as this cult laid the groundwork for Donald Trump to retake the White House.

Before attending Columbia, my understanding of modern world history was slanted. As a lifelong gay Democrat, the progressive politics I espoused were mostly just echoes of those espoused by my friends (mainly liberal women), left-wing news outlets, and slickly produced Hollywood films and television shows.

And yet, for multiple reasons, I believe I was uniquely positioned to grasp the depth and seriousness of what has occurred in academia and the broader culture over the last few years.

To begin with, when I started at Columbia, I was a thirty-three-year-old man with a fully formed prefrontal cortex, which (as I later learned) is the brain's main center for complex critical thinking, so I was capable of criticizing the theories and ideas that my professors, the college administration, and other students expected me to accept without question as fact.

And I already had a wealth of professional experience that had put me in daily contact with people from all walks of life, people whose values were drastically different from mine but with whom I nonetheless had to peacefully coexist. (This professional experience also meant I knew what it was to pay bills and put a roof over my head.)

World-changing events like 9/11 were visceral memories for me, not just stories I was told by biased news outlets and schoolteachers. Beyond that, I had experience working in LGBT activism, specifically on Maryland's marriage equality and transgender rights campaigns, so I understood a bit about how politics worked as well as the importance of pragmatism and compromise. I could recall what life was like for gay people in America when we still had to live in the shadows.

Finally, through my experience growing up in a Christian covenant community, I was intimately familiar with social groupthink, purity policing, and self-censorship. I knew what it was like to be excommunicated, to be shamed and judged, and to internalize that shame and judgment to the point of mental breakdown. I knew what it was like to be constantly afraid that I might inadvertently say, do, or think something wrong.

In woke parlance, you'd call this my "lived experience."

But the zealots I knew at Columbia would ignore that experience and focus instead on what's called my "positionality"—that is, my gender ("cisgender" male), my race (white), my citizenship status (American-born), my class (middle), and my ability (able-bodied).

"Intersectionality"—an academic framework for identifying how aspects of one's identity result in unique combinations of privilege and discrimination—has created a new moral hierarchy, one in which people are no longer seen as individuals but as members of identity groups, and in which the "privileged" are inherently depraved and the "marginalized" are inherently righteous and pure. In other words, in the hierarchy of intersectionality, my positionality meant that my opinions and perspectives were invalid. Worse, they were tainted, flawed, evil.

To queer cultists, it doesn't matter that I'm gay. I'm "cis" (that is, a male who still identifies as male), and for these cult members, "male" is a made-up identity not rooted in anything natural. To them, because I am cis, I am not properly queer. I am not properly radical.

It doesn't matter that I've suffered discrimination, or that I've worked damn hard for everything I have. I'm white: I enjoy white skin privilege, and any objections I may have to this illiberal dogma can be discounted as a sign of "white fragility."

It doesn't matter that I've battled and overcome mental illness and drug addiction. I'm able-bodied. Besides, being a survivor is *déclassé*. Victimhood is where it's at.

Queer cultists will say I'm just another "cis white gay" who needs to shut up and bow down to "transwomen of color"—those mystical figures who, they erroneously claim, are singlehandedly responsible for the progress of the gay and lesbian rights movement.

They will say I've wrongly interpreted some theorist or another; that they, the high priests of critical theory, are the only ones qualified to perform an accurate exegesis of the contradictory and incoherent ramblings of their gods.

They will say, "No one actually says that biological sex isn't real!" When that is exactly what they say, repeatedly, until they and their disciples believe it is true.

But this book wasn't written for them. It was written for those who remain freethinkers, for those whose brains haven't been washed by identitarian dogma, and especially for those who've been branded heretics for choosing sanity over the unhinged mentality of the mob.

I wrote this book, first and foremost, to combat this illiberalism and expose it for what it is. Columbia might be the source of this cancer, but it has now metastasized far beyond its wrought iron gates. Unbeknownst to many, for decades a Cultural Revolution has been underway in America, led by a motley crew of Islamists, Marxists, and Maoists. If we don't free our minds and institutions from the grips of its illiberal, regressive, totalitarian ideology, the very idea of a "free mind" will soon be a thing of the past. And, as Newton's third law of motion explains, for every radical action the New Red Guard takes, the MAGA counterrevolutionaries will react with equal and opposite force.

I do not consider myself uniquely smart or brave. I just hope that by telling the story of my liberation from the Church of Social Justice, I can help those who, like so many who have been cowed into silence, find the courage to boldly state what is actually true, what is actually liberal, and what is actually good.

Part 1

DISCIPLE

CHAPTER 1

I was a girly kid. My favorite toy was a My Little Pony. My favorite activity was spinning around in my grandmother's vintage gowns. I wanted to be just like my older sisters, Erin and Jess. Like them, I watched *The Bold and the Beautiful*, listened to Paula Abdul, and highlighted my hair with Sun In. I loved fashion, drawing, stickers, and choreography.

My gender-nonconformity posed a bit of a problem, given where I grew up: in a fundamentalist Christian community called the Lamb of God. Being a sissy meant that I would likely grow up to be homosexual. It was important for the adults in the community, therefore, to educate me about the gravity of my situation. That way, when I reached sexual maturity, I'd immediately recognize my inherent evilness and do all that I could to expunge it.

My first lesson came from my best friend's mother—when I was just eight. Mark and I had been kicking the soccer ball in his back yard when Miss Grace called us in for lunch: peanut butter and honey sandwiches and cut-up apples. Once inside, we kicked off our muddy shoes. Mark trotted down the hallway toward the bathroom while I walked into the kitchen.

"Have a seat, Ben," said Miss Grace. Her knife knocked against the wooden cutting board as she sliced through the green apples.

On the table sat my sandwich, a glass of milk, and a magazine. The magazine was opened to an article that stretched across both pages. "The Almighty's Retribution?" read a bold type title above an illustration of what looked like the squiggly amoebas we viewed through microscopes in science class. At the bottom of the page was a photo of two fat, bearded men, wearing leather vests and standing in the bed of a pickup truck that had been decorated with rainbow-colored feathers and looked to be part of a parade. I leaned in to read the caption: "Unrepentant homosexuals are dying from AIDS at an alarming rate—with no end in sight."

Mark's mom tipped a few apple slices onto my plate. Then she proceeded to explain the article to me.

"The men in the photograph are bad men," she said. "They defy God and follow Satan. See how the men hold hands, like they are a husband and a wife? These men are dangerous. They do bad things to kids. They are evil. They will get sick and die and spend eternity in hell."

It's possible I'm misremembering some of the details: The apple might've been red, for example, and I'm sure the words above aren't verbatim. But I know that was the gist of Miss Grace's lesson, because it has been encoded in my bones ever since.

The Lamb of God was what is called a covenant community, located just outside of Baltimore City. In covenant communities, members pledge fealty to a small group of self-appointed leaders. The male leaders are called "coordinators," and the female leaders are called (I kid you not) "handmaids." The leadership requires members to pay annual tithes, adhere to strict moral codes, and for all wives to obey their "husband-masters." Members must pursue moral purity, and they must police the purity of others. Among the covenant community's main enemies, along with homosexuality, are secular humanism and feminism, for these things weaken the integrity of the Church.

Covenant communities grew out of the Catholic Charismatic Renewal Movement of the late 1960s. Charismatics claim to be "baptized in the Holy Spirit" and to possess extraordinary gifts like the power of prophecy, healing by the laying on of hands in prayer, and "glossolalia," or speaking in tongues. In 1971, a twenty-something hippie turned charismatic named Dave Nodar began hosting a small prayer group in his mother's basement, just north of Baltimore City. By the end of the 1980s, the Lamb of God included over 250 families, living in what members called "the cluster," a fifteen-block stretch of the suburban neighborhood of Catonsville. Members gathered weekly at a community-wide prayer meeting and throughout the week at smaller, sex-segregated prayer meetings held in various members' homes. The children—including my sisters, my younger brother Bret, and I—attended the Lamb of God School, a kindergarten-through-eighth-grade institution located a few miles from the cluster. There were father-son retreats in the spring, sleepover camps in the summer, and in autumn, day-long festivals at the Farm, a ten-acre estate that the leadership had purchased with members' tithes. There we built bonfires, competed in potato sack races, performed fevered reenactments of the Israelites crossing the River Jordan (an irrigation ditch running through one of the fields), and danced around a maypole.

My mother and father found the group in 1976. They were twenty-one and twenty-seven respectively and engaged to be married. At their first prayer meeting, my mother was instantly attracted to the group's message, which seemed to be one of unconditional love and acceptance. Raised Catholic, she had been plagued by religious guilt since she was a young girl. The Church overflowed with harsh rules and regulations, but here was something different. It felt like grace.

My father, on the other hand, thought it was weird—the dancing around and singing, and the incoherent, trancelike rambling of the worshippers, who knelt on the floor with their hands lifted toward the ceiling. But he agreed to keep attending, if only to make my mother happy.

My parents were solid people. That's the word the leadership used in the beginning to describe attractive, upwardly mobile newcomers who could add a shiny veneer to the Lamb of God and attract more members. My mother, Nancy, a pretty physical therapist and the daughter of an optometrist and a homemaker, and Randy, my father, a handsome attorney for a midsized Baltimore law firm, were as solid as they came. Thus, it wasn't long after my parents joined the Lamb of God that Dave asked my father to become part of the leadership as the fifth and final coordinator. My father displayed little interest in the theater that was the weekly prayer meeting, never volunteering a prophecy or exemplifying the gift of tongues. But he had a sharp mind and a keen interest in theology. Together, his professional credentials and intellect made him a valuable asset for facilitating the growth of the community. He would go on to teach religious curricula to adult members and eventually at the school, where he would serve as superintendent and geography teacher.

My mother was proud of my father's quick rise in the community, but she also was confused: He had never been very spiritual. Besides, it had been her idea to join the Lamb of God in the first place. During private prayer time at home, after she had pored over scripture and emptied out her heart to the Lord, she'd wander into my father's office to find him flipping through the pages of *Sports Illustrated*. At first it didn't bother her, but when she was passed over for a role in the female leadership, her attitude changed. To her, rejection from the circle of handmaids meant she wasn't the model of Christianity that she hoped to be. This devastated her.

Despite her exclusion from the handmaids, my mother did maintain some authority. The Lamb of God operated hierarchically. Each coordinator and handmaid had a "district" of members they would preside over, and each district had a "head." My mother was a head, which meant that she would lead weekly prayer groups with the women in her district. At these meetings, each woman would share honestly about her transgressions, doubts, and fears. Afterward, the heads would report back a summary of the meeting to the handmaids. The handmaids dissected the gossip during their own private meetings and then brought the information to the coordinators. Meanwhile, on the men's side, the same exchange of information would occur. All of this allowed the coordinators to know precisely what was occurring inside the homes and hearts of all the community members. From their perch, they would pass down their judgments: Perhaps a man needed to watch less television and spend more time in quiet reflection, while another needed to purify his mind of lustful thoughts for another man's wife. Perhaps a wife needed to make her body more available to her husband. Up and down the hierarchy, the secrets would flow.

"It was like Stalin's communist system," a former member told a *Baltimore* magazine reporter, who in 1994 penned a six-page exposé on the Lamb of God. The image that accompanied the article—titled "The Cult Next Door"—was an illustration of Dave as a puppeteer, his marionette a dancing woman. The woman's eyes were closed and her open hands were extended toward the sky—toward Dave.

"The Cult Next Door" centered around the Catholic Archdiocese's investigation of the community after ex-members sent Baltimore's archbishop, William Keeler, dozens of damning letters about the psychological, spiritual, and financial damage they had suffered as a result of the leadership's cultish practices. One of those letters came from John Cignatta, who, along with his wife and children, had belonged to the community for thirteen years. He attached to his letter a thirty-nine-page report, meticulously detailing the leadership's "abusive control" of members' minds and behavior as well as their access to information. Instead of a rewarding lifestyle of Christian community and fellowship, Cignatta wrote that they experienced "the effective isolation of the individual, interference in our marriage, fragmentation of our family, confusion from the ever-changing new directions received from God by Mr. Nodar, alone, and an ever-increasing community bank account controlled solely by Mr. Nodar and a select few of other Coordinators."

The article was printed a little more than a year before my family left the Lamb of God, joining the ranks of the dissidents. (My mother, it turned out, wouldn't enjoy living in a patriarchal religious cult after all.) I was eleven when it was published, and I hadn't a clue about the controversy, which had been brewing for years. Yes, my classmates had dwindled in number as each new school year began—by the fifth grade, my penultimate year in the Lamb of God School, only four of us remained. But I assumed they had just moved away, and not, as I later learned, been removed from the school by parents who had sought help from Baltimore's Cult Awareness Network.

One ex-member told the reporter that the community had destroyed many marriages. My parents' marriage was one of them. As my father earned more power and distinction in the community, my mother grew resentful. My father became distant, even cold. Yet he would project to the community the image of a model husband, even calling my mother "lover" in public, when he hadn't touched her in months. In the years after we left, my guilt-ridden mother would share these intimate details with me, mostly in an attempt to justify her decision to uproot our lives from the only world we had ever known.

My father became distant from my siblings and me as well. When we were young, playing in the basement, he would sit nearby, reading the paper or watching a baseball game. When one of us wanted to show him something—a flawless execution of a somersault, perhaps—we'd stand in front of him, poised to tumble, and call out his name: "Dad! Hey, Dad! Dad! Look, Dad!" But his eyes would stay glued to the television, and he'd remain perfectly still, as if we'd lose sight of him so long as he didn't move. It eventually became a comedy routine: We would wave our hands in front of his eyes or tug on his ears. "Dad! Dad! Dad!" Still nothing.

In retrospect, it's possible my father was just following instructions. A 1989 covenant community handbook advised parents that it "ought not be their goal to spend the largest amount of time with the children. Rather, parents should be careful to use the time God gives them to best carry out their responsibilities." In case they felt guilty about ignoring their kids, it added that parents need never be afraid of "losing the children's love or of making the children feel bad."

The covenant community handbook included quite a number of child-rearing tips.

Children should be trained in "verbal restraint and indifference to self," it said.

Children should be "formed by other people as well as by their two parents."

Children should "learn to do what they are told to do, when they are told to do it," and "obey without arguing or resistance."

Children should be trained in "fear-respect."

We were raised, from the beginning, to be grown-ups. Apart from the spankings we received on our bare behinds—which our headmaster doled out behind the closed door of his office—discipline, as we knew it, didn't consist of two-minute time-outs or after-school detentions. That was kid's stuff. Our punishment was shame.

"When you get to the gates of heaven, a movie of every sin you've ever committed will be shown for all to see," our headmaster would preach in chapel, scaring the shit out of us.

I have no recollection of what, exactly, he told me the day I mischievously graffitied, with a red crayon, a small star on a corridor wall. (Perhaps I was caught in the act by a teacher, although it's more likely I immediately told on myself, since it was impossible to sit for very long with the knowledge that we had done something wrong.) But I'll never forget how ashamed I felt when my headmaster scolded me for defacing school property. Every sin, no matter how small, was equally grave.

Negative talk was absolutely verboten. Even negative *feelings* were sinful. If we felt sad, angry, or contrary, we were failing to be proper Christians. A good Christian is always positive, generous, humble, and most importantly, docile. He uncritically does and believes what his leaders tell him.

Our elders' endless guilt trips struck fear in our hearts that we might, if we continued to sin, fall short of God's glory. Which, of course, meant going to hell. But almost as concerning was that we had personally disappointed God. That we had lost his favor. To disappoint our headmaster and our teachers—these human proxies for the Lord—was bad enough. Anything beyond that was too terrible to contemplate. So we shaped up and amended our thoughts and behaviors.

After all, we had serious responsibilities: We were foot soldiers in God's army against evil. Our little sins had dangerous consequences. A weak heart meant a weak link in the chain of salvation. The Lamb of God—like the ungodly world from which it shielded us—was no place for the faint of heart.

But we were happy too.

Who wouldn't want to be raised inside a bubble and attend the same tiny school as all the friends they'd known since infancy, who were more like siblings than friends?

Who wouldn't want to experience, if only for a day, what it feels like to be relieved of the burden of having to think for oneself and determine one's own morals and convictions? (Very few, as I would learn throughout my life over and over again, for freethinking puts one at risk of being cast out as a heretic.)

How good—how *safe*—it felt to know that inclusion, acceptance, and salvation were guaranteed to us as long as we unthinkingly repeated the leadership's prescribed dogmas and scrupulously adhered to its ever-changing rules.

What very few people talk about is that life inside a cult is pretty great. Often, the real trouble doesn't come until after you leave—and have to figure out how to think for yourself.

CHAPTER 2

One Christmas, when I was about nine, my dad bought a video camera for the family. It was a giant monstrosity that my siblings and I struggled to balance on our shoulders while we filmed impromptu skits. Alone, I'd prop the camera on the coffee table and record myself modeling various outfits, explaining why this plaid shirt went with these cargo shorts, or why this teal Starter jacket perfectly complemented these acid-washed jeans. I captured on camera the dance I had painstakingly choreographed to Marky Mark and the Funky Bunch's "Good Vibrations."

Because the Lamb of God School was so tiny, there was no in-crowd, no separate cliques of jocks and geeks. Looking back, I'm sure my classmates were aware of my gender-nonconformity—all of our home videos prove that it was glaring—but it went largely ignored. In fact, it wasn't until after we left the Lamb of God, when I attended public school, that my gender expression was ruthlessly policed by my classmates. Within the community, the only thing that mattered was that we were good Christians, loved Jesus, and evangelized God's Word. When we learned about Sodom and Gomorrah in Bible class, or about AIDS, which God had created to punish homosexuals for their sins, I didn't think for a moment that these lessons pertained to me. Sure, my first real crush, when I was eleven, had been on a boy—Elijah Wood, an actor about my age whose performance in the 1994 B-movie, *North*, had captured my heart. But at the time, before sexual maturity, I mistook the longing I felt for Elijah with the more sanitized desire to simply keep his company and be his best friend. Besides, I also occasionally had crushes on girls. Thus, I indiscriminately absorbed all of the lessons I learned about homosexuals, as if they were and would always be irrelevant to my life.

WHEN I WAS in kindergarten, the school was located in an office building on the property of the Charlestown Senior Living Community in Catonsville. At the end of the school year, the lease on the building ended, so, in nearby Halethorpe, the leadership found another building—a red brick cube that was only slightly larger. It had already been used as a school, but it needed a lot of work. The site, for example, was crammed with exposed asbestos.

My father and others scrambled to get the building up and running before the new school year began, but like most construction projects, theirs ran behind schedule, so my first-grade school year began in various community members' houses and in the fields of the local state park. Our teacher, Ms. Kent, taped her lessons—how to add and subtract, how to write in cursive—to the rusted yellow panels of the Lamb of God's only school bus. It was great fun.

Apart from occasional lessons about the dark consequences of disappointing God, kindergarten had been mostly playtime. We splashed around with Tupperware at the water table, raked sand at the sand table, and, at Easter time, huddled around the incubator to watch slimy yellow chicks hatch from the eggs that the school's science teacher had gathered from the coop on his small farm. But in the first grade, the real preparation to become warriors in Christ's army began. Military bootcamp is known to be a place where recruits are broken down and remade into compliant soldiers. But my classmates and I were blank slates; there were no preinstalled ideologies to overwrite. Our teachers assembled us from the ground up.

Every day in school, a great amount of time was reserved for prayer and worship. Sometimes, a classmate would be "slain in the Spirit"; he or she would fall to the floor, seemingly in a fit of religious ecstasy—though this was rare the first few years I attended the school. We were taught to pray over each other by laying our hands on one other's heads and arms and legs, whispering for the Lord to reveal himself, or to give us the strength to beat Satan, the many-faced demon who hid around every corner, ready to coax us into sin. The Spirit would be so strong it would knock us to the floor. To be "slain" was a badge of honor, a sign that he or she was closer to God, or perhaps even in possession of some Divine Truth.

In school, we often tried to speak in tongues, like our parents, but we rarely sounded as fluent. We would cry too; it might start with a girl raising her hands in the air, saying things like, "Oh yes, Jesus, thank you Father Lord God, who is the maker of heaven and earth, yes Lord, praise you Lord," and she would drop to her knees and smack her forehead on the brown carpet and burst into tears. Some teachers said she had been "anointed" and others said "slain in the Spirit," but it was basically the same thing.

I loved getting prayed over. I'd sit in a metal folding chair in the school chapel—which also served as the cafeteria and an indoor gymnasium when it rained—or on the floor in a cozy spot next to the radiator. A classmate or maybe even our headmaster would lay a warm palm on the crown of my head and somebody else would stroke my thigh. I'd hear someone say, "Bless him, God, and give him your guidance," and I would feel so relaxed and safe, I'd want to curl up and take a nap.

It was in the third grade, under the tutelage of an especially zealous teacher, that my classmates and I began achieving deeper levels of communion with the Lord. With Miss Ellis, our worship would flow from the classroom and into the hallway, where the fourth- and fifth-grade classes would be invited to join in. We'd dance in circles and sing while our teachers played their guitars or tambourines (countless community members played these instruments), and then collapse onto the floor in fevered worship.

Miss Ellis's patience was as scant as her faith was abundant. One rainy afternoon, when my classmates and I failed to sing as loudly as she would have preferred, she became inconsolable.

"Jesus can't hear you!" she claimed, simultaneously frightening and confusing us: We were desperate to please the Lord, but we also knew that Jesus could do anything.

We sang louder. Perhaps a minute passed before Miss Ellis smacked her hand against her guitar strings, silencing them. "Kids," she said, her eyes filling with tears. "I don't understand why you won't *sing*." She stomped to the corner of the room and faced the wall. Strumming her guitar and weeping, she sang the next refrain alone.

The five of us guiltily looked on, eager for the struggle session to end.

Later, Miss Ellis forgave us, and the day ended well.

THE SCHOOL WAS small so the fourth- and fifth-grade classes were combined in the same classroom. Thus, for two years I remained under the influence of perhaps the most fanatical of religious zealots that ever crossed the school's threshold.

Miss Morehouse's faith was contagious. In her two-inch navy blue pumps, she bounced instead of walked into the classroom every morning.

"Praise him!" she'd shout spontaneously, whether it be during a math lesson or prayer.

We were instant disciples.

Miss Morehouse was well-versed in the coercive tactics of shame. Even an April Fool's joke warranted a response in this vein.

Our sin that April day was to place a plastic piece of poop in the center of the classroom. "Miss Morehouse, look, a dog must've gotten in here!" we giggled. She approached the fake pile of shit with a stern look on her face.

"You guys are so silly," she replied without smiling. She picked it up and placed it inside her desk drawer.

Shortly before lunchtime, Miss Morehouse called Miss Thomas, a part-time classroom volunteer, up to the front of the class. They had an announcement for us.

"We've decided that after lunch, since this is such a special day and you all are so wonderful, we're going to skip the rest of our lessons and go to Miss Thomas's house to make cookies!"

The class cheered. What a treat. Miss Thomas had hosted us at her house for activities like this one in the past, and it had been great fun. We commenced to the cafeteria, where we scarfed down our sandwiches, barely able to contain our excitement.

Twenty minutes later, as we lined up to return to our classroom—where, we imagined, we'd quickly grab our things and leave—Miss Morehouse and Miss Thomas announced they had another announcement for the fourth and fifth graders. The other teachers and students exited the cafeteria, leaving us behind.

"Guess what, kids?" Miss Morehouse said. "We're not going to Miss Thomas's today."

We exchanged confused looks.

"It's disappointing, isn't it?" she said.

We nodded.

"It doesn't feel good to be lied to, does it?"

Suddenly, we understood.

"The Lord tells us that we must never tell falsehoods," our teacher said. "They only lead us toward more sin. And that's precisely what Satan wants, isn't it? For us to be sinners, so that we might fall into his grasp."

The satisfied smiles splayed across her and Miss Thomas's faces looked pained, as if it hurt them to disappoint us just as much as it hurt us. But that, we knew by then, was just how it was sometimes. God's lessons were painful. And no one ever said that becoming a perfect Christian would be easy.

Even though Miss Morehouse was, in retrospect, a total whack job, it's important to give credit where credit is due. It's because of her that I discovered my love for writing.

Every day, during prayer time, Miss Morehouse instructed my classmates and I to take some time to write in our personal journals. It was my favorite time of the day. The blank page was a judgment-free zone, where the sinfulness of my unfettered thoughts was somehow nullified by the physical act of touching pen to paper. Writing granted me safe passage to another world, where the threat of hell—either here on earth, or in the hereafter—didn't exist. In my journal, I could write what I *really* thought of Miss Morehouse's outfit ("heinous"), and what I *really* thought about the Bible ("boring").

Until a few years ago, I hadn't read from the oldest of my collection of journals, which now number in the dozens since I wrote them. I finally unearthed them one day, eager to recall what had rattled around in my little brain. I knew the content would be unfiltered, but I was not at all prepared to discover, instead of Whitmanesque musings on human nature, a rich catalogue of vindictive (and homophobic) rants.

Here are some examples, which, for some, might require a trigger warning:

> December 20, 1993
>
> *Dave is getting on my nerves! We were playing basketball and he kept shooting airballs! Haha! He plays basketball like shit! Sometimes I feel like cussing him out!*
>
> And later that day:
> *Mark came over and we did homework the whole time. It was kinda fun. I'm taping Michael Jackson for Mark because he really likes the songs M.J. sings. M.J. is such a gay fag. M.J. really loves children, though. He is a Christian.*

A month later, most likely during prayer time, a moment of humble self-reflection:

> *"With his mouth the godless destroys his neighbor, but through knowledge the righteous escape."—Proverbs 11:9 (NIV)*

Alas, it was but a temporary reprieve.

> March 25, 1994
>
> *Mark asked Sarah out. It was a really dumb idea. Everyone knew she was gonna say no! Mark is gay anyway.*

Until I reread these old journals, I had forgotten how often my classmates and I casually slung around the words "fag" and "gay." One might suspect that, by calling my classmates (and Michael Jackson) gay, I was projecting my anxiety about my burgeoning identity onto them, but that wasn't the case. Again, I had no awareness of how different I was, nor did I ever suspect, before sexual maturity, that I'd grow up to be an actual homosexual. At the time, these insults carried no more weight than "freak" or "loser." But that would soon change.

IN THE LAMB of God, single newcomers to the community would live in various families' households, including ours, until they could find a husband or a wife with whom to start a family of their own. When I was four, there was Miss Denise, who, bless her soul, bought me my first My Little Pony—a white pony with emerald green hair and silver stars on its flank. (According to my mother, when she was pregnant with me, Miss Denise insisted I was going to be a girl. I guess she wasn't entirely wrong.) Later there was Miss Kay, a striking blonde whom my sisters followed around like shadows; Miss Evelyn; and Miss Esther. The latter two, after finding men in the community to marry, would move across the street.

A couple of months into my fourth-grade year, Miss Esther's husband, who we called Mr. Steve, was diagnosed with terminal cancer. On an Indian summer afternoon in late October, just after the final bell had rung, Miss Morehouse was compelled by the Lord to pack four or five of us into her station wagon and drive us the fifteen or so minutes to Miss Esther's house, so that together we could pray over Mr. Steve and heal him. When we arrived, we followed our teacher up the sidewalk and into the brick row house.

The house was dark—blackout shades were drawn—and smelled like something I couldn't identify—rubbing alcohol, maybe, and feces. Mr. Steve lay in the fetal position on a black leather couch in the living room. He wore red running shorts and a white T-shirt that was pulled up to his chest, leaving his belly, swollen with disease, exposed. We gathered around him, lay our hands upon him—upon his bare belly, his shoulder and hip—and closed our eyes. Miss Morehouse called upon Jesus to work his miracle on Mr. Steve. Her voice, a whisper at first, rose to its typical decibel, somewhere between a wail and a shout. When her English had turned to tongues, the four or five of us children chimed in. We said, "Yes, Lord, please heal Mr. Steve, Lord," our hands hot with purpose. Mr. Steve moaned.

The visit lasted less than ten minutes. When we returned outside, squinting in the afternoon sun, I felt dizzy and short of breath. What if I hadn't prayed hard enough, loud enough, humbly enough?

A couple of weeks later, Mr. Steve died. For weeks a black drape hung over the doorway of their home—a daily reminder of that day in Miss Esther's living room, and of our collective failure to heal him. Each day, as I passed their home on my walk to the bus stop, I prayed for Mr. Steve's soul, and vowed to the Lord that I would do everything I could to become a better, more effective Christian.

The Anointing occurred one school day in March, during my fourth-grade year.

We had only been praying for five, maybe ten minutes, when the Spirit struck.

I lay on my back next to my desk. Daniel, a fifth grader, sat at my feet, resting his left hand on my ankle. With his right hand he pinched the bridge of his nose, stifling tears.

"Bless Benjamin, Lord Jesus," Daniel said. "Bless your son, your soldier, your servant."

I watched him pray over me. His grip became tighter.

"Bless him, Father God," he said.

I shut my eyes.

I could see him. I could see God. There was what looked like silver vapor, and a dark gray shadow that shimmered gold in the center. The gold became eyes, and the shadow became a face. The golden eyes opened wider and wider, and wider still, and I knew that he loved me, but I was terrified, and it was perhaps then that I learned that God's love felt just like fear.

I sat up, looking for Miss Morehouse. I spotted her across the classroom, cradling Meghan in her arms. Meghan, a notorious brownnoser, repeated the same prayers as Miss Morehouse. Leslie lay nearby beneath a cluster of desks.

Sarah, who had been kneeling on the floor and facing the open window, suddenly rose to her feet. "Yes, Jesus!" she cried as she lifted her hands into the air. "Save me, Jesus God, my Father!"

Her tears were the most beautiful tears I'd ever seen, her wails like a siren's song, and I was overcome. I began to cry too.

Moments later, not a dry eye remained in the classroom, save for Miss Morehouse. We wept loudly and shouted. Someone banged their fists on the floor. A chair toppled over.

A frenzy had taken over us.

"Christ Jesus, forgive us," prayed Mark.

Elizabeth huddled with Rachel and Katie beneath the cubbies, their plaid jumpers blending into one.

Miss Morehouse eased Meghan from her arms and jumped to her feet. A laminated poster of multiplication tables slid down the wall. She stood high on her toes and reached for the ceiling.

"Praise him, children, praise his name!" she shouted. "We are anointed!"

With those words, it was official: My classmates and I had transformed into a morally superior corporate body. We were no longer individuals, but rather parts of a spiritual vanguard, an anointed elite. A righteous mob.

NEWS OF THE Anointing swiftly made its way around the school. A few days later, during chapel, our headmaster, standing at his podium, said, "Something special recently occurred in the fourth-and fifth-grade classroom." Miss Morehouse, sitting behind him with the other teachers, smiled, her spine lengthening.

"The students were baptized by the Spirit," he explained. "They were anointed by the Lord in prayer. This occurs often at our weekly adult prayer meetings. But it's never happened here, not quite in this way. So what I'd like for us to do today is to see if we can muster up the same type of passion for the Lord that our fourth and fifth graders summoned just a few days ago. I want us to reach deep inside our hearts, to locate the love we have for Christ, and to let it out as we lay our hands on one another in prayer. Let us invite the Lord to join us here today, to show us what he has in store for us, what he requires of us to realize his Kingdom here on Earth. Are you willing to try today, folks?"

In unison, we responded, "Yes."

Just like a few days before, it only took one of us to start crying before the rest of us began to weep. We had compassionate hearts, after all, and nothing stirred them quite like the sight and sound of a classmate's tears. And it was, we had learned, what true worship looked and felt like: chaotic, radical, even frightening.

Besides, it was what our headmaster wanted. And we wanted to be good.

In the spring of my sixth-grade year, my parents began talking about the possibility of moving to a neighboring, more rural county, which would put us out of reach of Baltimore City's urban sprawl. At least that was the reason they gave my siblings and me. Years later, I'd learn that it was my mother who wanted out—out of the Lamb of God and out of her marriage. Both bore little resemblance to what they had been in the beginning. My father had become a stranger. And the community had been transformed from quaint and Christian into a fundamentalist, top-heavy, and patriarchal church that coerced its members with shame.

For a while, my mother tried to stick it out. She appealed to the leadership for help and even inquired about marital counseling. But counseling outside the Lamb of God was forbidden. Psychologists were too worldly. Who knew what advice a therapist might give that would conflict with the coordinators' teachings? My father was the master, and my mother must submit. If this arrangement wasn't working for her, then it was up to her to get right with the Lord's plan.

It was in science class that I first broached with my three remaining classmates the possibility that I would be leaving. Years later, I learned that they, along with everyone else in the community, likely were already aware of this news; it was common practice to push out and eventually shun members who had begun to question the coordinators' authority. Since there were no secrets in the Lamb of God, by that time it was fairly widespread knowledge that my mom had become a doubter. Soon, my father would get a phone call from the leadership, telling him they no longer had it in the budget to employ him.

That day, in science class, for the first time since infancy, I felt an invisible wall come down between my friends and me. They would be carrying on with the Lord's mission in the Lamb of God, while I would be elsewhere, doing only God knew what. The only certainty about my future was that it would be a much less righteous existence.

What frightened me most about hell wasn't the raging fire or the perpetual torture; it was the total absence of love and community. In that moment, I got a small taste of what hell felt like.

My LAST SCHOOL year at the Lamb of God ended without fanfare. No big goodbye parties or emotional farewells from my cherished teachers.

Mark and I spent our days swimming at the local pool, as we had every summer before. A couple of weeks into summer break, some of the local kids started calling me gay. But their delivery of the insult was different from my classmates'; it was more accusatory, as if, because of the way I behaved, they suspected something deviant about me. They mocked my mannerisms—the way I fussed with my hair and put my hand on my hip, and my "Valley girl" inflection when I said how "totally annoying" so-and-so was. Because Mark and I were attached at the hip, they made fun of him too. But they didn't mock Mark's behavior like they did mine. They just taunted him for hanging out with someone like me.

I could have tried to deny what they were calling me, told them to shut up and stuff it. Instead, the gravity of what they were implying caused me to dissociate entirely. After all, I knew what happened to gay people and where they ended up—only a few months earlier our Bible teacher had included the word "sodomy" as a part of our vocabulary homework for our lesson on Sodom and Gomorrah. ("When a man puts his penis into another man's rear," I wrote as its definition, recalling what I had learned in Bible class. Funnily enough, we were never taught what sex between a man and woman entailed.) The thought that I might be destined for eternal hellfire and damnation was too frightening to consider, even for a moment.

Somehow, I managed to shrug it off and carry on. Occasionally, though, it felt like the earth was trembling beneath me.

CIS WHITE GAY

Every summer, my family vacationed for two weeks in Bethany Beach, Delaware. In the summer of '95, my parents rented a beach house for an entire month. Halfway through our vacation, my grandparents, Me-Mom and Pop-Pop, would come stay with my siblings and me at the beach while our parents returned to Catonsville for a few days to move us into a new house—and a new life.

In the weeks leading up to our vacation, it was odd to see our entire life reduced to a stack of cardboard boxes in the living room. I would be leaving behind the Lamb of God—my friends with whom I had been raised since infancy, my teachers who prayed over me daily, my childhood home, the cluster—all of it. For the first time in my life, the future was utterly blank.

Our vacation started off as blissfully as it always had. We spent all day on the beach, and at night, we walked into town. There, we shopped at the Five and Dime, played Skee-Ball and video games for prizes like glow sticks and slinkies, and then stopped for ice cream. I always got Chocolate Fudge Brownie, which tasted just like the kind Me-Mom bought whenever we spent the night at her house.

One night, during our second week in Bethany, I was exiting the ice cream parlor with a chocolate-smeared mouth when I ran into a girl I knew from the pool.

"Oh, hey, Ben," Carrie said.

It took me a moment to reconcile seeing someone from back home in this world, which, while only a three-hour car ride away, had always felt so removed and exotic.

"How's it going?" I asked.

"Not bad. I'm here with my family for the week." She nodded toward her older sister and parents. "Ice cream any good?"

"Yeah, it's the best," I said.

"Cool." She began to walk away and then paused. "By the way, everybody's still talking about you," she said.

"Oh yeah?"

"Yeah, like how you're gay and you act a lot like a girl, and sometimes you even look like one too."

"Whatever," I said. "I don't care. And it's not true anyway."

"Okay, well, I just wanted to let you know," Carrie replied, as if she was telling me that I had missed a phone call but it wasn't important so I shouldn't bother calling anyone back. She walked away and rejoined her family.

It was nighttime in downtown Bethany. The moon shone over the ocean, illuminating the waves that lapped peacefully on the shore. Children scrambled on the beach, tossing glow sticks into the air, while their parents mingled. Sounds of pinballs and Whack-a-Mole hammers drifted from the arcade. The sweet smell of caramel corn and a fog of sea spray blanketed familiar Main Street. When my teachers spoke of heaven, I always saw this place.

In seconds, a dark cloud had swallowed all of it.

When our vacation ended, our parents drove us to our new home.

A new world.

I did return to the pool with Mark, but only once. Things were different between us. Traces remained of our brotherly ease, but there were moments when he appeared to recoil from me.

One day, after a poolside ping-pong match, he got honest with me. "I'm embarrassed to be seen with you," he said.

I let out something between a gasp and a laugh—that sound you make when you're trying to pretend your heart hasn't broken.

My best friend since birth just looked at me, like he was trying to decide something. After a few moments, he put his paddle on the table and walked away, leaving me behind.

CHAPTER 3

At the close of the summer, my sisters—who had attended an all-girls Catholic high school after graduating from the Lamb of God—looked forward to being in a coed school. My brother, Bret, who was nine at the time, seemed altogether undisturbed by our recent uprooting. For me, my seventh-grade school year approached like an apocalypse. If that summer had taught me anything, it was that my obvious gender incongruence made me radioactive. Lord only knew what my new classmates would have to say about me.

On the first day of school, before I left for the bus stop, my mother prepared me for the day. "Place your tongue in the back corner of your mouth, like this," she said, demonstrating for me. She explained that it had always kept her from crying when she was a kid.

In the Lamb of God, there had been four kids in my grade, including me. At Mount View Middle School, there were over two hundred. No morning prayer, not a word about Jesus or about my special place in God's army. When the bell rang for first period, I still hadn't found where my classroom was in the massive school.

My tongue remained rooted behind my back molars all day long.

In homeroom, I was assigned to sit next to a girl named Amy. Amy had a twin sister named Jane.

Amy instantly liked me. I was sweet and relatively cute, with my thoughtful outfits and my short, wavy hair. Two weeks into the school year, Amy's friend Tiffany told me Amy wanted to go out with me. She asked me if I felt the same way. I said, "Sure."

A week and a half into our relationship—during which I can't remember ever exchanging more than a few words with Amy—I feigned a cold to stay home from school. In the afternoon, my neighbor, an eighth-grade boy named Tom, knocked on my door. He said that he overheard Jane talking on the bus about how Amy wanted to dump me. He said Jane was planning a cruel prank on me.

The following morning, as I climbed onto the bus, I heard Jane's voice say, "Three...two...one!" When I reached the top of the stairs, all of the kids on the bus lifted their arms, pointed at me, and laughed. "You're dumped!" Jane cried gleefully. Amy sat next to her, staring solemnly at the floor.

After I disembarked from the bus at school, Tiffany handed me a note. "It's from Jane," she said. I pocketed it and ambled inside. Once at my locker, I unfurled the notebook paper. *How dare you think that you could go out with MY SISTER. We all know your dirty little secret. You're disgusting.*

I wandered into homeroom, sat down at my desk, and wept.

Later that week, just before science class, a boy named Toby approached me. (Toby was one of the popular kids. He did things like cry when Kurt Cobain committed suicide, which made the girls swoon.)

Everyone was just settling into their seats. "Are you gay?" he demanded. My eyes darted around the room, at the two dozen or so kids who eagerly awaited my response. I shook my head no and exited the classroom, leaving my backpack behind.

The hallway was quiet. I slipped into the boy's bathroom, which was empty. I knelt upon the tile floor and folded my hands over my heart.

"Lord Jesus, forgive me," I whispered. I lifted my arms above my head in praise. "Lord God, please, please forgive me." My body thrummed like pounded metal. My cup, which once overflowed with Christ's love, was draining, and with it the certainty that I was guaranteed salvation. When I closed my eyes, in place of Christ's glowing countenance, all I could see was blackness. I was on my own.

As MY SEVENTH-GRADE year progressed, the bullying got worse. "Are you a boy or a girl?" my classmates would ask me between giggles. In one of the school's library books, I found "Ben is a fag" scribbled on the title page. Soon, everyone started calling me Ben-Gay. (To this day, I curse the inventor of that topical cream.)

To evade the bullying, I became a chameleon. I learned how to defeminize myself and conform to my classmates' definition of what a boy is supposed to be: I cut out the highlights from my hair, deepened my voice, and bought baggy clothes. I walked with my toes turned inward, because I read somewhere that that's how male athletes walk. I got rid of my Mariah Carey CDs and cultivated a disingenuous obsession with Nirvana, even though their music made me feel despondent and borderline suicidal. Every moment of every day, I scanned myself for signs of femininity, which I immediately expunged. The only reprieve I got was when I was alone. But alone, I was left with my thoughts.

In the seventh grade, I also began to drink alcohol and smoke cigarettes. The first time I got drunk was with my sister Jess and her friend, who had pulled down a dusty bottle of brandy from a cupboard one day after school. They fed me a couple of gulps and, after I became annoying, put me out on the back deck with a pack of cigarettes and a book of matches. I lay on my back, watching the clouds and smoking, stunned by the miracle elixir that slowed my racing thoughts and made all of my woes seem silly. Once I sobered up, I retreated to my bedside, where I knelt before the crucifix that hung on my wall and begged God to forgive me for indulging in vice. But I knew, deep down, that I would certainly be partaking again.

How swiftly my life had become a kind of mirror image of the one I had known. Except that now, instead of being prayed over and blessed, I was taunted and scorned. Alone, I felt incapable of accessing the Holy Spirit. If ever I felt the presence of God, instead of love, I felt disdain. I couldn't do anything to make it right. All I could do was pray and beg for forgiveness.

In April 1996, a couple months before my seventh-grade school year ended, my mother sat my brother and me down at the kitchen table. Dad was away on a business trip for his new job with a tax preparation company.

"Your father and I are divorcing," she told us. Tears filled her eyes.

If there was anything my brother and I couldn't tolerate, it was to see our mother cry.

"I just want you to be happy," I said.

"Me too," said Bret.

It was like spring break in Daytona Beach. My mother was finally free. Only yesterday (or so it seemed) she was pining to be a handmaid in a covenant community; now she was behaving like a first-semester freshman at Arizona State. She bleached her hair blonde, joined a gym, got her belly button pierced, and a butterfly tattooed on her thigh. She laughed more, drank more wine.

But she was angry too. Mostly at my father, whose wounded pride led him to totally withdraw from our family and eventually move two hundred miles south to Virginia Beach. ("For work," he insisted.) She was on her own with four kids, a full-time job, and a household to run.

My siblings and I dealt with this new version of our mother in different ways. My coping mechanism was to pray.

Late at night, as I lay awake in bed, wandering alone down the dark corridors of my mind, I realized that what the kids at school were saying about me was true. I was a faggot. So surely our excommunication from the Lamb of God—from my friends, but more importantly my teachers, who were the link between God's mercy and myself—and all the chaos that had erupted in my life since then was because of my abominable soul. I was certain things were going to get worse, and it was all my fault.

For hours, I would kneel before the pewter crucifix that hung above my bed, begging God's forgiveness for my innate evil. More than anything, though, I begged God to keep my mother safe, for I was certain that God was preparing to strike more vengeance upon me for my sins, and the worst punishment I could imagine was for my mother to die. Thus, it was up to me to win back God's favor, in order to guarantee not just my salvation, but hers. *I* was responsible. Every little sin I committed—I forgot to wash out my cereal bowl in the morning, I thought my teacher's new haircut was ugly—meant swift and severe punishment from God. No matter that we had a dishwasher for the cereal bowl or that my teacher's haircut was objectively hideous. The stakes were high.

Atop a tall bookshelf in the family room sat a white clothbound bible with a small portrait of Christ on its cover. Late into the night, as my family members slept soundly in their beds, I knelt behind the pink La-Z-Boy, lifted my head to the Bible, and repeated prayers of praise and repentance. *Please forgive me, God. I love you Jesus. Please keep us safe*, I pled over and over again. Because if I didn't, my mother would be raped and murdered or would perish in a fiery car wreck. After each set of prayers, I made the sign of the cross as many times as it took to get it right—perhaps I hadn't tapped the proper location on my chest, or my shoulder touches were asymmetrical, or maybe I needed to gaze more reverently at Christ's face.

The incessant need to pray baffled me. I simply couldn't stop.

Today, I know that I had developed a form of obsessive-compulsive disorder called scrupulosity. Typical compulsions like repetitive handwashing are basically an OCD sufferer's desperate attempt to exert some form of control over his life, particularly in areas where he is ultimately powerless but nevertheless feels entirely responsible. An individual with scrupulosity performs his compulsions—repetitive prayer, constant visits to confession, hours of genuflecting before religious iconography—to thwart God's retribution, which he, filthy sinner that he is, believes is imminent.

According to the psychiatrist and author Dr. Ian Osborn, who wrote the 2008 book *Can Christianity Cure Obsessive-Compulsive Disorder?: A Psychiatrist Explores the Role of Faith in Treatment*, scrupulosity first appeared in the early years of the Renaissance, when, along with an explosion of scientific discovery and humanist insight, came the rise of individual self-consciousness. This meant even greater responsibility for the fate of one's soul. Meanwhile, moral theologians devised ever greater purity tests for the faithful. Before long, the number of mortal sins went from only three (murder, adultery, and idolatry) to hundreds. Even entertaining an impure thought became sinful. Guilt-ridden Christians, their minds suddenly plagued by intrusive thoughts, now had myriad reasons to confess—and confess they did, over and over again. Osborn observed that scrupulosity, once a rare disorder, became a "virtual epidemic" by the end of the Renaissance.

I didn't learn about this disorder until I was an adult. Thus, for years, I navigated the turbulent seas of scrupulosity alone. Every day was an existential battle, a moral test that would determine the eternal fate of my soul.

"Please don't let bad things happen," was a prayer I can remember repeating by rote, over and over again.

It was my own personal holy war.

In the eighth grade, the bullies grew conflicted about me. I was a nice kid with a decent sense of humor. I could tell they enjoyed my company, though they preferred not to be seen with me. Girls continued to crush on me, most likely because I was unthreatening and sensitive, and because I treated them like equals. I finally did make a few friends—mostly girls, but also a few boys.

A few weeks into the school year, one of those boys invited me to a party at his house. His parents were out of town. A lot of popular kids, including many who regularly taunted me, were there. After we raided the liquor cabinet, I drank everyone under the table. I danced and goofed off, told jokes, and mimed the lyrics to everyone's favorite rap song. It was my entry into middle-school high society. I was no longer "Ben-Gay." But now, I was "Ben the Alcoholic."

I continued to drink. I even drank alone. Alcohol became my medication—my *solution*—and at the same time yet another transgression for which to feel remorseful and repent. There were times, during that last year of middle school, when I tried to curb my drinking, and not just because I felt guilty about it. Even at that young age, I knew that I was developing a drinking problem. Plus, there were kids who didn't approve of drinking and smoking, and I was desperate to please everyone. Any threat of abandonment—rejection, shunning, *excommunication* from a group—paralyzed me with shame and fear.

By this time—the summer before high school—my sexual and romantic desire for other boys had become an established part of my inner world. Soon came the intrusive thoughts. Now, I needed to launch into another repetition of prayer because, out of nowhere, the image of an erect penis had popped into my mind. The more I tried to force it out, the more I thought about it. My mind eventually became a visual landscape of pornography and religious iconography. While I prayed, I pictured Christ's face, and suddenly horns would sprout from his head and a serpent would shoot from his mouth. I saw penises fucking crucifixes, my mother being penetrated with the Jesus-shaped bottle of holy water that had sat for years on our living room table.

And there was the shame that accompanied my daydreams about my attractive male classmates. When I masturbated, a chasm of despondency would open up and swallow me the moment after I climaxed. I would pray myself to a fitful sleep.

During prayer time in the Lamb of God, there were always prophesies: "Jesus says…" and "I see the devil marching beneath the door with an army of demons. We need to pray him away!" On my own, I sometimes tried to resuscitate the emotions and sensations I felt back then. But when I saw those demons marching beneath my door, there was no one there to save me or help me pray them away. Alone, I didn't feel strong enough to keep them from entering my heart and my mind. I was a sinner, a homosexual. Even though it hadn't been my choice, I had left the community. I had abandoned God. I should have objected more loudly.

IN HIGH SCHOOL, my rituals no longer allowed for a trip to the bathroom as they had in middle school; I believed I had to pray, make the sign of the cross, and lift my hands in praise right there at my desk. Though I could recite my prayers silently, it had become necessary for me to say "Amen" out loud because the word had started to sound jumbled and incoherent in my head, as if it wasn't a word at all. This proved difficult since I couldn't interrupt my teacher and because I wanted to disguise what I was doing. Thus, when I lifted my hands in praise, I pretended I was stretching; to make the sign of the cross, I was merely brushing the hair off my forehead, scratching an itch in the center of my chest, and sweeping dust from my shoulders; and the word "Amen" was just a yawn or a cough with a little bit of song added to it.

Soon, I began covering the pages of my homework with faintly drawn question marks. This was because if I got one of the answers wrong but had answered affirmatively, I would be lying. By adding the punctuation, I was telling God and my teachers that my answers were merely conjecture.

In my journals, I stopped capitalizing all proper nouns besides "God," "Lord," "Jesus," and "Christ," along with their pronouns (he/him/his) because if I was capitalizing mere mortals' names I was giving them the same dignity as God. As with the question marks I wrote on my homework, I wrote "I think" and other qualifying words and phrases in the sentences that included any type of data, in case I had gotten the information wrong.

I also went through my old entries and crossed out curse words, negative statements I may have written about others, and any passages that suggested I was lacking in faith. I scribbled next to these entries "Forgive me, Lord!" and circled all the places I had written "God" and "Lord Jesus" to further emphasize my passion for his name.

In 1999, when I was sixteen and a high school sophomore, I got a job as a busboy at a local seafood restaurant. The restaurant had been around for two decades, some staff members just as long. Everybody partied together, slept together. Some even got married.

I started smoking pot with my coworkers. Pot was the new answer to my woes. It provided the best solution to my OCD that I had come across. It calmed my nerves, slowed my thoughts, and allowed me to detach from them. It also helped me sleep at night. Almost immediately I became dependent.

Sobriety was intolerable. When I was high, I was able to exercise my rational mind; I could intellectualize the reality of homosexuality, talk about it with my closest (female) friends, even trick myself into thinking I had accepted it. But my obsessions and intrusive thoughts were waiting the moment I came down or sobered up.

Years would pass before I understood that real mental, intellectual, and spiritual growth could only come from sitting with the anxiety, without the anesthesia of drugs or compulsive rituals, until it dissipated and lost its grip. But at the time, the cold reality that I was gay, and therefore an abomination in the eyes of the Lord, petrified me during my sober moments. Every day, the fate of my soul hung in the balance. The future depended entirely on my moral character and the purity of my thoughts. But living up to the moral standard my religious programming required was an impossibility.

Besides drugs and alcohol, the main solace I found was in writing. I continued to a keep a journal, and in 2000, during my senior year, I took a creative writing course called Advanced Composition. My teacher, Ms. Samuels, encouraged me to submit some of my work for a countywide scholarship contest. In my writing sample, I included a poem about my all-consuming crush on the star of the soccer team. I was one of three finalists nominated for the prize. I didn't win, but the experience encouraged me to keep writing.

That year, pot stopped working as well as it used to, so I began to dabble in heavier substances like MDMA, LSD, and opioids. The LSD, in particular, complemented the religious battle in my brain. It lit up my mind like a Bosch painting.

One gorgeous fall day, a friend gave me a Vicodin. I hadn't felt such an enveloping sense of peace and comfort since my religious teachers laid their hands on me in prayer and absolved me of my sins. It was heaven on earth.

In 2001, I graduated from high school. Despite my poor mental health and my daily drug use, I still managed to earn a fairly high GPA, and I accepted an offer to attend the University of Maryland in Baltimore County on an academic scholarship.

On the morning of 9/11, I drove from my mother's house to the campus with my sister Jess who was in her last year at the university. It was the second week of my freshman year.

In English class, we discussed an essay written by a woman balancing career and motherhood. After the class ended at 9:45 a.m., I drove home alone—my sister remained on campus for her next class—and listened to Howard Stern talk about crashing planes and collapsing towers. When I got home, I turned on the TV just in time to watch the North Tower fall.

I didn't know it then, but as I watched the burning towers on the television in my mother's living room, something shifted deep within my psyche, like the shifting of tectonic plates beneath the surface of the earth. As I watched the tower collapse upon itself, floor after floor, in a cloud of ash and smoke, I felt, deep down, like I was collapsing as well. Under the weight of my drug addiction and my ceaseless mental anguish, I was finally falling apart. But maybe it was okay, because the whole world seemed to be falling apart too.

As the news unfolded that day, for the first time in my life I understood the magnitude of the threat of Islamic radicalism as well as the true depth of our enemies' hatred toward us. That night, I watched members of the House and Senate break into a spontaneous rendition of "God Bless America" on the steps of the Capitol. Through the fog, I felt the stirrings of a patriotism born of real gratitude and a genuine understanding of just how lucky we had been, and hopefully still would be.

The next day, in my American Studies class, we discussed the cataclysmic events. A female student said she thought that the displays of patriotism around her were bullshit, as was everyone's sudden willingness to rally behind our Republican president. *Was she right?* I wondered. That evening, I shared with my sister Erin what the student had said. Erin, a Democrat attending law school, immediately contradicted the student, stating how important patriotism and bipartisanship were in times like these. Her conviction impressed me, but so had the student's. After some reflection, I decided I agreed with Erin, but that ended up being beside the point. The real point was my doubt that I would ever be able to assert a point of view as confidently as they had.

After my first semester, I decided to take some time off from school. Maybe I'd go to Europe or move to New York. I needed to "find myself."

Actually, my mental health was in a tailspin, and I needed the free time to anesthetize with drugs.

The following February, just after my nineteenth birthday, I traveled with some friends to New Orleans for Mardi Gras. We stayed at Le Pavillon, a beautiful hotel just south of the French Quarter with a rooftop terrace that overlooked the Crescent City Bridge.

All I remember from this trip are a few disconnected snatches: Heavy purple beads hurled from wrought iron balconies at hammered women revealing their breasts; breaded mozzarella di bufala smothered in chunky marinara sauce; tourists pointing toy guns at a life-sized cut-out of Osama bin Laden; crazed men screaming passages from the book of Revelations; losing forty dollars to a sidewalk scam artist performing magic tricks with red Solo cups; drinking with a man who I'm pretty sure was the rapper Ludacris; spotting the Naked Cowboy, of Times Square fame; and following a noisy jazz parade for a block or two.

I remember exposing myself on Bourbon Street and a San Franciscan named Tony cupping me from behind. I remember whispering in Tony's ear, "I've never been fucked," and being led by the hand through the raucous crowd to Tony's quiet hotel room. I remember that we showered together beforehand and that he wore a black condom, that it hurt at first and then it felt good, and that his roommates walked in on us while I was on top. I remember making out with Tony in between bites of beignet at the Cafe du Monde while the other patrons eyed us reproachfully.

I remember buying cocaine from a shapeless man who sat in the shadows of a gay bar. I remember his lips grazing my neck while I tipped more of his stash into my bag.

I remember snorting lines from a glass-topped buffet table and rambling for hours about how I was destined to be a star.

I arrived home from New Orleans a bona fide sodomite.

Two weeks later, I would break.

CHAPTER 4

"Chronic stimulant use can produce a paranoid psychosis that is similar to acute paranoid schizophrenia," says a 1991 paper, titled "Cocaine-induced psychosis," published in the *Journal of Clinical Psychiatry*.

For years, I had been binging on cocaine, alcohol, pot, and various opioids and hallucinogens, and I had severe OCD, anxiety, and depression, so who knows what it was exactly that caused me to lose my shit. All I know is that the signals coming to me through the radio seemed very plausible, as did the voices that told me to drive to an elementary school in the middle of rural Pennsylvania and announce to the ladies at the front desk that God had sent me. They were skeptical, of course, and instead of allowing me to continue down the hallway into one of the classrooms—where, I believed, my fifth-grade teacher, Miss Morehouse, was waiting for me—they called the police. I was taken into custody and, at the police station, handcuffed to a bench. Two or maybe four hours later, my mother came to pick me up. Crying, she drove me home to collect some of my things, and then to One North, the psychiatric ward at Howard County General Hospital.

IN THE PSYCH ward, they pumped me full of antipsychotics. Five days in, after coming down from the mania and being reacquainted with a terrifying new reality—which consisted of pure dread, self-hatred, and a persistent barrage of panic attacks—I needed to get out of there. I figured out what I needed to say to the people in charge in order to be released: "No, I'm not suicidal. No, I'm not thinking about harming anyone. No, I'm not seeing or hearing things."

The week after I got out, I slept as much as I possibly could. Soon, my body ran out of the need for sleep. The panic consumed me. The intrusive thoughts were nonstop. I didn't know what I was capable of. Like one who fears tall buildings because he's afraid he'll spontaneously jump off, or a new mother who has unprompted thoughts about harming her children, I felt dangerous, evil. I felt like I was in hell. I begged God to kill me.

In the kitchen, I rifled through the medicine cabinet to see if there was something I could take to end it all. Unable to find anything that would come close to doing the trick, I went upstairs to my mother's room, shook her awake, and told her I was going to commit suicide. She drove me back to the hospital.

This time, the doctors put me on antianxiety medicine, perhaps an SSRI. The relief was nearly immediate. Outside, in what the patients called the chicken coop—a fenced-in, ten-foot-square space with a cement floor, a few plastic chairs, and an ashtray—I smoked cigarettes and chatted with the other patients, feeling normal for the first time in years.

Hours later, after the sun had set and I returned to my room, the relief ended abruptly. Another panic attack ensued. I knelt by my bedside, hands folded and clasped against my forehead.

"God, forgive me," I pled aloud. "Please help me." But there was no reprieve.

Finally, at my wit's end, I screamed at God, "Fuck you!"

Everything was silent. The anxiety receded like seawater, taking with it all of the violent, sexual, blasphemous images that I was helpless to pray away. Hope washed over me.

Sometimes I wonder if the reprieve I felt was what they call "God's grace," that perhaps it was God's reward for finally being honest with him. That if he would have answered me directly, he may have said, "Why do you keep saying you're sorry? *You* are the one who is suffering. *I'm* sorry for the pain you have endured."

But these would have been the words and actions of a gracious God. And I knew of no such thing.

BECAUSE OF MY symptoms—paranoia, delusions, suicidal and homicidal ideation, intrusive thoughts—and my age, which is a common one for schizophrenic men to experience their first psychotic episode, I was diagnosed with schizophrenia. It was a relief to put a label on it.

One night, during a group therapy session in the common room, a nurse plucked another patient and me from the group and led us down the hallway to the "one-on-one" room. The room had glass walls, so I could see the two men already sitting inside, waiting. They were from a twelve-step program, the nurse explained, and they were going to share their stories with us. The other patient and I exchanged glances. He had shared in group about his crack cocaine use, and I had shared about my use of nearly every illicit drug under the sun. I didn't know how the other patient felt about it, but none of what she said surprised me. By that time, I had known for years that I was a drug addict.

I don't remember what the men said. But I knew there was a place I needed to go after I was discharged, a place that would help me to stop using drugs.

A WEEK LATER, I was released. The discharging doctor enrolled me in an outpatient mental health rehab not far from home, which I would attend every day for a month. She also advised me to go to AA.

I attended my first meeting at a church a few miles from my house. I raised my hand, said I was a drug addict and alcoholic, and proceeded to share way too much information with the group. The other members nodded their heads graciously. *Poor kid.*

At my second meeting, I met a cute guy named John. He said I should come with him to a meeting sometime in DC, where he lived. "There's a really great young-people meeting there," he said.

While I was in the psych ward, my mother had sold my car in order to pay the hospital bill, so John had to pick me up. On the ride to DC, he told me his story, about how long he used and how he eventually got sober. He then asked me to tell him mine. I divulged everything—the cult, the OCD, the bullying, being gay, the manic episode, the psych ward stays, the meds. He listened intently, occasionally asking questions. Nickelback played on his stereo.

The meeting was held in an enormous hall near Dupont Circle. The parking lot was full. We arrived to find nearly every seat occupied. Balconies stretched around the space. These, too, were filled. John led me to a row on the main floor, near the back, where a couple of his friends had saved two seats for us.

There was an unexpected amount of cheering during the meeting, and a lot of laughter, even when the speaker hadn't said anything particularly funny. He wore a shirt and tie, which, I learned afterward, was a requirement for men who were asked to speak at that particular meeting. Female speakers had to wear professional attire as well. "To attract newcomers, and to show that we can once again become upstanding members of society," they said.

The feelings the meeting aroused in me, being in a large hall with a congregation of young people, collectively gushing over the man's seemingly rehearsed speech—during which he testified about his faith in God and implored us to confess our faults to our fellows, if we wanted to stay sober—were quite familiar. I felt a strong pull to join in the laughter and cheers, even when I didn't get the joke or understand what exactly it was that we were celebrating, and to unquestioningly absorb the speaker's "suggestions," which my vulnerable mind immediately interpreted as rules. I didn't yet have the internal mechanism to critically evaluate the ideas espoused by a man at a podium with throngs of congregants. Here was a new community to which I could belong. One that would accept me and deliver some kind of salvation.

After the meeting, there was a sober party at a large home nearby, where a number of group members, including John, lived. There was loud music, board games, strong coffee, and cigarettes. John led me around introducing me to people. When he took me into his bedroom, I immediately remarked on how tidy it was.

"That's me," he said, smiling. "I'm a neat freak."

Then he told me that he wanted to show me something. He led me to his closet and opened the door. Inside were racks of clothes.

"See how I've organized everything?" he asked me.

I nodded.

"Look how the shirts are all organized by color. And if you held up a ruler, you'd see that they're each exactly two inches apart." He closed the closet door and sat down on his bed. I remained standing.

"You see, I have OCD too," he told me. "It's just something I've learned to accept about myself. It's okay to be OCD."

I told him I admired that.

"Thanks," he said. "I didn't ever think I would get over it. Like you, I thought I had to take medication to get better. But as it turns out, I don't. I want to be fully sober today. I don't want to take medication."

A long silence ensued.

"So, do you agree that you would probably be better off without medication? That maybe you could just rely on God instead?" he asked.

John's question overwhelmed me. *Forgive me, God, I haven't been relying on you,* I thought. *Even this man who's only known me for a week can tell.*

At the same time, the medication seemed to be keeping me relatively stable. If I stopped, would the panic attacks ensue? The crippling depression and the constant desire to die? Here I was, a total newcomer to a new spiritual community, and I was already failing to live up to its moral standards.

Little did I know that I was being seduced into another cult. In May 2007, *Newsweek* published a story about DC's "Midtown" AA group—also known as the Q group, named after a man named Mike Quinones, or Mike Q. According to the article, Mike Q had assumed leadership of the group in the 1980s and transformed it into a massive community of mostly teenaged and twenty-something alcoholics. Members shared homes, went on group vacations, and got jobs at the same companies. They were encouraged to cut off contact with nongroup members, discontinue psychiatric medication and talk therapy, and have sex with older members, including Mike.

The article, called "Critics Say Washington AA Chapter Is Cultlike," recounts various ex-members' personal stories. "You can't trust any of your own thoughts," one woman was told by her sponsor when she wanted to leave the group. "You can't go into your own head unsupervised."

The *Washington Post* subsequently reported that a woman who had been encouraged to go off her medication and discontinue therapy with a clinical psychologist eventually became suicidal and was hospitalized. According to her therapist, when group members found out she had resumed her medication, "she was ostracized."

I attended the Midtown Group in mid-2002, during the height of this activity. That first night, as John drove me home, he told me he would be my sponsor. I can't remember if I heeded his advice and discontinued my medication. But I didn't last long in the group, only a month or two. What ultimately cut my membership short was how closely the meetings resembled the prayer meetings at the Lamb of God, and how the members dismissed my objections when they told me I wouldn't stay sober unless I prayed multiple times a day.

"How can you fear God," they asked, "if AA allows you to choose your own conception of God?"

I didn't have the words to explain that my conception of God had been imprinted upon me so effectively and at such an early age that it may as well have been written into my DNA. So instead, I left AA and returned to drugs and alcohol.

I NEVER KNEW that heroin was brown. Or that it has a distinct smell. Or how simple it was to procure. Or how uncomplicated it was to find a vein.

People in recovery often talk about divine intervention. The DUI that leads to an arrest, which leads to court-ordered rehab, where the individual is finally able to get sober. The stranger on an airplane who absentmindedly tells her seatmate about her recovery from drug addiction, unaware that he is in the grips of the same disease.

If there is such a thing as divine intervention, mine came piecemeal. I was not struck sober after the first instance of what could be classified as divine intervention, but I do believe that the incident I am about to share is the reason I am still here, alive on this earth, typing these words.

I knelt on my bedroom floor, facing the window. The torn blinds filtered the yellow light of the streetlamp, casting jagged shadows on the objects spread across the carpet before me: Marlboro Lights, a lighter, a *Rolling Stone* magazine, a cup, my leather belt, a tin tablespoon, a syringe, a pencil-thin glass vial filled with powder. I uncapped the vial, tipped a fleck of powder into the spoon, and placed the spoon on the *Rolling Stone*. I reached for the cup of water, only to find it empty.

I was only away from my bedroom for five, maybe ten seconds, when I saw a shadow pass beneath the bathroom door. I shut off the sink. "Ben?" I heard my mother say.

I opened the door and entered the hallway. My mother stood in my bedroom door. In the upturned palm of her left hand rested my belt, looped into a circle slightly larger than my bicep. In her right hand, the syringe.

Three weeks. That's how long I had been shooting one of the most notoriously addictive drugs into my veins when my mother caught me in the act.

She screamed at me. I screamed back. But there were no lies I could tell to make it look like anything other than what it was. So I ran.

I ran for miles in the cold. I finally collapsed into the grass along whichever suburban road I had been tearing down and looked up at the sky. I could see my breath.

The sky was clear. The stars were blue.

And then the miracle, which came in a rare moment of absolute clarity: *If I ever use heroin again, I am going to die.*

I made a pact with the stars. And I kept it.

I GAVE UP heroin just in time. I did keep drinking, though, and smoking pot. Alone in my bedroom, I'd scribble morbid poems and angry, vaguely feminist diatribes in my journal while watching episodes of *Will & Grace* that I had recorded on videocassette. I yearned for a life like the handsome, successful, out-and-proud New York gay men on the show. The moment it would disappear from my screen, I'd encounter the glaring juxtaposition between their (fictional) lives and my real one and return downstairs to steal another glass of my mother's boxed wine.

The drinking made me erratic. On two occasions I woke up in the hospital with a catheter.

I had a couple more visits to One North too. These were voluntary; I was really just trying to escape the consequences of my drinking, like when I stole my mom's car and returned it with the sideview mirror missing, or when she finally kicked me out after I hosted what was technically an orgy in her basement.

All my anger came out when I was drunk; it was the only time I felt safe to express it. I'd scream at my mother. She'd scream back.

Some nights I would go to the local Catholic church, sit in the pews in the dark when the nave was empty, and cry and plead with God. He never answered.

IN FEBRUARY 2003, a few days before my twentieth birthday, I bumped into a former high school classmate at the grocery store. Margaret had been known for her infectious laugh, her magnificent singing voice, and her born-again Christian faith, which she proudly broadcast to anyone in earshot. She was very involved in the local Young Life organization, a sort of hip Christian youth group, which even a lot of the popular kids attended. For Halloween one year, her younger sister Cecilia, a freshman at the time, came to school as Margaret. Cecilia, who was not born-again (none of Margaret's siblings were), carried around a bible all day, quoting scripture and saying "Praise the Lord!" in a sarcastic tone. Margaret hated it.

When I ran into Margaret, I was slightly drunk and had just been kicked out of the house again. She asked me what I had been up to. I told her I was thinking about going to cosmetology school. College just wasn't for me, I said, but I had always been interested in beauty and fashion. Margaret, as chance would have it, was currently an apprentice at a local hair salon. She asked me then and there if I wanted to take her place in the two-year program; she was leaving to work in youth ministry full time and her mentor needed someone to fill in.

The next morning, she picked me up and drove me to my new job at the salon.

For the first three months, I barely hung on to the position. Miss Lisa—the office manager and the wife of Pastor Dan, a local Baptist minister—was always writing me up either for being late to work, trying to steal another hairdresser's muscle relaxers from her purse, or falling asleep on the job (they often found me snoring in a pedicure chair). Margaret stayed on for a few months to show me the ropes, like how to do blowouts and apply root-color touch-ups for Ariya, the four-and-a-half-foot Thai woman who owned the shop. We practiced haircutting and foil highlighting on mannequin heads, and Margaret had me apply her makeup and style her updos in preparation for the flood of local high school girls who would come in during prom season. I swept hair, shampooed clients, and applied toners out of plastic squeeze bottles. I brought my friends in to practice on them too: one of whom had a meltdown when I accidentally turned her hair pink, and my mother, who cried in the mirror at home when her hair began to fall out after submitting to my first-ever foil highlighting.

Each morning, I would resolve to not get high or drunk that day. But by 4:00 p.m., I would be calling my dealer for pot.

Each night, I would wrestle my demons. More pot, more wine, more television reruns depicting worlds in which there appeared to be no hell. The quippy dialogue, the catchy music, and the messages of love, hope, and acceptance would tickle my mind but never quite penetrate it. The drugs and alcohol formed a hard exterior, shielding my demons from anything that might arrest them, tame them, eradicate them.

On May 27, 2003, in my journal, I wrote:

> *I have continued to disappoint every single person in my life. I feel ashamed all the time.*
>
> *I am an alcoholic. I know that if I don't get help, I will probably end up dead.*
>
> *What makes me really sad is that I don't like myself at all. I hate so many things about myself. I look at myself, and I see shame and failure and frailty. I see a tiny little boy.*
>
> *I yearn for the comfort and knowledge that the greatest power in the universe is on my side and loves me for the person I am and the person I am growing into.*

But there is this other part of me that is so scared of that because it brings such a vivid image of my days in the Lamb of God. I'm not sure if I want to return to all that.

The next day I was blowing dry a client's hair when I overheard a conversation between another stylist and a young woman sitting in her chair. "I'm six months clean today," I heard the young woman say. "All the money I used to make I would put right up my nose."

When the woman went outside to smoke a cigarette, I followed her.

"What's your name?" I asked her.

"Stacy." She took a drag from her cigarette.

"Stacy, I'm a drug addict," I said. "I need help."

Stacy's eyes lit up. Globs of hair color ran down her forehead as she told me to take down her number and call her after work. She and her boyfriend would take me to a meeting.

That evening, I called my dealer. When he didn't answer, I called Stacy.

An hour later, a red Mitsubishi Eclipse pulled into the driveway. Stacy and her boyfriend, Chris, drove me to a Narcotics Anonymous meeting.

NA was very different from AA. There was more of an emphasis on fellowship than on working the twelve steps, which felt right for me at the time. And no one said "boo" about my psychiatric meds. In fact, it was the opposite; they encouraged members to seek professional help, often repeating the maxim that group members are not doctors and have no right to advise anyone on mental health treatment.

Of course, people talked about God—mostly they'd say "HP" for Higher Power—but here were heroin addicts, crack addicts, potheads, and pill poppers. They were young. Even the old ones seemed young. After meetings, we'd caravan to the Double T Diner, where we'd drink coffee and smoke, trading war stories and laughing, until the sun rose.

My memories of those first few months are blurry. But one memory is distinct: It was my sixteenth sober day. I couldn't believe it. For over two weeks, I had avoided drugs and alcohol, and somehow the sky hadn't fallen. I hadn't spontaneously combusted, and I hadn't killed myself or someone else. For the first time since that night in the psych ward, when I knelt by my bed and screamed at God, I felt hope.

This alien feeling soothed the obsessive thoughts. Maybe I thought that I was winning some morality points by getting clean and sober. I don't know. But I do understand why some addicts equate getting clean with being "born again." I had, after all, been saved. In this case, it was the fellowship of NA that saved me. Those kids were misfits. They were crazy, like me. And they, too, were fucked up about God. But they were also willing, eager, and desperate to believe in something. Anything.

Years later, after two decades in twelve step programs and numerous experiences in activism and academia, I would come to understand a very important axiom: Ideology, like nature, abhors a vacuum. No matter the secular context, dogmatism rushes in to fill a void formerly occupied by religious faith. AA, the "LGBTQIA+ community," social justice activism, politics, humanities departments—in these spaces, fundamentalism lurks and, in some cases, metastasizes. One person or group (or mob) establishes a doctrine that all others are made to feel they must follow to avoid exile. The rest quickly fall in line—because apparently, a sense of moral purpose, purity, and belonging are universal human needs.

Freethinking—going it alone—requires immense discipline and resolve. I would eventually develop the fortitude, but it would take years.

During the first few years of sobriety, my mental health dramatically improved and my schizophrenia diagnosis was rescinded. Eventually, my psychiatrist took me off the antipsychotics and, in their place, prescribed antidepressants, which soothed the OCD symptoms. I worked the twelve steps, made friends, and attended mental health counseling. My budding career in cosmetology took off.

Throughout my twenties, as a feeble exercise in "self-care," I sometimes tried to reconnect with the young boy I had once been—the boy whose interests expanded beyond what was typical for males. I experimented with bronzer and mascara and got French manicures and pedicures. These behaviors were liberating, though they occasionally just felt performative. I would eventually stop attaching so much meaning to these superficial things after I realized they weren't what made me my authentic self. My ideas, my voice, the way I treat other people—these are the things that make me the person I am.

But efforts to reconcile my sexuality with the fire-and-brimstone doctrine of my childhood continued to prove futile. Sex with men—even fantasizing about men—brought on the worst kind of fear and anxiety. Without drugs and alcohol, I was held captive by my paranoia. AIDS lurked around every corner. I was convinced it was my destiny to die from the disease. As I saw it, the seriousness of my "perversion" meant that, in all other areas of my life, I had to be as close as possible to perfect if I wanted a chance at salvation. Sex, more than anything, catalyzed the most persistent obsessions and compulsions. I'd ruminate over my sin and its possible consequences, then launch into prayer, sometimes for hours. But even the simplest mistake could send me into a tailspin.

I mostly attended meetings in the suburbs, where I lived. I continued to have mostly female friends, which felt natural. During conversations about relationships, our feelings, and insecurities, my ability to relate so intimately with women would sometimes come up. I'd joke, "Well, we all know I'm really a woman." My friends would chuckle, but we all seemed to be aware that I wasn't really kidding. I had masculinized myself since puberty, partly due to sexual maturity but mainly to avoid bullying and threats of violence. But emotionally and intellectually, I seemed to respond to the world and other people in a way that was more typical of women than men. In moments of introspection, I realized I even subconsciously perceived myself as a woman, often pushing behind my ear strands of long hair that weren't there. I had always preferred films with female leads and books written by women, about women. When I played sports, I frequently imagined myself as a female athlete.

The reality though, was that I was a man. A *gay* man. And if I wanted to have a full, sober life, I needed to meet and connect with other sober gay men.

I began to venture into Baltimore City to attend gay twelve-step meetings. It helped to listen to other gay people's stories, to hear them talk about their struggles with homophobia, being bullied as kids, and their conflicts with religion. In straight meetings, I felt, no one *really* understood the nuances of my problems. But in gay meetings, I realized that I was not alone. Many of these men had attended seminary schools. Some had been ordained priests. They had lived during a time when gay men were regularly harassed and arrested by police, publicly smeared as "perverts" and "queers." And almost all of them had endured the worst of the AIDS crisis. They had been wrestling their demons far longer than I had wrestled mine.

As much as the gay meetings helped, the program's emphasis on prayer and meditation continued to prove daunting for me. In meetings, one often hears the suggestion to ask God (or your Higher Power) to keep you sober that day, and to thank God every night for another day of sobriety. And we are encouraged to pray for those toward whom we harbor resentments. In the fourth edition of *Alcoholics Anonymous* (known in AA as the Big Book), AA cofounder Bill Wilson lists the steps he and other alcoholics took in order to recover. To work the eleventh step, the Big Book says, they had "sought through prayer and meditation to improve our conscious contact with God *as we understood Him*, praying only for knowledge of His will for us and the power to carry that out." The italicized phrase emphasizes the fact that twelve step programs are spiritual rather than religious; therefore, members are not required to have any specific understanding of who or what God is.

I wanted desperately to stay sober and continue to get better. I loved the idea of coming to my own understanding of God as one who loved me unconditionally. But as hard as I tried, I couldn't replace the angry God I had been programmed to believe in. The one who was perpetually disappointed in me. The one who was always ready to inflict the worst kind of punishment upon me. The one who hated the part of me I knew I couldn't change.

Sometimes prayer worked. There were occasions when I'd feel so overwhelmed by a particular concern, that I'd pray for God to help me, and a feeling of genuine peace would wash over me. Plus, I was staying sober—something I had never been able to do on my own. So who knew if the request I made to God every morning wasn't a vital part of my sobriety? But inevitably, the prayer would become repetitive, and I'd slip into my old habits.

It is in this regard that I compare spiritual abuse to sexual abuse. My teachers—those who laid their hands on me and rejoiced when I began to cry, who spoke of frightening prophecies and fed me bogus dogma that taught me to fear my own mind—emotionally and spiritually abused me. And they used spiritual practices, like prayer, to do so. Practices that can be healthy and fruitful, that can help an individual to attain a spiritual connection with a god of his understanding, and that can help him to discover the piece of God that is within him.

Maybe some of those prayer sessions in the Lamb of God did lead to something authentic—there was warmth and comfort and, who knows, perhaps we tapped into something that was divine. But most of it brought fear and guilt. We were shamed for our sins as if we were criminals and not children who made childish mistakes. They forever tainted the spiritual practice of prayer, and spirituality in general, just as sexual abusers taint sex and sexuality for their victims.

Education is power, and the more I read about the disorder of scrupulosity, the saner I felt. One famous religious figure who suffered from scrupulosity, I learned, was Alphonsus Liguori, the eighteenth-century founder of the Redemptorists Congregation. According to Dr. Ian Osborn, Liguori's scrupulosity began, like mine, during his adolescence, when he would compulsively confess to his priests. What intrigued me the most about his story was the surprising advice that his priests eventually gave him: They told him *not* to confess and to stop absent-mindedly repeating prayers. To back up their advice, they referred to Matthew 6:7 (NKJV), where Jesus says, "And when you pray, do not use vain repetitions as the heathen do. For they think that they will be heard for their many words." Today, the Redemptorists continue special outreach to those suffering from scrupulosity and publishes a regular newsletter, "Scrupulous Anonymous."

A pivotal moment came when I finally found a gay sponsor—a man who could guide me through the twelve steps and in whom I could confide my fears, resentments, and dark secrets. I was able to tell him about my childhood in the Lamb of God, the chaotic years that followed, and the odd and embarrassing disorder I had developed in the interim. Just as Liguori's confessors excused him from confession, my sponsor told me not to pray. He said that the steps and principles were just suggestions; they were not mandatory, and when we came into the program we were supposed to take what works for us and leave the rest.

His advice saved my life. It wasn't easy by any means. I had to call him almost daily to be reminded that it was okay not to pray. Then I would feel safe again…at least until the next time I felt I had done something wrong or my brain had been invaded by an image of my mother being sexually assaulted or I felt the familiar piercing in my chest.

But I also remember being flooded with relief after an entire day passed without prayer, and then an entire week, and the sky hadn't fallen and my mother hadn't died and I hadn't spontaneously combusted. It was very similar to how I felt after I gave up alcohol—I couldn't believe I was still functioning without it.

Before long, I came to realize that the prayer was perpetuating the anxiety, keeping me stuck in it. Like a load of T-shirts churning in a washing machine, or like a capsized kayak caught in what they call a "hole," where the boater becomes submerged in whitewater that has mysteriously reversed direction at the bottom of a fall. I was submerging myself in the shame and fear and tumbling around in it, obsessing about the sin I had committed—what it looked like, how it felt, its repercussions—and which punishment God might see fit to inflict. I was mistaken to believe that the prayer, if I could just say it correctly or repeat it enough times, would eventually ease my shame. Praying only made it more potent.

Eventually I realized that I wasn't praying to God. I was *playing* God. I was repeating prayers and rituals to get God to behave how I *wanted* him to: benevolently and generously. Ironically, it turned out that discontinuing prayer was the biggest leap of faith I could take. When I got anxious and obsessive, or when I felt ashamed and guilty, I forced myself to sit through the discomfort until it finally dissipated. I had to trust that everything would work out the way it was supposed to. And if bad things did happen, which of course they eventually would, I had to trust that I would be prepared to handle them.

The truth is, I can't think of a time in my adult life when what I most feared actually came to pass. Other difficult things happened, things I wouldn't necessarily have chosen. But I always had the strength and determination to walk through those difficult times. I put one foot in front of the other and tried my best to do the next right thing.

When it came to the idea of God, I didn't know what I believed. I still don't. The difference is that doubting the existence of God no longer feels like a bad thought that I have to avoid for fear of punishment. What I believed in then, and still believe in now, is grace and mercy. The kind my late grandmother gave me when she asked, "Do you think the reason you're so depressed is because you're gay?" When I nodded, she said, "Oh honey, you were born that way. Everybody knows that."

In that moment, I could feel my grandmother telling me that I could be different and still be good. I could be a unique individual and still be loved. I could still have a purpose. It's a gift she gave me. A gift I would come to believe that all people need, in one way or another. Everyone needs to feel that, on some level, they are good. That their life has meaning. That they are worthy of grace. Some turn to religion to be assured of their goodness, while others join political movements. In these spaces, they are guaranteed this goodness and this grace, so long as they follow the rules.

Eventually, though, every individual is faced with the challenge of determining his own values. Not everyone is strong enough to do that. Thinking for oneself runs many risks, including the risk of being wrong. Of making mistakes. Of erring.

The world is a condemning and punishing place. If a judge can't exact a debt from a sinner, he'll settle for that sinner to feel a sufficient amount of shame. And religious faith need not be involved for shame to manifest. Only dogma.

CHAPTER 5

Election Day 2012—a bright, blisteringly cold November day in Maryland. President Barack Obama and Vice President Joe Biden were running for reelection against Massachusetts's former governor Mitt Romney and his running mate, Wisconsin congressman Paul Ryan. The previous May, during an ABC News interview, Obama had publicly stated for the first time that he no longer opposed same-sex marriage. In three states—Maine, Maryland, and Washington—the question of whether gay couples should be allowed to legally marry was on the ballot.

I stood outside Elkridge Elementary School, somewhere between Baltimore and Washington, DC, holding a large blue sign that read VOTE YES ON QUESTION 6, which would settle the matter in Maryland. Some fifteen yards away stood my opponent, a black man alternately shouting VOTE NO! and IN JESUS'S NAME! I began the morning getting sick in the Elkridge Elementary School bathroom.

I was twenty-eight years old. If you'd asked me a year earlier what I thought about same-sex marriage, I would have responded that I couldn't care less. Sure, I wanted gay marriage to be legal for equality's sake, but I had no intention of tying the knot myself. Deep down, I didn't believe gay men were capable of truly falling in love, especially the kind that would make them want to enter a lifelong, legal commitment.

But on a summer night in 2011, all that changed. I was at the Hippo, a gay bar in downtown Baltimore, when a man whose upper body resembled Mark Wahlberg's walked in. We made eye contact across the bar—once, then twice. The third time the man returned my gaze, I knew he was interested, so I approached him.

The man said his name was Drew. He'd come up to Baltimore from DC to celebrate a friend's birthday. We chatted and flirted for a few minutes, then exchanged phone numbers and parted ways.

A week later, Drew and I went on our first date in Alexandria, Virginia, about a mile from the US Patent and Trademark Office where he worked as a trademark lawyer.

And that, as they say, was that. I fell fast and hard. Two months in, I told him, "I think I want to marry you." His brown eyes lit up. "Me too," he said.

Suddenly I had skin in the game: Marriage equality meant something real to me. When, in February 2012, the Maryland state legislature passed a same-sex marriage bill, I began to wonder if God or the Universe might actually be on my side. To secure conservative support, however, the legislation came with a caveat. The law wouldn't go into effect until the first day of the following year, which meant that conservatives would have a chance to overturn it at the November ballot box via referendum. I volunteered with Marylanders for Marriage Equality, an offshoot of the LGBT rights organization Equality Maryland, to ensure that wouldn't happen.

By that time, I was very familiar with the religious argument against gay marriage. "God made Adam and Eve, not Adam and Steve," and all that jazz. But I had no clue about the arguments against gay marriage that came from *within* the gay population. For decades, and especially since the rise of the New Left in the late 1960s, there had been a war raging between gay and lesbian "assimilationists" and queer radical "separatists." The former just wanted to integrate into society and have the same opportunities and rights as their heterosexual peers—the right to work, the right to marry, the right to serve in the military. In the late

'50s and '60s, Frank Kameny—an astronomer who was fired by the US Army Map Service after it was revealed that he was gay—famously appealed, arguing that the government's discrimination based on sexuality violated his civil rights. In the late 1980s, gay writer and former *New Republic* editor Andrew Sullivan made a novel and compelling case for same-sex marriage that was grounded in conservative principles. Five years later, the gay (and devout Christian) cultural critic, Bruce Bawer, deftly argued in his 1994 book that homosexuals just wanted *A Place at the Table*.

The radicals wanted no part of it. "What we need to do is overturn the table," said lesbian activist Donna Minkowitz. "What we need to do is build a new table." The way the radicals saw it, there was no distinction between sexual orientation and politics. To be homosexual in Western society was to be oppressed in the same way every other minority was oppressed—by capitalism and white male patriarchy. Institutions like civil marriage propped up capitalism and its middle-class mores. Therefore, any reasonable gay person—that is, any *moral* gay person—will desire revolution. To "overturn the table" was to overturn Western bourgeois capitalism. To "build a new table" meant to build a socialist utopia.

Today, we know that the pragmatic approach won. After decades of brave campaigning and bipartisan compromise, gays can get married, serve proudly, have jobs, own homes, and raise families. Like black civil rights leaders who preached nonviolent protest and a politics of respectability before them, gay and lesbian activists shrewdly took the long view. "We don't want to exist on the margins of society," they insisted, "we want *to participate* in it." Gays, they said, just like black Americans, are a vital part of the fabric of this nation.

But the queer radicals, I'd soon learn, wouldn't take this defeat lying down. Instead, they would work overtime to mainstream the most nonsensical and regressive ideas about gender and sex, and rabidly campaign for laws and policies that irrevocably harmed women and gay people.

ON ELECTION DAY, my polling location was a busy one. Some passersby shouted their support for our campaign, while others stated they "most certainly would *not*" be voting to legalize same-sex marriage.

Around noon, a young gay man, perhaps nineteen or twenty, approached me. "I just want to thank you for what you're doing," he said. "It means a lot to me."

I appreciated his words, but mostly they made me sad. I was certain we weren't going to win. Those kinds of happy endings were reserved for good people, righteous people, *Godly* people.

I electioneered at the elementary school until about 1:00 p.m., then went to work. I was a stylist at a hair salon in Columbia, Maryland, and I was fully booked with clients that day. When I walked inside, I bumped into Donna, a coworker in her sixties who had recently told me on Facebook that I needed to find the Holy Spirit.

"Your cheeks are so flushed!" she said.

I told her I'd been outside all morning, campaigning for marriage equality. She smiled curtly and walked away.

That night, I drove to the Baltimore Soundstage, an entertainment venue near Baltimore's Inner Harbor. Marriage-equality campaigners had rented out the space and were gathering to watch the results. Governor Martin O'Malley was there, as were a few state senators and congresspeople. Around 11:00 p.m., all of the televisions flashed an image of Obama with a headline stating he had won reelection. The room burst into cheers.

An hour later, Maryland Delegate Maggie McIntosh took the stage to announce the final results of the marriage vote: 52 percent of Maryland voters had approved same-sex marriage at the ballot box. For the first time in US history, marriage rights had been extended to gay couples by popular vote.

I was stunned. We had won. Balloons rained from the ceiling as Sister Sledge's "We Are Family" blasted through the loudspeakers.

Driving home in the early morning hours, I was so elated, I thought my car might take flight. I was desperate to keep chasing that feeling—the feeling of hope and empowerment that came with fighting for social justice. I had a new calling, one that felt almost religious. Here was my chance to forge a path of righteousness.

By that time, I'd been a hairstylist for nearly a decade. As the cold, November air rushed through my car windows, I resolved to do something more with my life.

ONE DAY, A few weeks later, as I blew her hair dry, a client asked me what was next for gay rights. Ignoring the fact that marriage equality did yet not extend nationwide (that would occur in 2015, after the Supreme Court's landmark ruling in *Obergefell v. Hodges*) or that I could still be fired in many states for being gay, I held up my hands to form a *T*. "Transgender rights," I told her. This, gay rights organizations and liberal media told me, was the natural next step in the fight for equality. We—that is, LGBT people—were a coalition after all, or so I had been led to believe.

At the time, I knew only one transgender person, a transwoman maybe ten years my senior, whom I'd met through sober friends. I didn't know a lot about her besides that she had once been married to a woman and had children. I didn't know if she was still married or how her family had reacted to her transition. I was years away from understanding the many different motivations for a person to identify as trans.

As far as transgender activism was concerned, I knew little about what rights trans people wanted that they didn't have. But that hardly mattered. All I knew was that I cared about transgender people, just like I cared about all "marginalized communities." The idea that someone, somewhere—anywhere—might continue to be unfairly oppressed and marginalized by our white, male, conservative Christian society filled me with righteous indignation. And more importantly, I knew that I wanted to keep chasing the high I had felt on the night we won the marriage equality campaign. I had a virtuous new calling.

Since 2001, Maryland's nondiscrimination law had included "sexual orientation" as a protected class, barring discrimination against gay people in employment, housing, and public accommodations. In January 2013, legislation was introduced in Maryland to amend the state's nondiscrimination law to include "gender identity," circularly defined in the bill as "the gender-related identity" of a person, regardless of sex, that he or she consistently asserts is a "sincerely held" part of his or her "core identity." An email from Equality Maryland stated that the organization would be hosting a public rally for the bill in Annapolis later that month.

My understanding of the legislation at the time was that, if it passed, transgender Marylanders would now be legally protected from discrimination. What I didn't know, likely because it was forbidden for any self-described liberal or progressive to even contemplate, was that because "gender identity" was to be given the same legal weight as "sex," its inclusion in antidiscrimination legislation would render the latter basically meaningless. This would lead to a major conflict of rights between women and trans-identified males, severely compromising the protection of women's spaces—like bathrooms, locker rooms, rape shelters, and prisons. I was also unaware at the time that this elusive concept of "gender identity" was a central part of a burgeoning ideology that attempted to render *homosexuality itself* meaningless.

On the night of the rally, a snowstorm had just passed through. Shivering in the cold, the forty or so of us who showed up cheered in front of the capitol building while a few people (I can't remember who; perhaps some of the bill's many Democratic sponsors) made speeches. Afterward, we disbanded in small groups to visit senators in their offices. We were there to lobby.

I met with a Republican senator from a conservative district north of Baltimore City. I told him how much the legalization of gay marriage had changed my life—how I finally felt like a part of society, like I could hold my head up higher. "Passing this legislation might do something similar for transgender people," I said.

The senator listened attentively, then asked me, "But what if a guy demands to show up to work in a wig or in something really inappropriate? We should take away an employer's right to tell him he can't?"

I rather smugly told the senator that he was confusing transvestism with transgenderism. Then, as I began to explain, I realized that I didn't really know the difference either. "A transvestite is a man who likes to wear women's clothes every now and then, and a transgender woman is a woman born in a man's body," I said, flushing with embarrassment.

How, exactly, could one be born in the wrong body? Aren't our bodies *ourselves*?

Perhaps we were really talking about the soul—that a soul could be female, and that, through some karmic mix-up, a female soul could mistakenly enter a male fetus.

Or maybe it was the brain. One had the *brain* of a female and the *body* of a male.

Even then, I instinctively knew that both explanations were absurd. Although, as I spoke, I did briefly wonder what the difference was between the hypothetical transgender person I was describing and myself, since for my entire life I had always "felt" more like a girl.

But it didn't matter whether any of it made sense. All that mattered was that there were some people who knew themselves to be the opposite sex *on the inside*, and that it was our job to validate them in their identities. Just like I was "born this way," so were they.

Well, rather, they were "born in the wrong body." But close enough.

Besides, only a terrible person would vote against legislation that protected a marginalized group from discrimination.

The senator smiled and nodded noncommittally, as senators do.

The bill failed to pass that year, but my passion for social justice grew.

On October 25, 2014, when I was thirty-one, Drew and I got married at the Belvedere Hotel in downtown Baltimore, two blocks from where we had met. Jane Wiedlin, the guitarist from the 1980s girl group the Go-Go's, officiated. We honeymooned in London and Paris.

Two months later, over Christmas Eve dinner, Drew and I spoke about our future. I found myself admitting how unfulfilled I felt in my hairstyling career. It was a wonderful creative outlet, and it had allowed me to interact and build relationships with people from all walks of life. It had provided a steady income for the first ten years of my sobriety. But now I thought it might be time for me to go back to college, to pick up where I left off all those years ago, when my addiction had derailed my academic studies. My desire for an education had never ceased, and my foray into activism, however brief, had given me a new perspective, a new calling. There was still so much I wanted to learn and know, so that I might be able to form strong opinions of my own, confident in my own perspective. I realized it might sound grandiose, I told him, but I also wanted to help create a world in which gender-nonconforming young people, like the girly little boy I once was, aren't shamed and bullied and pressured to conform, but rather accepted as valid minorities of their own sex. "I always wanted to be a writer," I said. "Maybe, if I pursue a career in that field and write about gay issues, I could make a real difference."

If my husband had balked or expressed an iota of doubt that I could do it, I might have given up on the idea there. But instead he said, "If that's what you want, you need to go for it." He added that the best place for a career like the one I imagined was in New York, a city we both loved. We finished dinner and drove home, and I started planning.

I searched online for college programs for "nontraditional" and "returning" students. There were numerous online options, but I was determined to study in person. That's when Columbia University's School of General Studies showed up in my Google search results.

The School of General Studies—or GS, as it's known on Columbia's campus—is one of Columbia's three undergraduate schools, along with Columbia College (CC) and the Fu Foundation School of Engineering and Applied Science (SEAS). A fourth, Columbia-affiliated undergraduate school is Barnard, a women's college located across Broadway from Columbia's Morningside Heights campus on Manhattan's Upper West Side.

Each school has its own requirements for degree fulfillment, but classes, I learned, are commonly filled with students from all four schools. That is, if I got into GS, I would be getting the same caliber of education as everyone else at the Ivy League university. This set it apart from other "continuing education" schools, where nontraditional students took classes separately from other undergraduates—classes often led by adjunct professors. The School of General Studies was exactly the program I was looking for.

Equally exciting was the thought of studying at a university that had such an impressive legacy of social justice activism. For years, the black-and-white images of the 1968 student-led protests at Columbia that circulated in popular film and media (often scored with John Lennon's "Imagine" or a Jimi Hendrix riff) and even school history textbooks had transfixed me. I was hazy on the details—I knew they had been protesting the Vietnam War and racial injustice, though I was unaware of the Marxist undercurrent—but I absorbed the intended message: These kids were on the right side of history. They were good and righteous. I wanted to be one of them.

I told Drew that Columbia had a creative writing undergraduate major with a concentration in nonfiction writing. After graduation, I could attend their famed journalism school or MFA writing program.

After further discussion, we agreed it would be best if I attended a local community college for a year to get used to being a student again and to build up a good resume for my application. Even though I worked full time, I could take classes in the morning or at night.

In January 2015, I enrolled in an online US History course and an in-person English course at nearby Howard Community College.

I loved being in school. During my first English class, my teacher, a black poet, told the class, "You are here to become the person you were meant to be." I felt like she was speaking directly to me.

In my history course, I inhaled the assigned text, practically cover to cover. I had excelled in high school, but my heavy drug use and preoccupation with morality prevented me from retaining most of what I had learned. Now, finally able to connect the dots between, say, President Truman's post-WWII foreign policy—in particular his recognition of the state of Israel and his pledge to defend it against hostile Arab forces—and today's ongoing conflicts in the Middle East, I felt empowered to form my own opinions. The world around me took on deeper layers of meaning. "Excellent idea for you!" my professor wrote in the margins of one my homework assignments, in which I mentioned my plan to attend Columbia. A subsequent course in US Government would fill in many of the remaining blanks in my political knowledge base. And then came the creative writing course in the fall, where I got to flex my muscles in various genres, including fiction and poetry. My professor's high praise of my work was a significant confidence booster, as was the college literary magazine's publication of one of my short stories.

A month or so into my first semester, Drew and I travelled to Manhattan with some friends to see a Björk concert at City Center theater. One evening, we split off from the group to visit Columbia.

We entered the campus through the wrought iron gates at 116th Street and Broadway. Trees wrapped in white lights lined College Walk, an asphalt and red-brick path that divides the northern section of the Morningside Heights campus from the southern third. Students in groups of twos and threes, some wearing sweatshirts bearing Columbia's insignia, passed by. I could barely contain my envy.

Eighty yards in, just past the line of trees, lay the campus's main quad—a huge open space, so different from any place I'd ever visited in Manhattan. It felt like we could have been anywhere. To our left, atop two flights of steps and facing south, was Low Library—now the home of the university's administrative offices—with its massive marble columns and limestone dome. In front of Low, a female figure in classical dress called Alma Mater sat regally on a bronze throne.

To our right, beyond the South Field, was Butler Library. It looked like the Parthenon. Etched in its frieze, above a long row of Ionic columns, were the names of great thinkers: Homer, Herodotus, Sophocles, Plato, Demosthenes, Cicero, Vergil. Facing north, the library's frosted-glass windows glowed with light, beckoning me inside.

"Come on," Drew said, nudging me along.

Together we walked north, ascended a flight of stone steps, and crossed another red-brick walkway to Lewisohn Hall, the home of the School of General Studies.

On the sixth floor, a friendly admissions officer named Dirk greeted us and led us back to his office. I told him about my plan to apply to Columbia the following year, after I'd taken some classes at community college. Dirk confirmed I was on the right track. He even told me that a few of my credits from the University of Maryland, way back in 2001, would likely transfer to Columbia.

On the subway back to our hotel, I flipped through the brochure Dirk had given me. Inside were testimonies of students that studied at GS. One of them was written by a former hairstylist. I showed it to Drew, who smiled. I started to feel like it was meant to be.

In June 2015, the Supreme Court reached its decision, which effectively struck down any remaining same-sex marriage bans in the US and legalized marriage equality nationwide. It was a grand finale to Obama's historic, eight-year presidency. The future looked impossibly bright.

Yet a dark cloud appeared on the horizon. That same month, Donald Trump announced his Republican campaign for the presidency. I was instantly terrified of what a Trump presidency might mean for gay and lesbian Americans, and for other minorities as well.

Just how invested was I in identity politics? To me, identity *was* politics. All that mattered were social issues. Not economic policy, not immigration policy, not foreign policy—just "social justice." This narrow political perspective gave me a sense of moral superiority over other people. In that respect it filled the place religion once held in my life.

"I don't vote only thinking about my bank account," I once said to a client after she criticized Obama's economic proposals.

How sanctimonious I was. Who knew what economic hardships this mother of young children was facing?

It never crossed my mind that there might be different approaches to effecting social change, or that perhaps some of the policies progressives had championed over the years had done more harm than good. In retrospect, I did harbor reservations about certain left-wing policies, but it was more important for me to conform and be accepted. As I had defeminized myself, I also eradicated any shades of conservatism, because I wanted to be "good."

All I knew at the time was that Democrats "cared about people," and Republicans didn't. I was always going to vote for candidates who claimed to support "LGBT rights" and "a woman's right to choose" while denouncing those who failed to do so. I was always going to support the party that nominated and elected racial minorities, and against the one that was predominantly white. I saw historically oppressed minorities as "better" and "wiser" and more virtuous—as the ones to lead the way into the future. I railed against black and gay people who irrationally voted Republican "against their own interests." I thought the term "black conservative" was an oxymoron. I had never even heard of Thomas Sowell, Glenn Loury, John McWhorter, and Shelby Steele—black intellectuals I would later come to admire.

In retrospect it's clear that my view of politics was solipsistic. I wanted a big and powerful government so long as that government intervened properly on my behalf. What mattered were *my* rights and the rights of people who thought the same way. Anyone who disagreed was simply unworthy of my respect.

At the end of 2015, I had completed six courses at Howard Community College and earned a 4.0 GPA. In January 2016, I uploaded my transcripts, my admissions essay, and my letters of recommendation to Columbia's application portal. A month later, I took the train to New York to take Columbia's admissions exam for General Studies applicants. That April, I received my acceptance letter.

Drew worked from home, so the move to New York would be a fairly easy transition. But we decided to defer my admission for a semester, so that we could save some more money before moving to one of the most expensive cities in the country. We would move in November 2016, and my first semester would begin the following January.

The excitement I felt about our new adventure was cut short that June, when an Afghan-American man named Omar Mateen shot up a gay nightclub, murdering forty-nine people. During the shooting, Mateen identified himself as a *mujahid* (one who engages in Islamic jihad) and pledged allegiance to ISIS leader Abu Bakr al-Baghdadi. While it was never confirmed that Mateen's hatred of gay people influenced his decision to choose Pulse as the setting of his massacre, it was a sobering reminder that religiously motivated homophobia was still deeply entrenched in our society, despite the progress we had made in recent years. More than that, it was a reminder of the continuing danger of radical Islamism in America, fifteen years after 9/11. At the time, Mateen's attack on Orlando's Pulse nightclub was the deadliest shooting in modern US history.

The shooting wasn't the only news headline that was causing me distress. Weeks earlier, Donald Trump had defied all odds by securing the Republican nomination for president. By the first week of July, I was smoking cigarettes again. I had quit the habit a few times in my early twenties and finally managed to give it up for good—or so I thought—in 2011. But as the election loomed, my nerves got the best of me. I was confident that Hillary Clinton would be our next president, but I couldn't shake the feeling that something was about to go terribly wrong. It was either take up smoking or gnaw off my right hand.

At work, I would sneak out the back door on my lunch break and hide behind a dumpster, wearing rubber gloves—the kind I used to apply hair color—so my clients wouldn't smell the tobacco on my hands.

Before I was halfway through every cigarette, I was already thinking about the next one. If it was 10:00 p.m. and I only had two left, I'd panic that I might want a third before bed.

Everywhere I went I was followed by a filthy cloud—kind of like the Peanuts character Pigpen, only mine was a mixture of cigarette smoke and shame.

Meanwhile the universe was torturing me, screaming at me to quit with the constant airing of the PSA starring the lady in the hospital bed with the tracheotomy, or the Spiriva commercial where the elephant sits on the chest of the old man with COPD.

But every time the 7-Eleven cashier handed me a fresh pack of Marlboro Lights, it felt like he was throwing me a life preserver.

Then, on a Friday in early October, as I maniacally scrolled through Twitter and chain-smoked, there finally came a moment in which I felt I could breathe for the first time in months. The *Washington Post* published its story about the infamous Access Hollywood tape, and I thought, *Surely this has to be it. Surely this recording of the Republican nominee for president boasting about grabbing women's genitals without their consent would be the last of countless nails in the coffin for the Trump campaign.*

I could feel the lactic acid draining from my shoulders and lower back while I watched the tape on a loop, utterly horrified and yet incapable of removing the grin splayed across my face. Our national nightmare was going to end.

Alas, I was wrong. The tape turned out to be nothing but a blip—a serious one, but still a blip—and with each passing day, Trump's path to the White House looked clearer.

I was up to a pack and a half a day.

THE MORNING AFTER the election, as I dressed for work, I was despondent. That the greatest strides in the history of the gay rights movement had coincided with my marriage to Drew and my newfound belief that I, a gay man, had just as much of a shot at a normal and happy life as any straight American, felt divinely ordained. I had begun to walk taller, fear antigay bigotry less, and, more often than not, see my glass as half full. I might've even started to believe that God was on my side.

Now I feared all of that could be taken away. Trump, to me, was a crass, narcissistic con man who brought out the absolute worst in people. Moreover, he had chosen as his vice president a virulently antigay politician—former Indiana governor Mike Pence. "It's our turn now, perverts," a Trump supporter had commented on a gay friend's Facebook post. We were in major trouble.

My first client that morning was a woman named Lynn. A staunch supporter of Trump, she hated both Obama and the Clintons. "Black lives matter?" she often said. "No, *all* lives matter."

As I applied her foil highlights, she talked about her upcoming trip to Italy, as if the world hadn't just ended the night before. Finally, she asked the question I had been dreading: "How about that election?"

My hands shook. I muttered, "Well, it turns out this country is a lot more racist than I thought it was." She promptly changed the subject.

The only thing that got me through that day, and the following month, was the knowledge that I would soon be leaving my benighted hometown, where Trump-supporting maniacs walked among us like flesh-eating zombies, and heading off to a radically progressive New York City college campus.

The week after the election, I was relieved to receive an email from the Columbia administration, sent out to all students and affiliates, that openly mourned the outcome. In this scary new world of MAGA rallies and evangelical prayer circles in the Oval Office, the university would be my safe space. There, I would #RESIST with other likeminded, peace-loving, righteously angry progressives.

In retrospect, I'm lucky I didn't know what awaited me. That soon I would be stumbling through the looking glass, where up would be down and left would be right, sex a meaningless fiction and gender a religion. That instead of liberalism, progressive students would be rallying for Marxism, Maoism, and even Islamic jihadism. That the group I had longed to unite with, dedicated to social justice and equality, would be more conformist and intolerant than the fundamentalist religious leaders of my childhood...and even crueler than my middle school bullies.

CHAPTER 6

Drew and I rented a two-bedroom apartment in Washington Heights, a multiethnic immigrant neighborhood a short subway ride from Columbia's campus. It was a new world—one I was immediately hungry to explore. Every day, I took off on foot, familiarizing myself with my new neighborhood, the New York City subway system, and eventually the entire island of Manhattan. What thrilled me, perhaps more than anything else, was the anonymity that the city offered me. I had spent the first three decades of my life in the same general area of Maryland. I rarely left the house without running into someone I knew. Here, in New York, I could begin again. I could be anyone.

In late November, I visited campus to meet with my academic advisor, Heather, a thirty-something English scholar, to discuss my plan of study.

"Things have been a little crazy lately," Heather said, obviously referring to the fallout from the election. Pretty and petite, her thick, blond hair formed a messy bun atop her head. Through the window, I could see a group of students protesting on the quad near Alma Mater, though I couldn't make out the slogans on their signs.

"I can imagine," I said. "Truth be told, I don't think I've been handling it all that well." In the weeks that had passed since the election, I told Heather, I had deactivated my social media accounts and avoided the news altogether. It was all too depressing.

"You're not alone," she said, smiling sympathetically. Then she turned to her computer to pull up my student account.

For nearly a hundred years, Columbia has prided itself on its Core Curriculum, which transcends disciplines by requiring all students—regardless of their majors—to take courses in history, philosophy, literature, science, and the arts. There was one small loophole, Heather informed me: Since General Studies students often come to Columbia with transfer credits, courses we've completed at other institutions can satisfy some of the requirements.

Nonetheless I told her that I wanted to take advantage of every learning opportunity the school had to offer. I was particularly intrigued by core classes like Masterpieces of Western Literature and Philosophy as well as Introduction to Contemporary Civilization, full-year surveys in which students read everything from Homer to Descartes to Virginia Woolf.

Heather's response surprised me. "Those classes are pretty tedious," she said, which I took to mean that they were basically a waste of time and that there was much more to learn at Columbia besides the Western canon.

Now I wonder if perhaps she was trying to protect me. For decades, a heated debate about the canon had been raging in the academy, and humanities and social sciences classrooms were the main battlefields. On one side were those who said that a knowledge of Western thought and philosophy was crucial to understanding the modern world and the myriad reasons why liberalism had prevailed over other political doctrines. The other side insisted that the canon was outdated and irrelevant; and worse, that by privileging "dead white men," universities were complicit in upholding white supremacy, patriarchy, and capitalism—ills supposedly specific to the West.

The latter view, it would turn out, was the "correct" one to espouse on campus. For the next three and a half years, I would be reminded again and again by various professors and classmates that there was very little to celebrate about the West. That in fact, Western colonialism had been the scourge of the earth for centuries, and nothing but violence and oppression had resulted from it. I'd hear and read about "decolonization"—decolonization of land, decolonization of education, decolonization of *thought*—more than any other word until I graduated.

Further, as a white man, I gathered I was somehow morally responsible for these past ills. Nor was being a member of a persecuted minority of any benefit to me in this regard. Gay or straight, I was just as guilty of white male supremacist privilege as the likes of Cecil Rhodes, a British colonist of southern Africa, or Teddy Roosevelt, the imperialist US president. I must therefore spend the rest of my life (or at least the rest of my time at Columbia) atoning for the sin of my immutable identity.

This cynical attitude, I would learn, was the fruit of something called Critical Theory (e.g., queer, postcolonial, and critical race theories), which as opposed to traditional theory, privileges subjectivity over objectivity and treats academia not as a locus of knowledge production but as a means to an end—the means being the deconstruction of existing knowledge, which had been conceived by the powerful few only to oppress the many. The goal of all this "deconstruction"? To destroy capitalism and cripple the West.

Some of this I would agree with, in an unexamined sort of way, and some of it would make me uncomfortable. But for a long time, I would feel like I didn't know enough to outright disagree. Besides, my need for acceptance in the group would lead me to suppress my misgivings and do my best to fit in—or at least not stand out as a dissenter.

For the time being, however, I decided to heed Heather's advice and enrolled in a creative writing workshop, which would satisfy part of my creative writing major; Beginner's Spanish, as part of the Core's language requirement; and University Writing, a required course that instructs students on how to write Ivy League–caliber essays. Each UW class has a different focus, like Climate Humanities, Race and Ethnicity, and Gender and Sexuality. The Gender section was already filled, so I chose Human Rights.

For my fourth course, one that would satisfy part of the Global Core requirement, I chose Contemporary Islamic Civilization. I told Heather that I wanted to learn as much about the Muslim world as I could, now that we had a president-elect who talked about banning Muslims from entering the country. She enthusiastically approved.

In early January 2017, I attended the new-student orientation for the School of General Studies. There I met students from all over the world, each one as interesting as the last. There were professional ballerinas, fashion models, US coastguardsmen, ex–Hari Krishna monks, yoga instructors, and flight attendants.

In the evening, a few of us walked off-campus to grab a bite at Tom's, a local landmark known in popular culture as the *Seinfeld* diner. I listened attentively while the others talked about the various signs and posters hung around campus, promoting the anti–Israel Boycott, Divestment, and Sanctions movement, known as BDS. Someone mentioned some past controversies at Columbia, when one or more professors had been accused of antisemitic behavior in class, though I didn't quite catch the specifics.

The BDS movement was represented on campus by Columbia University Apartheid Divest, a coalition of the student groups Students for Justice in Palestine and Jewish Voice for Peace. These and other activist student groups—of which, I was soon to discover, there existed a bewildering array—campaigned for the university to boycott and divest from Israeli businesses or foreign ones that dealt with Israel, on the supposedly self-evident grounds that Israel is an illegitimate nation of settler-colonialists guilty of racial apartheid.

"I mean, obviously," a female student said, nibbling on a French fry, "the progressive position at Columbia is to be pro-Palestine and basically, like, anti-Israel."

I hid my confusion by nodding along. As far as I knew, the Democratic Party had consistently made support of the state of Israel a big part of its platform. Clearly for my new colleagues this kind of thinking was out-of-date—insufficiently radical. I quickly realized that if I wanted to be welcomed into the progressive fold on campus, I had a lot of catching up to do. Voting Democrat wouldn't be nearly enough.

After dinner, I strolled alone around campus, learning its topography. As I walked, grainy images of the 1968 protests scrolled through my mind like a slideshow.

At the south end, neighboring Butler Library, was John Jay Hall, named for the first Chief Justice of the US Supreme Court, who in 1764 graduated from Columbia, then known as King's College. Flanking the vast South Field were more dormitories as well as Hamilton Hall—named for yet another Founding Father and King's College alumnus—which was occupied in April 1968 by student protesters for a week; and Pulitzer Hall, home of the university's famed journalism school.

Crossing Campus Walk, I climbed a flight of stairs into the small courtyard outside of Kent Hall, which houses the creative writing department, and Philosophy Hall. Further north was St. Paul's Chapel, a lovely little gothic church endowed by the Rockefellers. Then there was Avery Hall, the site of one of Columbia's most idyllic libraries; Schermerhorn, Mudd, and Uris halls; and finally Pupin Hall, where physicists during World War II had aided the Manhattan Project. Outside Pupin, the smell of chlorine permeated the air. Beneath my feet was the university's underground fitness center and swimming pool.

I returned south, walking past Havemeyer Hall and the Mathematics Building, and stopped in front of Earl Hall. It was there, at Earl, that the Student Homophile League, the first gay student organization in the US, had been founded in 1966.

I sat down on the building's stairs, unable to believe my luck. My previous tenure at college had ended with a cocaine-induced psychotic break. Now here I was, thirty-three years old, clean and sober, married to the man I loved, and a student at one of the world's most esteemed academic institutions and one of the birthplaces of gay activism.

After all this time, I had finally made it.

Part 2

DOUBTER

CHAPTER 7

The first day of the semester, January 17, 2017, fell on a Tuesday. That meant Spanish class at 11:40 a.m. in the International Affairs Building, located just across Amsterdam Avenue from the main campus. With barely a minute to spare, I finally found the classroom tucked away in the northeast corner of the building's labyrinthine basement.

There were about twenty students in the class. As expected, most of them were traditionally-aged college students, save for one black man with long dreads who wore a thick, beaded necklace and a colorful dashiki. Our professor, Francisco Meizoso, who instructed us to call him Fran, said that he would be teaching the entire class *en español.* I counted myself lucky that I had taken two semesters of Spanish at Howard Community College—the first as a student, the second as Professor Bauer's teaching assistant.

A very long seventy-five minutes later, I exited the classroom at the same time as the man in the dashiki.

"GS?" he asked when we made eye contact. Instead of a backpack, he wheeled a small suitcase behind him.

I smiled. "Yep, how'd you know?"

"Lucky guess."

The man, whose name was Shaun, told me he was majoring in English. It was his third semester at Columbia. He appeared to be older than me, perhaps in his mid-forties. He said that he planned to attend Columbia Law School after graduation from GS.

"What's your major?" Shaun asked.

"Creative writing."

"Oh wow, so cool!"

Shaun lived in Brooklyn, but on weekdays he'd typically spend all day on campus. "We should grab food sometime," he said. "And maybe you can help me in this class. That dude spoke fast!"

I laughed. "For sure," I said.

We exited the International Affairs Building on Amsterdam Avenue. "See you Thursday," Shaun said. He crossed Amsterdam, wheeling his suitcase behind him.

THAT NIGHT, DREW and I had dinner at 181 Cabrini, a neighborhood bistro where we would quickly become regulars. Over nachos and burgers, I talked excitedly about my first day.

Hours later, as a *Friends* rerun played in our living room, I opened my MacBook to review my schedule. The following day, I would have University Writing in the morning with Rebecca Wisor and Contemporary Islamic Civilization in the afternoon. An online search revealed little about Professor Wisor other than that she had been an English professor at West Point Military Academy and had written her doctoral dissertation at Rutgers on Virginia Woolf.

Contemporary Islamic Civilization would be taught by Hamid Dabashi. His Google search produced countless web results and images. In the first photo that came up, Dabashi wore a collared shirt, a dark blue jacket, and a thick silver beard. He tilted his head and squinted at the camera through his spectacles, as if scrutinizing the photographer's very soul. I was instantly intimidated.

An Iranian born in 1951, Dabashi had received his college education in Tehran before earning a dual PhD in Sociology of Culture and Islamic Studies from the University of Pennsylvania in 1984. The author of more than two dozen books, including *Islamic Liberation Theology: Resisting the Empire* and *Shi'ism: A Religion of Protest*, he had cofounded Columbia's Institute for Comparative Literature and Society and its Center for Palestine Studies (CPS). Launched in 2010 and lavishly funded through Columbia's Middle East Institute, CPS was created to honor the legacy of the late Edward Said, the Palestinian-American professor and activist who is widely considered to be the godfather of postcolonial studies, which analyzes colonialism and its consequences through a quasi-Marxist lens. It was Said and his acolytes who turned Columbia into the nerve center of Palestinian activism it is today. Rashid Khalidi, a familiar media figure who once worked as the director of the PLO's press agency and has framed terrorist acts against Israeli civilians as justified "resistance," currently holds Columbia's Edward Said faculty chair.

Dabashi, it turned out, had been the subject of *Columbia Unbecoming*, a 2004 documentary that sought to expose alleged intimidation and harassment of Jewish students by professors in the Middle East and Asian Languages and Cultures department. Produced by The David Project, a pro-Israel campus group, the film also profiled professors George Saliba and Joseph Massad. Saliba, a historian of Arabic and Islamic science who earned his first M.A. in Beirut and his second at UC Berkeley, had been teaching at Columbia since 1978. Massad, born in Jordan and of Palestinian descent, received his doctorate in political science from Columbia in 1998 and began teaching at the university a year later.

Students interviewed in the film said Massad had once demanded that an Israeli student confess how many Palestinians he had killed in the IDF, while Saliba allegedly told a Jewish student that she personally had no claim to the land of Israel because she had green eyes and was therefore "not a Semite." In a subsequent grievance report, Barnard student Deena Shanker testified that after she pointed out in a classroom debate that the IDF warns Palestinians before bombing certain areas, enabling innocent civilians to escape, Massad yelled, "If you're going to deny the atrocities being committed against the Palestinian people then you can get out of my classroom!"

In the end, *Columbia Unbecoming* would do little to calm the simmering tension between Jews and Palestinian activists on campus, which would reach a full boil two decades later. Nor would the film dissuade Columbia professors from involving themselves in the conflict. After October 7, faculty members would not only defend Hamas's barbarism, but they would also participate in the anti-Israel protests that erupted on campuses around the country.

I was surprised to learn that, according to the *New York Times*, in 2007 the Alavi Foundation, a nonprofit linked to the Iranian regime, had paid Columbia $100,000 only months before the university invited Iran's former president, Mahmoud Ahmadinejad, to speak at its World Leaders Forum.[1] I seem to have missed this episode entirely, but at the time it was hugely controversial, and many students were outraged. Under Ahmadinejad, Iran was guilty of some of the world's most horrific human rights abuses, particularly against women and gay people, not to mention his financial support of the terrorist organization Hezbollah. *Columbia Magazine* reported that "photocopied images depicting hangings of gays and unchaste women in Iran" were posted in building windows around campus.

When Columbia's president Lee Bollinger introduced Ahmadinejad to the audience, he listed the Iranian president's numerous misdeeds and said, "Mr. President, you exhibit all the signs of a petty and cruel dictator.... I feel all the weight of the modern civilized world yearning to express the revulsion at what you stand for."

---

1 The Alavi Foundation, which has poured millions of dollars into American universities for Middle East and Persian studies programs and owns several US properties that house mosques, has been the subject of federal investigations for decades. In June 2017, a New York jury ruled that the foundation had violated US sanctions law by funneling millions to Iran and therefore must forfeit its thirty-six-story Fifth Avenue building as well as other real estate and funds. It was the largest terrorism-related civil forfeiture in US history. Later, an appellate judge overturned the action on procedural grounds. According to a report from George Washington University's program on extremism, the legal battle is still ongoing.

Reading Bollinger's words, I felt proud of Columbia's president—even more so after I watched Ahmadinejad's speech and the question-and-answer portion that followed on YouTube. To a question about Iran's practice of executing gay men, Ahmadinejad responded, "In Iran, we don't have homosexuals like in your country."

At the time, Ahmadinejad's response rightfully drew boos from the crowd. But if this were to occur today, an audience of Columbia students, now properly indoctrinated in queer and postcolonial theories, might just nod along. In a very strange way, these theories, I would learn, actually agree with Ahmadinejad.

Dabashi felt quite differently than Bollinger. He wrote in *Al-Ahram* that Bollinger's principled and passionate affirmation of Western liberal values exemplified "the most ridiculous clichés of the neocon propaganda machinery" and "the missionary position of a white racist supremacist carrying the heavy burden of civilizing the world."

Two hours later, I finally closed my MacBook. As I got ready for bed, I felt uneasy. In my mind, the archetype of the antisemite was the tattooed white skinhead. Throughout the 2016 campaign, I gaped in horror at the endless headlines about the Trump campaign's white-supremacist dog whistles, its courting of neo-Nazis, and its blatant broadcasting of antisemitic tropes about nefarious Jews controlling the world. I knew that conflicts between Jews and Muslims were as old as the Islamic religion itself, and that tensions in the Middle East were perpetually high. But I had always assumed that, in the US at least, white supremacy was the far greater threat to Jews than radical Islam and its sympathizers on the left.

Trump, I thought, was a xenophobe and an antisemite, and in response, I was appropriately outraged. But in the conflict between Muslims and Jews on campus—or more specifically, between those who were anti-Israel and pro-Israel—which side of history was the "right" side to be on? If I hoped to keep my leftist bona fides—and I intended to—where would I be required to come down on this issue?

The next morning, I arrived on campus with plenty of time to spare before my 10:00 a.m. class. I grabbed a latte from Joe's, a popular coffee shop sandwiched between the J-School and an undergraduate dorm, and made my way to the Philosophy Building, where University Writing: Readings in Human Rights would be held twice a week.

The twelve-person class consisted entirely of GS students, some of whom I recognized from orientation. We sat around a large rectangular table in a small classroom, looking over the syllabus. Among that semester's readings would be Michelle Alexander's *The New Jim Crow*, about the mass incarceration of black Americans; Edward Said's "Identity, Authority, and Freedom;" and "Teaching Trayvon: Race, Media, and the Politics of Spectacle," in which UCLA professor and *Algorithms of Oppression* author Safiya Umoja Noble writes about critical race theory's contribution to the study of "protecting white property, including whiteness itself as property."

Professor Wisor was no-nonsense but friendly. She explained that we would be expected to complete four pieces of writing, known for some reason as "progressions." P1 would be an argumentative essay. For P2, we would need to put two writers in conversation with each other. P3 would be a 3,000-word research paper, and for P4, we would distill that paper into an 800-word op-ed. The assigned readings would serve as examples of these essay forms. The point of the class, she said, which was required of all Columbia undergraduates, was to equip us with the skills to write essays worthy of both scholarly and popular publication.

I suspected, judging by most of the class readings as well as the focus of the various other UW sections, that it would also be a moral education in the proper way to think about these complex issues. But this didn't worry me; I was certain that I thought the right way about them already.

I would soon find out that I did not.

CIS WHITE GAY

Contemporary Islamic Civilization was held in the International Affairs Building, in a large lecture hall on the main floor. I chose an aisle seat in the seventh row and took out a pen and a blank notebook. There were about eighty students in the class, all from various years and schools. While we waited for Professor Dabashi, a few students spoke quietly to each other, but most scrolled through their phones.

At 2:40 p.m. on the dot, Dabashi entered and took his place at the podium. He was shorter and slightly rounder than I had imagined. His beard, whiter than the picture I'd seen online, shimmered in the fluorescent spotlights that hung overhead.

"Hello," he said.

I uncapped my pen.

"Before we begin, I would like to honor the Lenape people, the indigenous tribe that held this land before Europeans colonized it."

I was bearing witness to my first land acknowledgement, which, similar to a prayer that a pastor recites at the beginning of a sermon, had become a ritual for leftists to perform at the beginning of lectures, rallies, and even casual business meetings. It was a new shorthand, a way for a speaker to communicate his belief in decolonization and his dedication to the Marxist project of overturning capitalism.

For a few moments, the room was quiet. I wondered if perhaps I should bow my head and close my eyes. I glanced around me. The other students looked ahead, seemingly unfazed.

"In your spare time," Dabashi told the class, "I call on you to visit the plaque commemorating the Lenape." He said we could find it in front of John Jay Hall.

Lenape people—see monument on campus, I wrote.

I hadn't expected a sacred pilgrimage to a holy relic to be one of our first assignments.

For the next hour, Dabashi paced the front of the hall with his hands folded over his protruding belly. He spoke in nearly incomprehensible academic jargon—a habit, I would soon learn, that was common among academics whose scholarship is centered in critical theory.

"Islam," Dabashi said, "collapses upon any synthesis that it reaches, whereupon it becomes a thesis waiting for an antithesis, an antithesis expecting a thesis."

The task of the course would be "to make the foreign familiar by making the familiar foreign." He was doing a good job already.

"Dialogical heteroglossia is like a game of chess."

"Gender is an illusion."

My pen flew across the page.

"Gay people in what we call 'the West' can now get married," he said. "And, so what? Gay people shouldn't want to get married. That is not their political project."

Why was he telling us what gay people should or shouldn't want? I tensed, tempted for a moment to interject, or at least to ask him to elaborate. It was true that marriage might not be right for all gay people. But I would've been a lot better off growing up if I had known that gay people would have the same opportunities as straight people. Instead, I was given the impression that people like me were incapable of lasting love, or that the love we felt was inferior and wrong. This interjection, I now know, likely would have been seen by Dabashi and many upperclassmen who were present as shortsighted. As an oppressed minority, I should desire to destroy the system, not change it. I should be a revolutionary, not a reformer.

Referring to the course's title, Dabashi asked, "What even *is* civilization?" He said something about the millions of hungry and homeless people around the globe and the increasing threat of climate change. "If we can't define ourselves, how can we define a civilization?"

In his class, Dabashi told us, we would learn about the history of Islam. Yes. But we also would be challenging what the Western university—a "corporatized medieval institution"—had told us about Islam and, more importantly, about ourselves. It was clear that whatever positive ideas we might be clinging to about the West would be discredited, right here, in this lecture hall.

Along with Karen Armstrong's *Islam: A Short History* and *The Autobiography of Malcolm X*, we would read plenty of Dabashi's own work as well as that of Joseph Massad and other Columbia faculty, like Middle Eastern Studies Professor Timothy Mitchell and the feminist anthropologist Lila Abu-Lughod (also Mitchell's wife). Our grades would depend on attendance at Dabashi's lectures, participation in weekly discussion sessions with Dabashi's graduate teaching assistants, and two papers in which we engaged with the assigned texts.

For a considerable stretch, Dabashi spoke about his former colleague, Edward Said. His personal connection to Said was clearly a source of extreme pride for him.

Said was indeed a significant figure with a massive legacy at Columbia. An accomplished literary critic and classical pianist, the Egyptian-born Said graduated from Princeton and Harvard before joining Columbia's English and Comparative Literature department in 1963. He was also, until his death from leukemia in 2003, the most prominent US advocate for Palestine, writing numerous books, giving impassioned speeches, and building a global reputation as a hero of the anticolonial movement.

In his seminal work, *Orientalism*, published in 1978, Said claimed that Europeans, through cultural and academic knowledge production, had constructed an idea of "the Orient" as backward and barbaric in order to justify colonization as a "civilizing" project. Through this construction, "the West," in turn, crowned itself as the East's superior and benefactor.

Orientalism, I would eventually learn, was pivotal in undermining Western scholarship and knowledge, a central purpose of critical theory. Framing scholarship as a question of morality, in which the approach was to treat the West as an evil, oppressive empire and formerly colonized nations as its virtuous victims, led universities to hire scholars who refuted so-called Western constructs of knowledge—which, these scholars insisted, were developed by straight white men to maintain supremacy over women as well as racial and sexual minorities.

Said's *Orientalism*, Dabashi explained, was inspired by the work of the French philosopher, Michel Foucault—a name I would be hearing frequently during my time at Columbia. Foucault, who had authored some of the most widely read books in the academy including *Discipline and Punish* and the four-volume *History of Sexuality* is perhaps best known for his theories about knowledge and power. To Foucault, the control of "discourse"—the way we talk, write, and think about things—is how dominant groups (read: straight, white, male capitalists) maintain a monopoly on what society considers to be true. By controlling knowledge production, these groups maintain power by imposing their ideas upon the groups they dominate.

Foucault referred to this dynamic as "power/knowledge." Said saw Orientalism as an example of it. It was how "the West" justified imperial domination of "the Rest."

This concept was totally novel to me. Nonetheless, I didn't hesitate for even a moment to accept it as self-evidently true. And I don't think my classmates did either. Dabashi had delivered a persuasive sermon.

"'The Orient,'" Dabashi said, making scare quotes with his fingers, "is a discursive construct. It is the West's civilizational 'other'—a means to an end."

The concept of "the other" would come up again and again at Columbia, both as a noun and as a verb, not just in the curriculum but in everyday campus culture. If, say, a student athlete from Nebraska remarked on a cultural difference between himself and an engineering student from Pakistan, he might be accused of "othering" the Pakistani. That is, he would be suspected of pointing out the difference in order to say, "I belong here, and you do not" or "my ways are superior to yours and, therefore, you should assimilate."

Of course, most of the time—more likely, always—the Nebraskan student intended no such thing. But "impact matters more than intent," we were told. Therefore it was the student's duty to always prioritize the feelings of those around him before he spoke instead of "centering" his own. After all, with "white privilege" comes great responsibility. In the meantime, while the Nebraskan was busy "doing the work to deconstruct his privilege," he would be known as the "ignorant white guy who 'others' black and brown people" until he had effectively proven otherwise.

Today, Foucault's theories about power and discourse are applied to nearly all academic disciplines in universities across the country. Critical theorists, who refer to him as "the godfather of queer theory," consider his work to be a key ingredient in the antidote to Western colonization.

Foucault was an extremely persuasive and intelligent man—maybe even a genius—but his preoccupation with power and his dogged insistence that the West had oppressed more than it liberated has bred a deep cynicism among his acolytes. Rather than create new knowledge and continue to build upon the revolutionary philosophy and science of the last three hundred years, their priority has been to interrogate existing knowledge and relitigate the past. It has been to pull apart, "deconstruct," "reimagine."

Worse than cynicism, this has bred nihilism. For the endless peeling of the onion, the constant dissection and reanalysis of long-established truths, ultimately ends with everything meaning nothing. It is because of this cynicism in the academy that, for the three and a half years I spent at Columbia, I was constantly reminded of an acid trip I took when I was eighteen. After swallowing tabs of LSD, my friends Cara and Stephanie and I sat for hours in Stephanie's basement, discussing the meaning of life and speculating about the building blocks of the universe. Round and round we went, sucking down cigarettes and bong hits, always ending up in the same place: Life is meaningless. There is no rhyme or reason to any of it. Everything humans have built is one giant cope.

Over time, as I learned more about Foucault, among the many things I would be surprised to discover was his support of the 1979 Iranian Revolution, which birthed today's Islamofascist regime. In a 1978 interview, Foucault stated that capitalism, born out of Enlightenment philosophy, was "the harshest, most savage, most selfish, most dishonest, oppressive society one could possibly imagine," for it expanded the power of the state (a "monstrosity," he called it). He said that "any Western intellectual with some integrity" should look to Iran, where they were in the process of building "a different way of thinking about social and political organization, one that takes nothing from Western philosophy [and] from its juridical and revolutionary foundations." Foucault believed the West should "question one by one the validity of all the principles that have been the source of oppression," meaning Enlightenment principles, especially where reason and science were concerned. Out with the old, in with a new "political imagination," which presupposes that what we've created is a disaster, an oppressive society that must be dismantled.

This praise of Iran's theocratic regime would be hard for me to square with Foucault's openly gay lifestyle. What state of mind do you have to be in to see the Iranian revolution as somehow good for women, gays, and religious minorities who are openly oppressed and murdered? How is this superior to their treatment under Western civilization? But Foucault's hatred of Western mores evidently outweighed those concerns. And he, like so many others, mistakenly believed that the Marxists leading the revolution would be allowed to participate in the reimagining of Iran after the ayatollah had returned to power.

Wrapping up his lecture, Dabashi admitted to having a few qualms about Said's work. In his opinion, the man was too soft on Enlightenment humanism. (He was, after all, an accomplished pianist and lover of classical music.) *Orientalism* was a revolutionary work, Dabashi said. But it didn't go far enough in exposing capitalist modernity for the "monstrosity" that it is.

After class, I stayed in my seat for a few moments, attempting to distill the notes I had taken into some kind of comprehensible narrative. I desperately needed a coffee.

My phone buzzed. It was a text from Molly, one of the GS students I'd met during orientation. She invited me to meet her at Butler, where she was studying in one of the library's many reading rooms.

Twenty minutes later, I walked through the double doors and scanned my ID at the security desk. Not for the first time, I felt a surge of pride as I imagined all of the distinguished Columbia alumni who had been here before me: young Barack Obama, heading to the stacks to retrieve a source for a political science paper; playwright Tony Kushner, in search of a quiet corner to write; or the Beat poets, Allen Ginsburg and Jack Kerouac, blowing off class.

I grabbed a coffee from Butler's Blue Java Café and passed through the adjoining lounge before returning to the lobby. Tacked to the walls were more BDS flyers as well as others advertising the myriad student groups on campus, which all seemed to be concerned with politics and activism as they pertained to identity: the Columbia Queer Alliance, Columbia Queer and Asian, Proud Colors (for "queer and trans students of color"), GendeRevolution, ChicanX Caucus, LatinX Heritage Month, Alianza ("pan-Latinx"), the African Students Organization, the Black Students Organization, the Caribbean Students Organization, Students for Justice in Palestine, and the seemingly innocuous Columbia Vegan Society. I didn't see the words "gay" or "lesbian" on any of the flyers, so I assumed (correctly) that these identities had been slotted under the "queer" umbrella.

Back in the lobby, at the foot of the stairs, two female students sat on a blanket they had spread across the floor. As I moved past them, I heard them explaining to a passerby that they were demonstrating in support of climate justice. One of them, a young woman with frizzy hair and a pale, gaunt face, said she had been fasting for two days. Uncertain how starving herself would help reverse climate change, I ascended the stairwell thinking about Hannah, a schoolmate in the Lamb of God who had regularly fasted so that she might become more dependent upon the Holy Spirit for nourishment. When I ran into Hannah at the mall, some years after my family had left the community, her face was as sallow as ever. We exchanged pleasantries, and as we parted ways, she called after me, "I'm praying for you!" Hannah was on the path of righteousness. I was a wayward lost soul.

The enormous Lawrence A. Wien Reference Room, located on Butler's third floor, is arguably the most beautiful space on Columbia's Morningside Heights campus. Books line all four walls, and from the ornate ceiling hang two massive, three-tiered chandeliers, which are responsible for the warm glow that seeps through the frosted-glass windows onto the main quad below. In the room's center are about a dozen long wooden desks with gold reading lamps. Etched high in one of the stone walls are the words of Francis Bacon, one of the founders of modern Western science: "A man is but what he knoweth."

I spotted Molly sitting at a table to the right. Molly was in her mid-twenties, a lifelong New Yorker, and a lesbian. Bearing a resemblance to a young Diane Keaton, she made unflattering turtlenecks and ill-fitting jeans look chic.

My new friend looked up and smiled. I whispered my thanks for saving me a seat.

As I opened my MacBook, a text from her appeared on my screen. "So quiet in here!"

I turned and smiled.

"We'll choose a noisier place next time," Molly's next text read. "Things good?"

"Yes, lots of reading to do already."

"OMG same!" she replied.

Molly was considering a major in anthropology, but she was also interested in psychology. During orientation, we had been warned that the amount of reading our professors assigned would be humanly impossible to complete. They weren't lying.

Figuring I might as well get ahead of it, I opened CourseWorks, the online portal for course files and readings, and clicked on Contemporary Islamic Civilization.

For our next class, Dabashi had assigned two readings. The first was a 1993 *Foreign Affairs* essay by the late Harvard professor Samuel P. Huntington, written four years after the fall of the Soviet Union. In the post–Cold War world, Huntington predicted a "clash of civilizations" would dominate international relations; one of these would be a conflict between the secular West and radical Islam. Western values like "individualism, liberalism, constitutionalism, human rights, equality, liberty, the rule of law, democracy, free markets, the separation of church and state often have little resonance in Islamic...cultures," he wrote. Any efforts by Western powers to propagate these values globally on the grounds that they are universally valid would be viewed by non-Western cultures as "human rights imperialism." In response, Huntington wrote, those cultures would likely reaffirm their commitment to indigenous values, "as can be seen in the support for religious fundamentalism by the younger generation in non-Western cultures."

Unabashedly pro-Western, Huntington concluded with recommendations for the West: promote greater unity, strengthen institutions that reflect Western interests and values, "identify elements of commonality" between the West and other civilizations, and maintain robust economic and military power.

I nodded along with nearly all of what Huntington had written. Though it sparked a major controversy at the time, less than a decade elapsed before his thesis was proved horrifyingly correct in the terrorist attacks of 9/11. Hence, it was considered prophetic.

The second reading was Dabashi's own response to Huntington's essay. It was nothing short of scathing.

In "For the Last Time: Civilizations," itself fortuitously published in *International Sociology* on September 1, 2001, Dabashi wrote that Huntington's essay "reads like a State Department policy directive." Accusing Huntington and other "reactionary intellectuals" of having "impeccable racist records dating back all the way to the Vietnam War," he went on to reduce his highly nuanced discussion of global civilizational dynamics to an imperialist argument that "Islamic civilizations ought to be confronted with full military might." Dabashi held in contempt any narrative that praised the West for any reason while ignoring or downplaying its "catastrophic consequences." "The Enlightenment," he wrote with undeniable flair, "had the Holocaust in its belly and colonialism in its trail."

I was taken aback by Dabashi's vitriolic tone and attitude of utter certainty. I was well aware that European history was rife with atrocity and other misdeeds—just like all of world history. But I also knew that the Enlightenment had produced some of the most consequential philosophical, cultural, and scientific advances known to mankind. Moreover, it was thanks to Enlightenment thinkers that modern liberalism, in particular the concepts of individual liberty and religious tolerance, had taken hold in the first place.

To that extent, Dabashi owed his own freedom to preach against Western imperialism from his tenured perch at Columbia University to these very values, and to the revolutions that had enshrined them in our politics.

Besides hypocritical, Dabashi's polemic was irrational. Ten days after its publication, Islamic fundamentalists had hijacked airplanes full of passengers and crashed them into the Pentagon and the World Trade Center. The ensuing decades had seen the rise of ISIS and nearly endless military conflict between Western forces and Islamic jihadists. In 2013, two jihadists would detonate bombs at the Boston Marathon. Three years later, one jihadist would shoot up an Orlando gay bar.

Yet in a few more years, universities would be overrun with students praising Hamas for the genocidal murder of 1,200 Israelis on October 7, and city streets would be filled with protesters calling for an "intifada" to overthrow the US and other democracies. The convergence of left-wing anti-Western capitalism and Islamic fundamentalism—two movements that seemed to have nothing in common except for their enemy—would surprise nearly everyone. But not me.

When I had entered Columbia's gates for the first time, I had been overwhelmed with excitement, but I was also intimidated. Would I be able to keep up? I was so preoccupied with how smart and accomplished the other students were, I forgot one very important thing: They were *kids*. Unlike any of them, I had ideas and opinions that had formed from adult life experiences. I wasn't just old enough to remember 9/11, I could remember what life in America was like *before* 9/11.

This would be an advantage, but it would also create a major challenge for those who were so desperate to indoctrinate me. For refusing to fall in line and conform to their way of thinking, I would become a frustrating inconvenience. But it would create a challenge for me too. It meant I would have to figure out what I actually thought—and summon the courage to say it out loud.

LATER, AS I headed home on the subway, I wrestled in my mind over Dabashi's lecture and the readings he had assigned. It wasn't that I didn't sympathize with some of his views. I, too, had often thought of the West, the US in particular, as a bully from the perspective of gay and minority rights. I, too, had cynically suspected that it used a supposed commitment to "spreading democracy and human rights" abroad to disguise its ulterior motives, which I assumed had more to do with maintaining power and controlling access to resources. And we all knew that the Iraq War had been a disaster.

Looking back, however, I can see that my antipathy toward the West wasn't entirely based on evidence. Rather, it was reflexive—the consequence of a standard-issue liberal education and the generalized attitudes of the prevailing culture. As far back as I could remember, at least in public school, the educational curriculum—and of course, the media and popular culture at large—had always displayed an anti-American bent, a lurking antipathy toward the West and the US in particular. Regardless of whether teachers and professors were themselves anti-American, it was like it was almost their job to denigrate nationalism and prevent jingoism, which were considered animating forces of the right. Somehow, patriotism got lost.

My own anti-Americanism, if one can call it that, had softened a bit with the election of a black president in 2008 and the strides that were made in gay and lesbian rights during his administration. Besides, there had to be a reason why millions of immigrants still wanted to come to the US, and why they were known to be among the most patriotic of Americans.

In Donald Trump, of course, Dabashi and I definitely had a common enemy. My opposition to Trump was mostly about his divisiveness and ugly rhetoric. I had always believed that a president's top priority should be encouraging national unity, and I feared Trump would do the opposite. But to Dabashi, Trump epitomized basically every negative thing he seemed to believe about America itself. And that is where we parted company.

I could agree with Dabashi that America was a flawed and sometimes ugly place. Unlike him, however, I still believed in its fundamental goodness and continued to feel, on some level, that our way of life was better, freer, and more just than anywhere else on earth. Here, with the help of so many Americans who had shown up for me along the way, I was able to overcome mental illness and drug addiction. Here, I was free to be who I actually am.

Maybe the other students, so many of them on their maiden voyage into society—a society that civil rights activists had worked tirelessly to improve—would find it easy to accept Dabashi's opinions as fact. But I knew how far we had come. And I knew how far non-Western nations still had to go. That wasn't just jingoist fervor.

Two days later, on my way to Spanish class in the International Affairs Building, I noticed a number of students huddled around a television in the lobby. Before I could see what was on, I remembered the date: January 20.

Inauguration Day.

On screen, a camera panned over the crowds gathered on the National Mall. When the president-elect appeared, my heart rate surged unhealthily.

I couldn't bring myself to watch another second of it. I was too exhausted to be outraged. Besides, I didn't have any more time to waste, feeling helpless about what was happening in our country. I had work to do. So I turned and kept walking.

CHAPTER 8

As one of his first official acts, President Trump signed Executive Order 13769, commonly known as the infamous "Muslim ban." After provoking a national outcry, the order—which banned people from seven Muslim-majority countries from entering the US for ninety days—was blocked in court in early February. In March, a second, more narrowly defined Muslim ban replaced the first one.

The ban as initially worded was clearly too broad, and it predictably drew an angry response from the Democrats and the liberal press who denounced it as proof of Trump's hatefulness, stupidity, and racism. This gave rise to a new wave of revulsion and visceral hatred for Trump—revulsion and hatred that were easy, even cathartic, to get swept up in. I was on the side of good. And when you're certain you are good, that kind of rage and bloodlust against evil doesn't seem unreasonable. Maybe it's even necessary.

The response on campus to Trump's actions was immediate and palpable. Emails from the administration pinged my inbox, affirming solidarity with Columbia's Muslim community and lamenting the president's deplorable Islamophobia. Protests—as they did at the drop of a hat—immediately erupted on campus.

On the steps of Low Library—the site of so many epic protests since the Vietnam War—I shouted in protest of the ban along with the other students who had gathered. At first it was exhilarating—almost like a religious revival. *I am good! I am virtuous! God will bless me!* Moments later, though, I felt ridiculous. Who, exactly, were we shouting at? I slinked away and headed to my next class.

In the weeks that followed, I became very attuned to what was the collective attitude toward Muslims on campus. It was as if they were shrouded in holiness. The hijab, rather than a consequence of patriarchal oppression, was now a symbol of resistance. What I understand today is that, in the ever-shifting hierarchy of oppression, Muslim students had claimed the top spot.

Around this time, members of a campus Muslim group invited students to participate in their afternoon prayer as a way of showing solidarity with the Muslim community. Kneeling on giant blue tarps they had unfurled onto the quad, we bowed in the direction of Mecca. As I touched my forehead to the ground, I felt truly radical. What was more subversive than a gay former Christian performing an Islamic ritual?

Remarkably in retrospect, everything I had learned about Muslim persecution of gays briefly went out the window. It was like the Pulse nightclub shooting had never happened. Anti-Islam sentiment—"Islamophobia"—had been framed by the academy and the media as solely an issue of racism, rather than as opposition to a harmful ideology—and I was falling for it.

Afterward, a Muslim student wearing a shirt and tie gave a short speech. He told each non-Muslim student to introduce him or herself to one of the Muslim students after prayers had ended, and to ask them questions about themselves.

I did as I was told, reaching out my hand to various students. "What's your name? Where are you from? What are you studying?" The students' answers all blended together, as I was preoccupied with adopting an air of proper deference.

When I was in the Lamb of God, I had been part of God's army. The righteousness was baked in. So long as I remained in the fold, I was, in modern social-justice parlance, "on the right side of history." After we left I felt unmoored, despairing, and ravaged by feelings of guilt and self-blame. It's no surprise that I fell prey to drug abuse and mental illness. It was hard going to rebuild my life from the ground up, but moving from a victim to a survivor is what gave me self-esteem. And yet it wasn't until I latched on to gay rights activism that I found myself on a path to full recovery. Feeling like part of God's army again was incredibly fulfilling. It gave me a sense of belonging, of meaning and purpose—feelings I had sorely missed since leaving the tight-knit world of the cult.

Now, as a social justice warrior, I was tethered to a new righteous cause, one that transcended my identity and limited concerns as a gay man. I had found a new sacred community, pledged to the unending task of purifying the world of its hatred and bigotry. It soothed my lingering scrupulosity—the nagging feeling that I was inherently "bad"—and my persistent fear that "bad things would happen" if I failed to perform enough virtuous acts. It also restored the belief, for the first time since I was twelve, that I was one of the good guys.

Yet even then, in those first weeks and months at Columbia, I harbored an indefinable skepticism about just what, exactly, I was signing up for. After all, my entire adult life had been about battling a religious fundamentalism that sought to control my thoughts and regulate my life, trying to find the courage to think independently and define myself as an individual apart from a religious or social community. Yet here I was, once again, kneeling in prayer. Only this time it was to honor the inherently political religion of Islam. A religion which, as currently practiced in many places around the world, seriously threatens the lives of women and gay people as well as punishing anyone who dares challenge its orthodoxy.

I also knew that a massive Christian worship service on Columbia's quad would never be seen by the student body as a "progressive" exercise in the fight for social justice. Rather, there would likely be a large outcry, with students claiming that "right-wing conservatives" were trying to convert them to Christianity.

What did not cross my mind at the time was whether the afternoon prayer was an attempt by Muslims to convert students to Islam. It would have seemed ridiculous. Now, after years of witnessing Islamism being advertised to impressionable young progressives as an exotic way to rebel against Western imperialism, I don't find that possibility ridiculous at all.

Was it really "progressive" to be championing Islamic culture? Was it progressive to champion the veiling and patriarchal domination of women? I couldn't help asking these questions. After all, I knew that many Muslim women around the world viewed the Islamic mandate of the veil as oppressive and sexist. Those who dared to defy it often suffered extreme violence at the hands of men. Veiling is not even a universal practice in Muslim societies, but only in those where radical Islam holds sway. So why were we on the left identifying with the most radical form of Islam instead of with secular reformers of it?

These hesitations—the seeds of later heresy—began as a chafing sensation, as my burgeoning need to think for myself rubbed up against the orthodox views of my new activist community.

Samuel Huntington had warned Americans about this coming clash between Western values and Islam. But even he could not have predicted how significantly it would reverberate on campuses like Columbia's, where professors and students would openly denigrate Western ideals and proselytize non-Western ones amid a general attack on Western "ways of knowing." At Columbia, students were taught that the enlightened scholar's job was to "decolonize" our thoughts. Truths established via the scientific method, born out of the Enlightenment and the ensuing scientific revolution, were tainted with whiteness and colonialism. All black and brown people were, by virtue of their oppression by Western colonial powers, purer and more principled—more culturally authentic—than white people were. And how they behave must be judged differently—that is, if their behavior can even be judged at all.

But this perspective, I eventually noticed, was reifying the very thing it aimed to destroy. It recreated around people of color, regardless of their nation of origin, an air of exoticism, of unknowability, of irreducible "other"-ness. It painted Western history—not only its tragedies but also its discoveries and triumphs—as singularly white, denying the vital roles that so many black and brown historical figures have played in this project. And it reimagined non-Western and indigenous peoples as a single-minded, innocent monolith, denying the diversity of thought, experience, and morality within these groups—as well as their own historical sins of conquest, slavery, and repression—thereby effectively dehumanizing them.

Nor did it escape my attention that these radical critics of Western enlightenment cloaked themselves in Western traditions of freedom of speech while doing their best to silence, marginalize, and drive out alternative perspectives.

At the end of February, I witnessed my first annual "Israeli Apartheid Week," sponsored by SJP, Columbia-Barnard Jewish Voice for Peace, and Columbia University Apartheid Divest along with Barnard Columbia Socialists and the Columbia Queer Alliance. Every day on Low Plaza, a "mock apartheid wall" was erected—giant gray banners tacked to plywood, covered with anti-Israel slogans and illustrations. Programming events were titled, "No Peace on Stolen Land," "50 Years of Occupation: The 1967 Nakba with Professor Rashid Khalidi," "Natives and Colonists: Pasts & Futures of Palestine with Professor Joseph Massad," "Teaching Palestine: Scholarship and Resistance," and "Zionists are Racists."

Six weeks into the school year, I had already met dozens of Jewish students, some of whom were Israeli. Even then, I found it strange that the administration, which was clearly adamant about making the campus a "safe space" for minorities, seemed to expect this tiny minority to peacefully tolerate naked calls for the destruction of the world's only Jewish state. And SJP, I learned, was supported by American Muslims for Palestine, a radical anti-Israel group that grew out of the Islamic Association of Palestine, which, until 2004, was the main propaganda arm of the terrorist group Hamas.

Again, I wondered: *Why the rigid orthodoxy and unrelenting moralism? Why were no alternative views allowed? Why the selective outrage aimed at only one side in the conflict? Just what, exactly, was I signing up for?*

The semester sped along. I was relieved when my midterm paper in Dabashi's class, a book report on Karen Armstrong's *Islam: A Short History*, earned an A. The book provides an illuminating history of the religion, though clearly its main purpose is to counter Western claims that Islam is inherently violent and misogynist. (Armstrong blames Islam's misogyny on the influence of Greek Christians in the centuries after Muhammad's death.) The book, which was one of the assigned texts, provided one of the only opportunities that semester to learn about the actual history of Islamic civilization, since Dabashi was primarily focused on preaching postcolonial theory.

For my final paper, I chose to explore the compatibility of feminism and Islam, since that question seemed to come up frequently in class discussions and in many of the readings. I used as a source a 2002 article called "Do Muslim Women Really Need Saving?" by Lila Abu-Lughod, a Palestinian-American professor of anthropology at Columbia and a leader within the BDS movement.

Like Dabashi, Abu-Lughod seemed to believe that attempts to liberate women in the Muslim world and Global South since the eighteenth century had mainly been a way to justify Western colonization and military intervention in these regions. Postcolonial scholars refer to this as "colonial feminism."

Gayatri Spivak, a Columbia professor and scholar of feminism and Marxism, gave a cynical description of this phenomenon in her 1988 essay, "Can the Subaltern Speak?" by writing, "White men are saving the brown women from brown men." (In postcolonial theory, the British military term "subaltern," which describes a junior officer, refers to colonized populations excluded from power.) Oddly enough, this sentence appears during Spivak's discussion of Britain's abolition in colonized

India of *sati*, a practice in which Hindu widows—willingly or otherwise—self-immolated atop their dead husband's funeral pyres. I do not know what, if anything, Spivak has had to say about the actual documented oppression of women by both Hindu and Islamic patriarchalism.

In her paper Abu-Lughod argued, somewhat convincingly, that First Lady Laura Bush's November 2001 speech, in which she stated that "the fight against terrorism is also a fight for the rights and dignity of women," was part of a Bush Administration strategy to dress up the war on terror as a humanistic effort to free Muslim women from oppression in Afghanistan. But she lost me when, downplaying the oppressiveness of the burqa, she described the mandatory head-to-toe coverings as "mobile homes" for women, enabling them to move about freely in the public sphere while remaining in the "inviolable space of their homes."

First of all, as I pointed out in my paper, a woman's need to hide her physical form in order to remain safe in the presence of men did not reflect well on Afghan culture. It basically shifts the burden of assuring female safety from men to women themselves. But this sentiment, I also wrote, directly contradicted what Dabashi had stated in his lecture, that the "public sphere" is a place where ideas are exchanged, where "public reason" develops from communicating with each other "eyeball to eyeball," and where participation gives people the feeling of being part of something bigger, which in turn creates "public happiness."

That may be the norm in Western liberal societies, but when women in Afghanistan and other Muslim countries are hidden beneath their burqas—and even eye contact is discouraged—can they participate in the development of public reason as men supposedly can? If not, doesn't this deny them Dabashi's "public happiness"? In the same lecture, Dabashi stated that a nation is ultimately composed of public space and the public sphere. *If that's the case*, I wrote, *then Muslim women are effectively excluded from citizenship in countries operating under Islamic law.*

Another source I used was one that Dabashi had not assigned: Ayaan Hirsi Ali's memoir, *Nomad*. Ali, a Somalian refugee and vocal critic of Islam, is a survivor of Islamic forced marriage and female genital mutilation (FGM) who went on to become a member of the Dutch parliament, a bestselling author, and the founder of a nonprofit organization for the defense of women's rights. I didn't know about Ali until Dabashi instructed the class to watch a recent interview with her. As I watched the interview, I found myself agreeing with Ali's perspective. It wasn't until our subsequent class discussion that I realized we were supposed to disagree with it.

In *Nomad*, Ali wrote that blaming oppression in Muslim countries on Western colonization "excuses formerly colonized peoples from scrutiny and criticism for their own failings" and ignores the fact that, since these nations have become decolonized, the quality of women's lives has worsened. Western scholars of Islam and left-wing activists have harshly criticized Ali, alleging she portrays her experience as representative of all Muslim women. In the videos and interviews I viewed, I saw them accuse her of failing to mention the part that economics, class, war, imperialism, and religious law play in the oppression of women in the Muslim world—*an argument*, I wrote, *that took the onus off the perpetrators of FGM, honor killings, rape, and child marriages and attributed blame to their circumstances.*

After reading Ali's memoir, I found her perspective even more reasonable. And yet to postcolonial leftists, she was a heretic. (One of Ali's books, in which she argues for the liberal reform of Islam, is actually titled *Heretic.*) Over time, her example—and that of others who were unafraid to challenge prevailing orthodoxies—would be the one I followed. Just as Ali asserted the moral and ethical primacy of women's rights based on the universal application of Western liberal principles, I would do the same against queer theory.

Somewhat surprisingly, this paper also earned me an A. But Dabashi's TA graded our papers, so I doubt he actually read any of them.

One of our course requirements was to attend a weekly, TA-led discussion during which we'd review Dabashi's lectures and the readings he had assigned. During one session, about halfway through the semester, we discussed gender norms in the Muslim world. At one point, a student suggested that Muslim society is harsher on effeminate men than it is on masculine women.

I raised my hand.

"I think that's because it's more acceptable for a woman to act like a man than it is for a man to act like a woman," I said, "since societies often believe that if a man behaves like a woman, he is degrading himself." I was basically quoting a line from Madonna's 2000 feminist anthem, "What It Feels Like for a Girl." I knew it was a reductive statement, but I thought it was true nonetheless.

An Asian female student's hand shot up. "Excuse me," she said, "but there is nothing easier about being a woman in society than a man."

Heads swiveled toward me. "Right," I muttered, even though that wasn't at all what I had said.

A tense silence ensued.

"Let's move on," the TA said.

My heart pounded. What had I done wrong?

When the class ended, I gathered my things and caught up with the student in the hallway. "Excuse me," I said, "I'm sorry, but I was just curious to hear more about why you objected to what I said."

"Um, I don't know," she answered impatiently. "What was it you said again?" She genuinely seemed to have forgotten the whole thing.

I attempted a good-natured shrug. "Oh, it's not important," I said. "I'm Ben, by the way."

She smiled flatly and walked away.

This seemingly innocuous exchange rattled me. I had always seen myself as an accepted member of the progressive world I had embraced. I was gay. I was an activist. I spouted all the approved cliches. But even when evincing a progressive point of view, my perceived identity—white, male, and conventionally masculine in gender presentation—meant that I was privileged and hence ideologically suspect. More to the point, I had no right to speak for any other group, especially one that was marginalized and oppressed by cis white males like me.

This would become a pattern. Students would frequently interpret my words in a way that was the exact opposite of what I'd intended—and sometimes *of what I had actually said*. And if I dared to offer an unorthodox perspective, they'd quickly react as if it was made in bad faith. For white guys like me—no matter my life experiences, my sexuality, my history of gender-nonconformity, or the complexity of the topic we happened to be discussing—it was best to toe the radically progressive line, using only approved language. Otherwise I should keep my mouth shut.

Soon, I found myself declaring my sexuality whenever I spoke, since my right to have an opinion clearly depended on whether or not I had ever experienced identity-based "oppression."

"As a gay man…" I'd begin, loathing myself for conforming to this culture of extreme identitarianism.

But equally demoralizing was the way the university clearly expected me to partake in the practice of reducing people to their identities, in particular their race, which felt, well, racist. Whereas previously I had evaluated a person's ideas on their intellectual merit, now I was expected to judge a person's ideas based on their identity. That is, I was being encouraged to judge people not by "the content of their character" but by "the color of their skin." Therefore, whenever a student spoke, I first needed to consider his or her race or "gender identity" before I thought about what he or she had said. And the proper way to do that, I gathered, was to evaluate a black or brown person's words on a different scale than a white person's. Better yet, I should just accept whatever they said as true, especially when it came to matters related to social justice.

"It was really Benjamin Franklin's slaves who discovered electricity," a black student said during a writing seminar. Apparently, she had learned this from her young cousin, who had learned it on social media.

"How interesting," my classmates and professor responded, not daring to challenge the veracity of this outrageous claim. For to challenge it would be to uphold white, Eurocentric, Western epistemology, to deny that there are "other ways of knowing"—ways that are, by virtue of the interlocutors' identities, closer to the truth. Or rather, "their truth," since

Truth with a capital T was confidently declared to be an artifact of white male European culture.

I resented it. I resented what these ideologues were asking of me: to dehumanize my peers. It felt immoral. And rather than improving the way I connected with people of color, it atrophied my interactions with them by triggering my moral scrupulosity. Before long, whenever a black student spoke, I would clam up in fear of not knowing how to respond. If I nodded as they were speaking, I was "actively listening," which was good. But what if it came off as patronizing? No, better to keep my head still. But now I'm unreadable, and possibly threatening as a white person if I'm just staring at them while they talk. I should look down. But if I'm looking down, it looks like I'm not listening. No, better to look at them and smile while they're talking. But what if they're talking about something tragic? Then it looks like I'm making light of it.

On and on it went. It was like I was no longer seeing black students as equals or even as individuals, but rather as an oppressed, disadvantaged monolith. It was generally the same with women, or any other minority.

Paradoxically, this validated the way I had been raised. Race and sex, I was taught, were irrelevant to a person's character or their intelligence. I was taught it was *wrong* to make assumptions about people based on their identities. Those lessons, thankfully, had stuck.

Now, it was if identity was *the only thing* that mattered.

In our discussion about gender norms, the Asian female student's identity automatically trumped mine, making her "right," no matter the merits of her argument. But even so, I didn't resent her for correcting me in a publicly humiliating way. In fact, I suspected she felt just as much pressure to play by these rules as I did. To be righteous, it was her duty to call out the white guys who dared to speak about feminist issues in class. It was a religious act she must perform in order to prove her faith.

Everyone was under *so much pressure.*

The most disorienting aspect of the ordeal was being accused of thoughtcrime by a woman. I was primarily raised by my mother and two older sisters, and nearly all my closest friends had been females. Since I was young, girls and women had gravitated toward me because I was "safe," "kind," a "good guy," "like one of the girls." For a young woman to suggest, in front of a room full of people, that I had said something regressive, even sexist, left me feeling ashamed, as though I had sinned and needed to atone.

After the discussion ended, I couldn't let go of the fear that I had done something wrong.

In my head, a familiar tape began to play. *Forgive me, God. Forgive me. I'm sorry. Please forgive me.*

I didn't know who or what I was praying to. I only knew how necessary it felt to try and quiet the obsessive thoughts that rattled my brain.

What had I done wrong? Who else thinks I'm bad? How will I be punished?

God, forgive me.

I said it again and again.

On a warm afternoon in March, Shaun and I finally had lunch. After Spanish class, we walked to the café inside Uris Hall, where I'd occasionally study in the Business and Economics Library. The library was big and spacious, and the biz school guys were often cute to look at, which was a nice distraction from the endless reading. I got a turkey sandwich and a coffee, and Shaun got some pasta, then we grabbed a table on the patio outside.

Shaun was from the Midwest. He currently lived in Brooklyn with his partner, James. Like me, Shaun was an anxious student; he constantly agonized over his grades. He was determined to get into Columbia Law School—no other school would do. "I know, I'm a snob!" he joked. He had a family member who had struggled within the criminal justice system, and he hoped to improve it as a public defender.

"How are your classes going?" Shaun asked.

"Pretty well," I said. I told him I had thus far gotten A's on all of my assignments. "If only I could take a second to pat myself on the back for how well I'm doing," I said. "But all I can think about is the next thing. The next exam, the next paper, summer internships, et cetera."

Shaun nodded. "That's Columbia," he said.

Three students sitting at the next table began gathering up their things. After they left, I said to Shaun, "Can I ask you a question?"

"Sure."

"Are the people around here a little, I don't know...weird?"

Shaun furrowed his brow. "What do you mean?"

Suddenly, my mouth was dry. I took a sip of my coffee, which burned my tongue. "About certain topics," I said. "Like, topics that have to do with...race, and whatnot."

"Dude," Shaun said, and began to laugh. "I cannot wait to tell James you said that."

"Why?"

"Because I often try to explain how it is here, but I can never find the right words."

I must have had a worried look on my face, because finally Shaun said, "Yes! The answer is yes! These kids are *weird*!"

It was as if I had taken a Xanax. My shoulders felt like they dropped three inches.

"You're definitely not crazy," Shaun said, and he proceeded to tell me a little bit about his experience at Columbia.

Shaun had been around white people all his life. Some of his closest friends were white, he said. So it was weird to see people denigrating "whiteness," as if that would actually do anything to solve racism. In fact, it was probably making things worse.

I told him I agreed. "But it's not just that," I said. "It's how others expect me to treat black people. Like they're helpless or something. It just doesn't feel right."

Shaun nodded.

"To tell you the truth," I went on, "it actually feels wrong. Like, really wrong."

"I totally get that."

We were both silent for a while. The sun had disappeared behind Uris, and it was starting to get cold.

"You need to talk about this stuff," Shaun said. "In class, I mean. Either that, or you need to write about it."

I shook my head. "There's no way…."

"No, you have to," Shaun said. "Like, we *need* you to."

I wasn't sure who Shaun was referring to. If he meant black people in general, I doubted there were many who would agree with my perspective. Yet, if I thought about it, the students who typically spoke with such passion in class about racial justice were white. I actually had *no idea* about the diversity of perspectives within the black population. In fact, just the previous week, a black student in class had surprised me (and probably everyone else) when she said she often found herself agreeing with Trump's talking points.

"I don't know," I said to Shaun. "We'll see."

CHAPTER 9

About halfway through my first semester, I attended an information session for students who were interested in writing for the student newspaper, the *Columbia Daily Spectator*. The session was held a couple blocks from campus at the *Spectator*'s headquarters, inside a second-floor walkup on Broadway.

The *Columbia Daily Spectator* was founded in 1877, but its service as an organ of student activism didn't really begin until the 1930s, when its editor, a wealthy student named Reed Harris, developed a new class consciousness and steered the paper in a more radical direction. From there, *Spectator* reporters began to adopt an adversarial approach toward the administration, holding it up to ever-increasing scrutiny. In 1968, after campus protests erupted into chaos, *Spectator* reporters accused local newspapers of exaggerating the mayhem and overestimating student opposition to the protesters' radical tactics. Their April 1968 article, "City Newspapers Distort Protests," stands in sharp contrast to some of the letters printed just below it. "Despite the validity of some of the Students for a Democratic Society's demands...we loathe the tactics used to secure these ends," wrote one group of four current students. Classes had been "effectively cancelled," they complained, warning that the protests could "lead to violence and the destruction of University facilities." Another group of students wrote that the protests did not reflect "the views of what we feel is the vast majority of concerned students who will not sacrifice rational order for emotional expedience. SDS by its coercive actions has denied our right to attend classes." They concluded, "Authoritarian solutions, left or right, are not solutions."

In 1985, the cause du jour was South African apartheid. At the time, *Spectator* editors praised "the peaceful actions of the Coalition [for a Free South Africa] members who plan to fast in protest of Columbia's South African investments." In the 2010s, hot button issues like the BDS movement, Columbia's gentrification of Harlem, and fears of campus rape began to overwhelm print space. "Israel is an apartheid state," wrote Columbia Students for Justice in Palestine member Tanya Keilani in 2011, comparing it to South Africa. "Racism, colonialism, and settler-states are not complicated." *Spectator* ran Keilani's op-ed during "Israeli Apartheid Week," a new campus event that would be held annually by Columbia SJP.

In May 2014, *Spectator* controversially chose to print the name of a male student accused of rape by an art student named Emma Sulkowicz. Sulkowicz famously demonstrated against the university's failure to expel her alleged rapist from campus by carrying around her mattress as a performative art piece for her senior thesis. Even though a seven-month investigation found the accused fellow student not responsible, he became a campus pariah and, last I read, relocated to Germany.

ABOUT THIRTY STUDENTS were at *Spectator*'s headquarters when I arrived. Some sat in chairs or on the floor, while the rest stood near the windows. Moments later, *Spectator*'s editor in chief, Catie Edmondson, a senior at Barnard College, addressed the room. She now works as a congressional correspondent for the *New York Times*.

Catie said that *Spectator* was looking for people who had a thirst for investigative reporting. "We know there's a lot of fuckery that goes on at Columbia," she said, "and we intend to expose it." She spoke proudly about how many professors *Spectator* staff had managed to get fired, though she didn't mention any specifics.

Catie's speech unnerved me. Journalism, I knew, was about speaking truth to power. But the thought of being involved in any type of controversy that could jeopardize my place at the university terrified me. I wasn't there to cause problems.

I think it was then that I really began to see just how different I was from the other students. Obviously, I was older and had more life experience. But we also seemed to have grown up with very different expectations of what our lives would be. Looking around me, I realized that most of these students probably came from immense privilege, from homes run by wealthy parents who shielded them from any and all discomfort. Columbia was merely the manifestation of their preordained destinies. Whereas, for me, an experience like this had always seemed beyond my wildest dreams. And just as they had probably rebelled against their overbearing helicopter parents, I supposed it was only natural that they'd want to rebel against the university—to exploit the cracks in its foundation and take it down a few notches as proof of their own moral superiority.

Over time, I would see that my observations had been right: The posture of many students toward the university was exactly the one a teenager would take toward an overbearing parent. Often, privileged teenagers demand from their parents whatever they desire—new iPhones and wardrobes, Ivy League educations—but resent the cost of continued obedience and the insecurity that comes with knowing they haven't achieved anything on their own. Students were quick to roll their eyes at the university and smear it as a racist, out-of-date, and corrupt institution. Yet at the same time they demanded the administration make the campus a "safe space" by regulating the behavior of everyone around them. It was as if they expected the campus to be an extension of their childhood bedrooms. And just as they probably pitted Mom against Dad to get what they wanted, they'd pit the administration against the faculty, and vice versa. They wanted to bring down the big, bad institution and at the same time uphold the existence of its bureaucratic Thought

Police, to whom they could report incidents of supposed "bias" or anything else they deemed "unfair" and that needed to be remedied at once.

Literally. At Columbia, the Thought Police are known as the Bias Incident Resource Team. A "bias-related incident," its website states, is when "language" or even "behavior" communicates "prejudice and is motivated in whole or in part by a negative judgment about an aspect of a person's (or group's) perceived identity." If a student reports a bias-related incident, a team member will review the report and then "offer to meet and discuss the incident in detail and explore a plan for resolution." These "remedying solutions" might include "facilitated dialogue and/or educational opportunities"—that is, struggle sessions and intersectional reeducation for the offender.

The bias-reporting website insists that its methods do not suppress free speech. However, in its 2023 college free-speech ranking list, the nonpartisan Foundation for Individual Rights and Expression (FIRE) ranked Columbia dead last in the nation, deeming its speech climate "abysmal."

By the time Catie finished talking, I had decided investigative reporting wasn't my thing. Besides my aversion to ruffling feathers, I also liked to think that "New Journalism," in the vein of writers I had long-admired like Joan Didion and James Baldwin, was more my style. However, *Spectator* did have a weekly arts and culture publication, *The Eye*, which featured more personal essays in its "View from Here" section, where students wrote about everything from working as a Subway "sandwich artist" to a semester studying in New Zealand. *The Eye* was the place for me.

I filed out of *Spectator*'s office with the rest of the students and headed back toward campus to attend another information session, this one for Columbia's LGBT student organizations. My friend Molly had texted to say she would be there, and we agreed to meet in front of Lerner Hall a few minutes beforehand. Like me, she was hoping to get involved with some of the LGBT groups on campus, and we were curious to see what they were working on. I imagined it would be a hive of activity, what with Trump in power and a right-wing evangelical serving as his second-in-command.

As it turned out, things were rather chill. Molly and I entered the room to find games, toys, and arts and crafts materials spread across the desks. On the agenda were not protests or petitions but slumber parties, at which students would watch movies and decorate posters for their rooms. Yes, I was over a decade older than the other attendees. But as I looked around me, I was startled by how young and vulnerable my classmates—some of whom literally wore pajamas—appeared.

Memorably, it was also the first time I heard LGBT people exclusively referring to themselves as "queer." I was rather indifferent to the word, but I knew that many other gays and lesbians found it offensive, since it had historically been used as a slur.

What I did not yet understand was that "queer" was much more than a reclaimed synonym for "gay"; it was a specific form of radical politics. I was also unaware that some of these students were neither L, G, B, or even T, but were adopting the identity of "queer" as a way to gain entry into a marginalized group and earn social cachet. I would become much more familiar with these trends over the summer as an intern at GLAAD, the LGBT rights organization, and during the fall semester, in George Chauncey's US Lesbian and Gay History course.

"That was weird," said Molly after we had returned outside, where we each sparked up a cigarette.

"Thank God you said it. They all just seemed so…"

"Fragile," said Molly.

"Yes. Like if you said something to upset them, they'd literally break."

Molly laughed.

Evidently, LGBT campus activism wasn't for me after all. If I wanted to make a difference, I was going to have to focus on my writing.

Beginner's Fiction Workshop was held in a classroom on the top floor of Kent Hall. The class was small, about eleven students altogether.

The instructor, Nancy Brown, a physically powerful woman with a pixie cut, was a graduate student in Columbia's MFA program, working on a memoir about female bodybuilding.

My first workshop experience was a lot less enjoyable than I had hoped. In those early days, I never for a second thought that anything I said or wrote could be considered "problematic" (an adjective university students and professors often used to identify a possible thoughtcrime). After all, I was one of the good guys—a gay, feminist, Democrat-voting activist in the making. If anything, I spent my time in class on the lookout for conservative opinions I could smugly dismantle. But those opportunities never came.

For workshop, drawing from my own history, I submitted a short story I had written from the point of view of a woman having a psychotic break. In retrospect, this utterly tone-deaf decision amuses me to no end. At the time, I knew nothing about "cultural appropriation" or the burgeoning controversy in literary publishing, where seemingly overnight it became a punishable offense for an author—especially a white male—to write from the perspective of anyone belonging to a different identity group. (In my story, I had even had the protagonist say something like, "He couldn't stop staring at my tits.")

In workshop, the author sits quietly while the rest of the students discuss their story or essay. I waited in eager anticipation of the praise that I was sure my classmates were about to heap on me.

Instead, they were mostly dead silent. When one finally complimented the story arc, another rushed in to say that my "diction was unsophisticated." Ouch. What a putdown.

Things got worse when it came time to workshop another student's story, a piece of historical fiction about the day the Manhattan Project team detonated the first atomic bomb. In the story, the writer—I'll call her Lauren—had included characters with German accents. The way she wrote made them leap off the page, almost like I was watching an *Indiana Jones* movie.

So that's what I said: "I loved it. It reminded me of an *Indiana Jones* movie."

A few of my classmates laughed.

"The *Indiana Jones* movies are crazy racist," said one.

"Totally," said Nancy.

I nodded my head in understanding, though I didn't have the faintest idea what was racist about the *Indiana Jones* movies, two of which depicted the hero defeating literal Nazis. Now I know that they were likely referring to their portrayal of the protagonist as a "white savior," in particular the second installment in the series, 1984's *Indiana Jones and the Temple of Doom*. The film has been criticized for its "racist tropes," particularly its depiction of Hindu Indians, who eat monkey brains and practice human sacrifice in the film. "Its racism has become positively disquieting to modern eyes," wrote Robert Vaux for *Comic Book Resources* in 2023.

In retrospect, I'm just glad I didn't get around to telling the class that *Temple of Doom* was my favorite film in the franchise.

Ten minutes later, I left the classroom shrouded in shame. *They all think I'm racist!*

Even worse, they all seemed to be more enlightened than I was.

What the hell was going on?

It was, in fact, my first encounter with critical theory—Edward Said's theory of Orientalism in particular—in praxis. The students and my instructor were properly "woke" to social injustice and racial inequality; I was not. Indians eating snakes and monkey brains? That just reinforces the idea of Indians as the "other"—a strange, backward, primitive people unlike us civilized Westerners who consume only "dignified" cuisine. To undermine whiteness and combat racism, fictional people of color must be portrayed as virtuous and white people as spiritually flawed. After all, art is not there to reflect reality, which is often very ugly. Art's purpose, like all critical theory, is to *generate cultural change*. Its purpose is to *balance the scales*.

Unfortunately, what many fail to realize about this well-intended artistic approach is that it actually dehumanizes people of color by flattening them into two dimensions and denying them moral complexity, which is part of what makes us human.

A minute later, I found myself exiting Kent Hall at the same time as Lauren. "That wasn't as fun as I thought it would be," I said. Lauren agreed. "By the way," I added, "I really didn't mean anything by that *Indiana Jones* comment."

"No worries," Lauren said, seeming sincere. Though her words did nothing to soothe my shame.

AT OUR FIRST staff meeting for *The Eye*, the team gathered in one of the small offices at *Spectator*'s headquarters. Among the ten or so writers and editors present were the managing editor, Fiona, and Alexander McNab, who wrote for *Spectator* about racism at Columbia. In 2019, McNab would garner national media attention after refusing to show his student ID at Barnard's entrance late one night, causing security guards to corner him on campus minutes later—an incident caught on video that naturally went viral on social media as an example of racial profiling—though the story would turn out to be much more complicated than it was initially reported.

The staff meeting was the first time I heard people state their pronouns when they introduced themselves. They said it was to make the space more inclusive for transgender people, though I don't recall any trans-identifying people being there. At the meeting, all the declared pronouns were traditional male or female, which makes sense, since in early 2017, neopronouns like "fae/faer" and even the plural pronouns "they/them" weren't yet widespread.

I stated my name and said I was a first-year GS student majoring in creative writing. "Oh, and he/him/his," I said.

"What beat would you like to cover?" Fiona asked me. She reminded me a bit of Lena Dunham's character in the HBO series, *Girls*—inquisitive, quirky, and noticeably insecure.

"Where can I write about gay issues?"

Fiona paused, thinking. "Maybe the Health section?"

For my first assignment, I wrote a long-form essay about the ongoing stigmatization of HIV-positive gay men. I knew that Columbia had been at the center of the AIDS crisis, both because of its location in New York City and also because, in 1985, it had opened the Gay Health Advocacy Project (GHAP), the first university health clinic to offer HIV testing for students, faculty, and staff. I was eager to learn more.

For selfish reasons, I also wanted to write about the culture of fear that AIDS had fomented within the gay population. Ever since I was a kid, when I was told that AIDS was God's punishment for gay people, I had harbored an obsessive fear of the disease. I hoped that by confronting the topic head-on, through conversations with other gay male students and alumni, I might deaden its potency. In retrospect, it's easy to see how much of my writing and activism was an attempt to deprogram myself from the antigay dogma I had learned in the Lamb of God. Activism is a collective fight for a better future, but often it is also a personal vendetta against the past.

For the piece, I interviewed Paul Lerner, a gay alum who attended Columbia in the early 1980s and had written about gay visibility in a 1983 *Spectator* op-ed. He now lived in California with his husband, who coincidentally he had married on the same day I married Drew. On campus, I spoke with two other gay GS students—Michael Pacitti, thirty-eight, and his friend Stephan Trano, forty-eight. Trano had lived in Paris when the AIDS epidemic began, but it was his older brother who contracted the disease, likely through intravenous drug use. It was cathartic, speaking with them about the fear and the stigma of HIV/AIDS, and how growing up alongside the epidemic had affected their worldviews. As a result, I felt less alone.

My last subject was a twenty-year-old visual arts major named Davian Flores, whom I found through Columbia's Queer Alliance website. In his dorm room, portraits lined the walls, and nearly every surface was littered with half-empty tubes of paint. When we spoke, I asked him if his perception of HIV had changed since coming to Columbia.

"I've learned more about the social stigma surrounding it and how racial prejudices shaped the way that people look at HIV," he said. "You see these advertisements about HIV testing and PrEP [the HIV antiviral] around the city, and they're always [featuring] black individuals." Davian said this contributed to "misinformation about all of the black bodies that contract HIV."

I, too, had noticed these advertisements posted on bus stops and in subways, which typically featured black or Latino men. But I wondered why Davian would call it "misinformation" to feature black people in advertisements for HIV testing, when the black population is, in fact, disproportionately affected by HIV. Rather than a sign of racial prejudice, I saw it as purely pragmatic. Davian did talk about racism in his hometown, and how people would often speak about the prevalence of HIV among the black population. *But were they actually speaking derogatorily about black people*, I wondered, *or were they simply stating something that was true and urgently needed to be addressed?*

In retrospect, I realized that Davian was discounting facts as "misinformation" because they reflected what prejudiced people had told him about the black population. Thus, advertisements that were meant to create greater awareness about HIV among the gay black population in order to *help* it were viewed by him as evidence of racism.

As a campus newbie, I hadn't yet adjusted to this bizarre culture, where students are indoctrinated to see evidence of racism everywhere—even where it clearly is not. Nor was I familiar with the common practice of prioritizing narrative over facts in academia and activism. Optics, it would turn out, were more important than truth, even if it could actually lead to more effective policies.

I also was thrown by Davian's use of the term "black bodies"—which, despite the antiracist sentiment it sought to communicate, sounded reductive and ultimately dehumanizing. Weren't we more than our physical bodies? The way the term rolled off his tongue made me suspect he used it often. I filed it away, reminding myself to research it later.

As it turned out, I didn't need any reminders. As the semester progressed, I would hear the term used constantly in relation to race as well as in gender-related contexts ("trans bodies," "queer bodies"). Mind you, no one could ever tell me how or why this had become the norm in academia. But I would eventually learn that, like so much of today's social justice discourse, it was likely inspired by Foucault. In *The History of Sexuality, Volume 1*, Foucault defined "biopower" as "an explosion of numerous and diverse techniques" that the modern state purportedly uses to achieve "*the subjugations of bodies* and the control of populations" (emphasis mine). The phrase "black bodies" likely surged in popularity after Ta-Nehisi Coates used it in his best-selling book, *Between the World and Me*—a work critical social justice activists treat as gospel—in which he writes about the ways our systemically racist society exploits and controls black people, particularly through policing.

This talk of "bodies" is meant to communicate not only the dehumanizing tactics of the state, but in some cases, to suggest the *social construction of actual bodies*, ideas that are central to the framework of critical theory. To critical theorists, bodies in themselves do not matter as much as the meaning that society applies to them and how they are viewed and talked about. It's the postmodern belief that language, rather than simply reflecting and describing reality, actually *creates* reality—or at the very least, creates the impression that a stable reality exists.

Weeks later, after I had submitted my draft to *The Eye*, I received an email from Fiona, asking me to stop by the office. "This is really strong writing," she said when I arrived.

I beamed with pride.

As a topic for my required research paper—or "Progression 3"—for University Writing, I chose the antigay discourse of the Christian Right. I was intimately familiar with scriptural arguments against homosexuality, but I wanted to explore the movement's influence on politics since its rise in the 1970s and to map the evolution of antigay political discourse since then.

The gay rights movement—and religious opposition to it—began decades prior to the 1970s, I learned. But Anita Bryant's 1977 Save Our Children campaign marked a turning point in this particular culture war. Bryant, a former beauty pageant winner and brand ambassador for the Florida Citrus Commission, launched a campaign to overturn a Dade County measure that protected gays and lesbians from discrimination in employment, housing, and public accommodation. Her tactic, which ultimately proved successful, was to paint the gay rights movement as a threat to children in order to attract nonreligious people to the cause. If we allowed the law to protect homosexuals, Bryant argued, then homosexuals would be emboldened to recruit children into their lifestyle. As a result, Bryant's name became a byword for bigotry and hate among liberals.

Learning about Bryant's campaign—and about the Moral Majority, a political movement founded in 1979 by Baptist minister Jerry Falwell Sr.—filled in some of the gaps in my childhood memory. I vaguely recalled Lamb of God members mentioning their names, but it helped to understand the specifics. Mostly, it answered the questions I had about the origins of antigay arguments that linked homosexuality with pedophilia. This association had always haunted me, and it became even more relevant after the births of my four nephews. I had never known a love like the one I felt for them, or such a fierce desire to protect them from harm. To my dismay, I would soon learn of the many queer theorists and activists who gave credence to Bryant's concerns.

In my research paper, I also wanted to compare Islamic and Christian beliefs about homosexuality, and to explore the possibility of the US enacting antigay laws like those in nations governed by Islamic law, where homosexuality was (and still is) punishable by death. My interest in this topic was sparked in the weeks after the 2016 Pulse shooting. At the time, Texas Republican Senator Ted Cruz, a vocal opponent of gay rights in the US, blamed the attack on the inherent homophobia in Islam, stating, "ISIS and the theocracy of Iran…regularly murder homosexuals. This is wrong, it is evil, and we must all stand against it."

Like nearly everyone else at Columbia, I disliked Cruz intensely. But he was correct about Iran. Article 234 of the Penal Laws of the Republic of Iran states that the "insertive/active party" in the act of sodomy between two men (*livat*) is punishable by death if this party uses force or coercion, or if he has a "permanent" wife (temporary marriage exists in Shia Islam). Otherwise, he receives one hundred lashes. The punishment for the "receptive/passive party" is death. Iran puts more people to death per capita than any other country, and many of these executions are issued for crimes of sodomy. And yet Iran's president had the temerity to claim in his speech at Columbia that there were no homosexuals in his country.

Still, I found it hypocritical of Cruz to condemn Islam's hardline stance against homosexuality when he himself practiced a religion that was arguably just as antigay. Iran's penal laws are influenced by the story of Lot in the Quran, which is the same narrative—known in the Bible as the story of Sodom and Gomorrah—that Christians use to justify their opposition to homosexuality. And while progressive activists in Muslim-majority countries organize for Westernized, liberal reform of Islamic law that emphasizes individual freedom and equality, Christian fundamentalists in the West campaign for reforms that threaten the rights of women and gay people.

In late 2015, at the National Religious Liberties Conference, Cruz was introduced by radio host Kevin Swanson who stated his support of the death penalty for homosexuals in the US (though he does think they should be given time to repent before the executions begin).[2] Phil Kayser, the pastor of Dominion Covenant Church, also spoke at the conference. Kayser once authored a paper advocating for the implementation of biblical law. "While many homosexuals would be executed," he wrote, "the threat of capital punishment can be restorative."[3]

What I discovered about US evangelicals' work abroad was most troubling. At the time Cruz made his remarks about the Orlando shooting, evangelicals had for years been traveling the globe, encouraging local

---

2 Michelangelo Signorile, "Why Is the Media Ignoring Ted Cruz's Embrace of 'Kill the Gays' Pastor?", *The Huffington Post*, Nov. 12, 2015, https://www.huffpost.com/entry/post_b_8544540.

3 Luke Johnson, "Phillip Kayser, Ron Paul Endorser, Called For Executing Homosexuals Under 'Biblical Law,'" *The Huffington Post*, Dec. 28, 2011, https://www.huffpost.com/entry/phillip-kayser-ron-paul-gays-iowa-caucus-2012_n_1173338.

political leaders to criminalize homosexuality. Many Christian leaders in the Global South already viewed the gay rights movement as a form of Western neoimperialism. US evangelicals exploited this viewpoint by warning leaders that they'd lose converts to antihomosexual Islam if they didn't take a harder stance against gays.[4]

For my last UW "progression," I distilled my research paper into an article about US evangelical Scott Lively's involvement in Uganda's 2009 "Kill the Gays" bill and Russia's 2013 outlawing of "gay propaganda." With Professor Wisor's encouragement, I published the article on *HuffPost.*

It was thrilling, seeing *HuffPost* share my article on social media. *People were actually reading my work.* I had not known a natural high like that.

All of this led to my becoming identified on campus as something of an authority on gay rights issues. Eventually, the assistant director of the undergraduate writing program and the editor of its online journal, *The Morningside Review,* invited me to speak on a panel to incoming freshman about my *HuffPost* op-ed. Even more flattering, I learned from Professor Wisor that my work in her class was now being used in University Writing classes as examples of successful progressions (although the fact that I was writing from a Columbia-approved point of view probably helped).

At *The Morningside Review* panel, along with five other students whose op-eds had also been published, I described to the hundreds gathered in one of the university's large lecture halls my own creative process of extracting a topical opinion piece from a larger work of research. It felt wonderful to be recognized for excelling at a craft I loved and empowering to speak on a topic I was passionate about, although I was

4 Kapya Kaoma, "How US Clergy Brought Hate to Uganda," *The Gay & Lesbian Review Worldwide,* 2010, https://glreview.org/article/how-us-clergy-brought-hate-to-uganda/.

disappointed when, as I spoke into the microphone, that old feeling of shame washed over me. *Now all of these people know I'm gay. Who among them thinks I'm bad, evil, dangerous?*

And yet I pressed on. Like the martyred Christian saints after whom I was taught to model my own character as a child, I would defend my faith in social justice—consequences be damned. It was, after all, my new shot at salvation.

CHAPTER 10

At the end of my first semester, I already felt miles away from the person I was when it began. My worldview, which I had thought quite broad, turned out to be narrow, and that narrow worldview had been blown wide open. I was getting exactly what I had asked for: The opportunity to learn and to do independent research so that I could figure out for myself what I thought about the world. It was as exhilarating as I had imagined, but also far scarier. As much knowledge and information as I finally had at my fingertips, there was simultaneously an immense pressure to conform—a pressure unlike anything I had encountered since childhood. Freethinking was problematic—even dangerous, especially when practiced by someone "privileged" like me.

Thankfully, my professors (or in Dabashi's case, my TA) rewarded me for my hard work: After completing my first four classes at Columbia, I earned a 4.07 GPA, something I didn't realize was possible before Professor Wisor gave me an A+ for my work in University Writing. I might have felt proud and relieved if my fears of transgressing weren't so constant.

What had become abundantly clear was that the education I received at Columbia wouldn't only be an academic one; it would be moral and political as well. And it would go far beyond reciting land acknowledgments in class. Every topic was to be sifted through a social justice filter. Every shred of knowledge was to be scrutinized, pulled apart to determine which aspects belonged in the "good" column and which in the "evil" column. Did this essay or book perpetuate colonization or did it support decolonization? What was the source of this so-called fact you just pronounced to the class? Was it a white man? A descendent of slave owners perhaps? If the source was black, it was good. Indigenous, even better.

Before long, my OCD was, once again, nearly in full swing.

Over the semester, I had applied for about a dozen summer internships. In the late spring, I received word that I had landed one at the New York City headquarters of GLAAD, a legendary gay rights organization I had long held in highest esteem. As GLAAD's sole News and Rapid Response intern, I would aid the Trump Accountability Project, a fledgling initiative that reported on the new administration's LGBT-related policies. It was exactly the type of activism I had longed to get involved in.

GLAAD used to stand for Gays and Lesbian Alliance Against Defamation, but is now officially known only by its acronym, so as not to exclude transgender, bisexual, and "queer" people along with the myriad gender and sexual identities made up in recent years by teenagers on the internet. Founded in 1985, its original mission was to "fight for fair, accurate, and inclusive representations of gay and lesbian lives in the media," particularly in news coverage of the AIDS epidemic. Today, it aims to actively "shape the narrative" and "provoke dialogue that leads to cultural change." Sarah Kate Ellis, who became GLAAD's president in early 2014, founded GLAAD's Media Institute, which advises individuals and companies on how to tell stories about "LGBTQ+" people "responsibly." Under Ellis, GLAAD sends consultants to review production materials for news segments, television shows, movies, and Broadway plays to ensure they are in-line with GLAAD's increasingly radical vision. It essentially boils down to the prioritization of political propaganda over art and free expression. Every year, GLAAD hosts a star-studded awards ceremony, where it awards arts and media professionals for adhering to its preapproved narrative.

In 2017, I had no idea just how out of touch organizations like GLAAD had become with the average gay American. After the 2015 Supreme Court decision in *Obergefell v. Hodges*, which made marriage equality the law of the land, radical activists had pounced. "You got what you want," they seemed to say. "Now it's our turn." GLAAD and the Human Rights Campaign, under the influence of far-left ideologues and in an attempt to stay relevant (i.e., donor-worthy), refocused their mission to trans people. But it was not just trans people who took hormones and underwent surgeries to soothe their gender dysphoria that they focused on. They also were concerned with trans people who evangelized trans identification as a sort of postcolonial project, a rebellion against the established order, against Enlightenment ideals, "whiteness," liberalism, capitalism, and the "bogus" notion of the sex binary. Every LGBT organization became an extension of a university Gender Studies department, whose purpose was not to produce new knowledge but to interrogate—or *queer*—the knowledge we had achieved through the hard sciences, since all of that knowledge was tainted by whiteness, colonialism, and the Western patriarchy. GLAAD and HRC would so badly lose their way that they would soon begin advocating for so-called sex changes for children and adolescents—kids who are a lot like the girly little boy I once was.

The next three months of my life would be one long sojourn into *The Twilight Zone*. I would only begin to make sense of this upside-down world over the years that followed, when I learned the dark truths about queer theory and the dystopian medical scandal known as "gender-affirming care."

That summer, there were about eight interns at GLAAD's New York office. We were cordoned off in a small room, separate from the full-time employees, who worked in offices and cubicles elsewhere on the same floor. The other interns—early twenty-somethings, most of them—worked on things like special events and graphic design, though a few of them mostly chatted and scrolled through social media.

In 2017, state legislatures around the country were introducing "bathroom bills" that mandated transgender people only use restrooms that correspond with their sex. There was a lot of media attention about how this legislation would negatively affect so-called trans kids, particularly in schools. Not yet aware of how GLAAD was misleading the public about this issue, I got firmly behind its mission to defeat these bills, especially after I read reports in liberal media about kids who were getting urinary tract infections because they weren't allowed to go into the bathroom of their choosing. As the News and Rapid Response intern, I assisted with research for GLAAD's press releases on this issue and on President Trump's recently announced transgender military ban and contributed reporting for its website.

Occasionally, as I pored over articles in *The Advocate* and *LGBTQ Nation*, I wondered how these trans kids differed from the gender-nonconforming little boy I had been. How could anyone confidently assign that kind of label to a child who still had years of maturing to do? *Besides,* I thought, *"trans" describes something a person* does *rather than something that they* are. That is, a "trans" person is an adult who medically "transitions" to attempt to live and pass as the opposite sex—right?

The internship ultimately proved invaluable, for it gave me a behind-the-scenes look at the tactics activist organizations use to effect social change. In GLAAD's case, there was a lot of boycotting and deplatforming. Sometime that spring, Roseanne Barr had voiced concern about policies that would allow anyone who merely "identified" as a woman into female-only spaces, a development she feared would increase the risk of sexual assault. For her views, Barr was labeled by trans activists as a TERF—a trans-exclusionary radical feminist, which, I learned, was basically the worst thing a woman could be.

Roseanne—a loud, often tactless comedian with a vocal affinity for Trump—was easy to hate. Certainly no one at GLAAD spoke up for her right to free speech and opinion. "We're calling for a boycott of Roseanne's new show. I need you to research every problematic thing she's tweeted about trans people," said one of my supervisors. Basically, I was being tasked with oppo research.

Whatever happened to having a civil conversation? I thought. Was this really the best approach to a controversial issue? While I agreed that Barr was obnoxious, I couldn't help but think she had a point. Obviously, not all transwomen are sexual predators. But they are biological males, after all. It didn't seem all that outrageous for a woman to speculate that predatory men might take advantage of lax policies in order to invade female spaces.

I found myself even more sympathetic to Barr after a quick Google search revealed that the overwhelming majority of transwomen don't undergo vaginoplasty, a castration procedure during which the remaining genital tissue is fashioned into something that resembles a vagina. So, basically, we'd just be opening female restrooms, locker rooms, fitting rooms, rape shelters, jails, and prisons to any man who claimed to "feel like" a woman—penis, balls, and all. If that was the case, then what even was the point of sex-segregated spaces?

Along with a behind-the-scenes look at the work of special interest groups, the internship gave me a crash course in Gen-Z political correctness, or what would soon be called "wokeness."

"How can you like Katy Perry when she totally appropriates black culture?" a fellow intern interrogated me during my first week.

One intern at GLAAD identified as straight—we'll call her Christine. One afternoon, Christine posted a selfie on Instagram in which she wore her gay best friend's sweatshirt. "I miss my BFF so much, I'm wearing her clothes," read the caption, followed by a string of pink heart emojis.

That's sweet, I thought.

"That's queerbaiting," said the interns.

"Queerbaiting," I learned, was when straight people are suspected of acting gay in order to get what they want from gay people, whether it's love and affection or something else. Another example would be producers of a television show hinting at, but never depicting, gay romance in order to attract a larger audience.

A couple of the GLAAD interns introduced themselves as "nonbinary," which, I was told, described someone who identifies as neither male nor female—or as both. This may be hard to believe, since 2017 doesn't seem like that long ago, but it was my first encounter with the concept.

It was also the first time I learned that I myself was something called "cisgender." Cisgender is a nominally neutral term used to describe a person who "identifies" as their biological sex. In other words, "cisgender" means anyone who is not transgender or nonbinary. While researching for this book, I learned that the use of the prefix "cis" (Latin for "on this side of," as opposed to trans, which means "on the other side of") in relation to sex and gender can be traced back to early twentieth-century Germany, when sexologist Ernst Burchard contrasted "cisvestitismus" with "transvestitismus"—that is, dressing in gender-conforming clothing versus cross-dressing. The English word "cisgender" was reportedly coined by a graduate student named Dana Leland Defosse in a 1994 post on the Usenet newsgroup alt.transgendered, though its usage became more widespread after the transgender writer Julia Serano used the word in the 2007 book *Whipping Girl.* "Cisgender" was added to the Oxford English Dictionary in 2015. In discourse, it is commonly shortened to "cis."

What most intrigued me about the word was the way the other interns enunciated it: with disdain, as if it were a slur, which reminded me of how my seventh-grade classmates called me "fag." Curiously, "cis" also mimics a hissing noise and sounds like it could be short for "sissy," another taunt gay men have endured for decades.

It felt strange, to suddenly be antagonized by my peers for what they seemed to be perceiving as conformity—and which was ultimately just my respect for the reality of biological sex—when for so many years I had been bullied for being gender *non*conforming. It looked like I was never going to be able to get it right.

In the end, "cisgender," I think, can be a useful term—it's easier than saying "not transgender." But over the years I've noticed that its addition to the lexicon has given a lot of shitty people cover to express their contempt for gay people, in particular the much-maligned designation "cis white gay."

"Cis white gay men are the weakest links and [I don't care] who knows it."

"Behind every bad man there is an even worse cis gay white man."

"We need to realize that gay cis white men are still cis white men."

"Maybe homophobia against cis white gay men is valid."

"I love it when white gays erase the trans and black side of this flag [...] You faggots deserve to get hate-crimed to death."

Those are just a few examples of social media posts shared by purportedly progressive and "queer" people. This attitude, which has permeated much of LGBT media in recent years, offers one explanation for the sharp uptick in the number of gay men and women who now identify under the umbrella of "trans/nonbinary." As I've told close friends, if I were to dye my hair purple, start painting my nails and wearing eyeliner, and change my pronouns, I would experience less antigay hostility in the "queer" community, since I would have visibly rejected cisheteronormativity. In fact, my change would also be taken as a signal that I'd adopted a whole set of acceptable politics and beliefs, including the belief that people are attracted to others on the basis of their internally felt gender as opposed to their sex. In the process, however, I would be denying who I really am. While gay men are many and varied, just like every other population, we all share one common trait: exclusive sexual attraction to other men, full stop.

When it came to the concept of "nonbinary," I was immediately thrown off by the plural pronouns. I went along with it as best I could, although I couldn't help but bristle whenever I had to use the grammatically incorrect language. (I no longer bristle, but only because I no longer participate in this farce.) Though I didn't say so, besides being kind of ridiculous, I thought the whole concept regressive and in direct conflict with what the gay and women's movements had been about.

Why should someone who defies rigid gender norms have to identify *out* of their sex category? If a woman who shaves her head and a man who wears makeup say they're nonbinary, then what they seemed to be communicating is that, to be a woman, you must have long hair and wear makeup, and to be a man, you have to have short hair and wear no makeup at all. As far as I had always understood it, the goal was to *expand* what was possible for the sexes and to recognize that inherently gender-nonconforming people were natural variations of their own sex. "Nonbinary" just made the categories of male and female *smaller*. In the end, it seemed to add up to nothing more than a funky haircut, a nose ring, and a gender-bending wardrobe.

As an activist, I had always supported transgender people's basic rights. But it was starting to become clear that my allyship would be insufficient so long as I failed to endorse the trans-radical view of human nature. I would have to deny the reality of the sex binary and sex differences. And I would have to abandon my identity as a homosexual man—since, if sex isn't real, then neither is homosexuality—and define myself as part of the problem. Because I wasn't willing to do this, I would soon suffer the consequences.

One GLAAD intern, Morgan, was a white female who alternately identified as trans and nonbinary, though her pronouns were consistently "they/them." I have neither the credentials nor the expertise to diagnose mental disorders, but I am certain Morgan was a textbook narcissist. Whenever the interns were chatting, if the attention happened to drift away from her and land on someone else, she would noticeably wither.

But I empathized with Morgan, because almost immediately I could tell how much her identity depended on the validation of others. Sometimes, as she proselytized nonsensically about gender (her favorite topic), I would find myself thinking about Henry David Thoreau and his two-year-long retreat into the woods. I had never read *Walden* in its entirety, though I knew it to be a reflection on individualism and self-reliance that resulted from living outside of society's constraints. Thoreau's story had always intrigued me, mostly because I wanted little more than the courage to simply be myself. The only time I ever came close was when I was alone.

I tried to imagine who or what Morgan would be, living alone on Walden Pond. Would she still claim to be trans/nonbinary if (like the proverbial tree in the forest) no other people were around to validate her identity?

Of course I kept these thoughts to myself. Besides, I was so preoccupied with speaking and behaving "correctly," there was no room left in my brain to distill my heresies into coherent sentences. All I knew for sure was that I objected to so much of what was occurring around me. And that terrified me. Not only because it meant I might be a terrible person but also because, if I were ever to truly be myself, I would need to be honest with myself and others about what I actually thought.

Morgan regularly preached that, to claim a transgender identity, one need not suffer from gender dysphoria, a condition the DSM-5 describes as a "marked incongruence between one's experienced/expressed gender" and one's natal sex. In fact, according to Morgan, you didn't have to medically transition, or even *want to*, in order to be trans.

Well, what the fuck is trans *then?* I remember thinking.

Most confusing of all, Morgan had a serious boyfriend, but she spent a lot of time on Grindr, the hook-up app for gay men.

"Cis white gays are so racist," she said once as she scrolled through Grindr. I sat nearby, compiling a Google Doc on a state senator who had voted in favor of a bathroom bill. Minutes earlier, Morgan had been taking a poll on whether her latest Instagram post was too risqué. It was a photo of her on her bed, wearing spandex shorts and a sports bra. Her breasts looked enormous.

"Cis gays are so problematic," she added. As though I weren't sitting right there.

Since I was not yet inured to these broad generalizations about "cis white gays," I bristled at Morgan's aspersions. Over the years, I had occasionally heard people claim that gay white men's dating profiles often included cruel and exclusionary statements about other races, although I had never seen anything like this myself. Not to suggest, of course, that these profiles didn't exist, or that some gay white men weren't racist. But to paint the entire population this way was obviously ridiculous.

Morgan's Grindr membership perplexed me. While she sometimes identified as trans—which I assumed meant she identified as a man—I knew she hadn't done anything to transition physically, besides perhaps abstaining from shaving her legs and changing her pronouns.

But even if she *had* modified her secondary sex characteristics with testosterone and/or surgery, she would still have been technically female and therefore not a gay man. I wondered why Morgan didn't find it even a little bit gauche to invade an online space that had been created specifically for gay men looking for sex and companionship. Her seeming disregard for the whole concept of homosexuality irked me. To make it worse, she thought it was actually okay for her to police the space!

My momentarily unfettered mind immediately summoned an analogy: Morgan's behavior was not unlike that of a white person claiming membership in a black community, then proceeding to call that community out for not being "black enough."

I finally sinned one August afternoon, when I said to Morgan, "Hey girl, you ready to go to lunch?"

Morgan scrunched up her face to indicate her evident distaste at being labeled female. I was instantly mortified and babbled, "I'm so sorry, I call all of my friends, 'girl!'"—which was actually the truth and probably had something to do with the fact that most of my friends were women. It also may have had to do with the fact that, apart from her moderately hairy legs and short haircut, everything about Morgan screamed "woman"—from her feminine wardrobe to her large breasts, high voice, bone structure, and all the other myriad ways in which humans distinguish females from males.

"That's such a 'cis gay' thing to say," Morgan scoffed.

I ruminated on my transgression for days.

DURING MY LAST week at GLAAD, I came across an *Out* magazine article in which writer Rose Dommu aired her frustration with gay men who had complained to her about bachelorette parties at gay bars. This might seem like a minor issue in the scheme of things. But the fact is, many gay men do in fact resent straight women for invading their communal spaces in this way. Some feel like the women are only there to gawk at them, like exotic animals at a petting zoo. Moreover, gay bars are a space for gays and lesbians to let loose, flirt, and behave like actual human beings—human beings with sexual drives and desires. The presence of straight people getting a weird high off their uninhibited behavior can be strangely, well, inhibiting.

Yet for some reason, Dommu was incensed by this "exclusionary" attitude. "Women in gay bars are not limited to bachelorettes," she wrote. "Did you forget that queer women exist? Trans women? Straight women with gay friends or straight women who just like gay bars or drag queens?"

I actually thought Dommu made some valid points, until I reached her concluding diatribe against gay men: "If you can't dance to some shitty house song or go down on a stranger just because a woman is in the room, you need to examine what that says about you."

Well, what *does* that say about me? Because, no, I really *don't* want to have sex in front of women. I'm gay!

Further, no matter how long we've been out of the closet, many gay men still struggle with feelings of shame after having sex with other men, regardless of whether it takes place in an accepting space. One reason we have historically sought out gay bars and bathhouses is because many of us don't feel entirely safe anywhere else. These were the only places where we could feel entirely free. In some places, they still are.

I turned with an annoyed expression to the intern sitting to my right. That day, it happened to be Morgan.

"What is it?" she said.

I summarized the essay and explained my objections. Morgan furrowed her brow. "But I think that writer is trans," she said.

Her response left me speechless. Apparently, trans people were so oppressed that it was verboten to even disagree with one. But didn't this attitude ultimately dehumanize trans people by locating the worth of their ideas in who they *are* rather than what they think or say? What did someone's trans-ness have to do with the merit of his/her argument?

After a few more semesters at Columbia, where I would see more and more people variously identifying as queer, nonbinary, or transgender, it would all make sense. Morgan and others like her were just trying to survive the intersectional hellscape in which we found ourselves by embracing the new orthodoxy and becoming an enforcer of it. As an official member of the "LGBTQ+" community, she no longer had to worry about saying and doing the right things, since her membership in an "oppressed" and "marginalized" group meant she was inherently better and more enlightened than straight, white, "cis" men or women. "LGBTQ+" identity even brought professional opportunity, what with the sudden proliferation of DEI departments across the country, which prioritized minorities in hiring. It was a genius capitalist enterprise. Plus, as a bonus, if she harbored any homophobia, she could now express it without fear.

It legitimately bummed me out to see how eager these privileged young people were to be viewed as persecuted victims. I had spent the better part of my adult life doing everything I could to heal from mental illness and addiction so that I could rise to their level of social and economic opportunity. I wanted to be a survivor, not a victim. I knew I didn't have a choice; I could either get help and get better or give up and die. Besides, taking responsibility for myself as an addict in recovery was what gave me self-esteem. It's what empowered me to make my own life.

Instead, what I saw happening around me was the exact opposite. People were doing everything they could to disempower themselves and each other. This illusion of helplessness allowed them to climb up the greasy pole of the new inverted status hierarchy. Not only that, but it also seemed to reinforce dependence on the state, which exponentially empowered the state—especially after this mindset invaded the bureaucracy and intersectional ideologues gained control of the levers of power. Being a survivor was lame. Being a victim was fucking cool. And lucrative!

Along with the benefit of identifying into a supposedly marginalized group, there was yet another reason so many people were identifying as "LGBTQ+." It was to be a part of a radical queer political project, a total rebellion against anything considered "normative." Eventually, "queer" would become a stand-in for "anti-Western," a development epitomized by the activist group, "Queers for Palestine," which, after the October 2023 terrorist attack in Israel, would gain notoriety for its bizarre inconsistency during the pro-Palestine demonstrations that erupted on campuses and in cities nationwide.

EVERY DAY, I left the GLAAD offices completely drained of energy. Not because the work was particularly tiresome, but because I was exhausting so much mental energy making sure I didn't misspeak or accidentally misgender someone. I was so desperate to be good and so afraid of being exposed as a heretic.

When the internship finally ended in mid-August, I spent the rest of my summer vacation indoors, watching bad TV and nursing my resurgent OCD.

CHAPTER 11

I met Nathan at orientation, during a meet-and-greet when we wound up in the same small group. We were surprised to learn that we had grown up in the same general area of Maryland, though he was about six years younger than me. Equally interesting was that, in the 1970s, his parents had also joined a cult. But rather than a charismatic Christian covenant community, it was the International Society of Krishna Consciousness, commonly known as the Hare Krishnas.

When Nathan was eighteen, he joined an offshoot organization called Sri Caitanya Sangha, where he served as a personal assistant to the group's leader, Tom (or "Swami," as he would come to be known), and also as a group manager and preacher. During his first year with the group, Nathan spent four months in the jungles of Costa Rica, where, through hard physical labor, sleep deprivation, and indoctrination, he was molded into a member of the group's "inner circle."

Until he was twenty-four, Nathan lived in a yurt at the end of an unpaved road in northern California, surrounded by redwoods. He left the Hare Krishnas in 2015. At Columbia, he planned to major in psychology and to eventually work in abuse and influence prevention.

Nathan was a godsend, especially during my first year, when I was having a hard time articulating, even to myself, just how disturbed I was by some aspects of the campus culture, particularly the purity policing and groupthink.

One night near the beginning of the Fall 2017 semester, standing outside of Lewisohn Hall, Nathan and I smoked cigarettes and talked about "wokeness." I told him I generally agreed with what self-identified woke people claimed to stand for, like equality and social justice, but was wary of how they were going about it, which reminded me of the community I had grown up in. I also said that all this talk of "equity," rather than equality of opportunity, seemed authoritarian—like its aim was to put power in the hands of those who don't have it through nonlegal means. It's one thing to oppose racism and sexism, and to want to make opportunities to succeed available to everyone. But to enact a system that discounts merit and denies certain groups opportunities based on their immutable identities? That seemed inherently discriminatory and therefore un-American. Not just that, but I feared it would inevitably invoke mass resentment and only fuel division.

Nathan, too, was passionate about social justice and broadly agreed with woke politics. What worried him about the discourse, he said, was its binary nature: You were either woke and therefore totally enlightened, or you were not and thus totally ignorant. In Krishna Consciousness, one must fully believe that the community has a monopoly on the highest truth and that, with this truth, they can save others. Indeed, they have an obligation to do so. "Wake up, souls!" was the first line of a Bengali song that Nathan had regularly recited before sunrise. That was his mission: to "wake up" and help others do the same. What Nathan saw occurring within the woke social justice movement was all too familiar to him.

A week or so after Nathan and I spoke, in early October 2017, a protest erupted after the Columbia College Republicans invited Tommy Robinson to speak at the university via Skype. Robinson, a controversial British activist who cofounded the English Defence League, opposes "global Islamification" and has called Islam inherently "violent" and "fascist." A central figure in publicizing the existence of Muslim rape gangs in Britain, he has served multiple prison terms for his political activities.

Though Robinson was still fairly obscure in 2017, he has since become something of a folk hero on the American right. On the left, he was just well-known enough to turn out a sizeable protest at Columbia.

Over thirty protesters, some of whom held signs that read HATE SPEECH = VIOLENCE, stormed the Lerner Hall auditorium to disrupt Robinson's virtual speech. Outside, 250 more people gathered in protest, among them members of Refuse Fascism (led by the Revolutionary Communist Party, USA), Black Lives Matter of Greater New York, the Muslim Students' Association, the International Socialist Organization, and Southern Poverty Law Center's Columbia chapter. (On Facebook, SPLC at Columbia writes that its job is to "push back against" the "unchecked white supremacist ideology" that "pervade[s] universities everywhere.") Some banged on the doors of the auditorium while others, like Durrell Washington, a student at Columbia's School of Social Work, addressed the gathered crowd. "Being a black body on this campus who looks the way I do—I don't conform in the way I dress, I don't conform in the way I talk—I get looks," Washington said, as reported in *Columbia Daily Spectator*. "We have to be made comfortable."

The protest against Robinson was held on a Tuesday, the only weekday that I didn't have classes that semester. I wasn't aware that it had occurred until two nights later, when I overheard a Barnard student boasting in my nonfiction writing class about her participation. During that particular class, this student had accused me of improperly sexualizing my oldest sister for mentioning in a personal essay a tattoo she had on her thigh. Another classmate said she was offended by the way I had described people in a park. The offending paragraph read: "When I arrive at the park, I'm happy to see that it isn't crowded: only a young white couple chasing their two small children, three elderly Korean women taking pictures, and a homeless man sitting on a bench and speaking to no one."

After class, I shared the paragraph with Nathan via text message and asked if he found anything problematic about it. He responded with a series of question marks.

"I'm being policed by radicals," I replied. "Never in a million years did I think that would be an issue in my life."

Nathan responded, "Dude, it gets so out of control. I see nothing racist, and I think they'd be hard-pressed to persuasively argue how."

"It wasn't even so much about race as it was about me degrading the homeless person or something," I wrote. "I don't even know anymore."

A couple of weeks later, Nathan and I met at the Starbucks just off campus. I told him more about my writing class, and he commiserated. I then asked him if he knew about the Robinson protest. He said yes, adding that some friends had actually invited him to attend. At the time, he had no idea who the guy was, so he looked him up. In the end, he declined his friends' invitation, explaining that he didn't feel the need to protest the speech of someone he was largely unfamiliar with.

For refusing the invite, Nathan's friends began jokingly calling him a "Nazi." Nathan's mother, though she practiced Hinduism, was Jewish, and his father was black and of Middle Eastern descent. Nathan told me he initially thought it was funny—he couldn't be further from a Nazi. "But after a while, it just got old."

Nazism—like "violence," "harm," "white supremacist," and myriad other concepts—was now applied so broadly, it was beginning to lose its original meaning. Soon, even Jews would be Nazis.

THAT SEMESTER, I enrolled in a course called US Lesbian and Gay History, taught by George Chauncey, a preeminent scholar in the field. Chauncey, the author of a celebrated history of gay people in prewar New York, had served as an expert witness in more than thirty gay rights cases, including 2003's *Lawrence v. Texas*, which struck down laws criminalizing gay intercourse, and 2015's *Obergefell v. Hodges*. He had previously taught at Yale, where he chaired both the History Department and the Committee for LGBT Studies. Chauncey, along with Sociology Professor Tey Meadow and Gender Studies professor Jack (Judith) Halberstam, were, I had read, part of a $3 million "LGBTQ faculty-diversity initiative" recently devised by the vice provost for faculty diversity and inclusion. This was Chauncey's first semester at Columbia.

The class was held on Monday and Wednesday mornings on the top floor of Hamilton Hall. The building had only one small elevator, and students lined up early to use it, so most mornings I had to climb the seven flights to get there. But it was worth it. Courses like this were the reason I had wanted to go back to school in the first place. I needed to learn as much as possible about gay history so that I could be a more effective writer and activist. I couldn't wait to get started.

I was happy to see that Molly had also enrolled. I grabbed the empty seat next to her and together we looked over the syllabus. In Chauncey's class, we would cover an extensive period of gay history, from Colonial England to the present day, with a significant focus on pre- and post-WWII America; antigay policing and the purge of gays from the US government during the Cold War, otherwise known as the Lavender Scare; the post-Stonewall movement; the rise of the Christian Right and culture wars of the 1990s; the AIDS crisis; and the fight for marriage equality. Besides numerous essays, news articles, and primary sources, required readings would include intersectional feminist Audre Lorde's *Zami: A New Spelling of My Name* and staunch anticapitalist John D'Emilio's *Sexual Politics, Sexual Communities: The Making of a Homosexual Minority, 1945–1970*. Both were not just gay activists but political radicals as well. In her famous poem, "East Berlin 1989," Lorde lamented the triumph of capitalist democracy over communism after the fall of the Berlin Wall, while in 2014, D'Emilio told *OutHistory* that the fight for marriage equality was "a sad misdirection of a social change movement's limited resources."

Chauncey's syllabus promised that we would explore "the social, cultural, and political history of lesbians, gay men, and other socially constituted sexual and gender minorities, primarily in the twentieth century." Attention would be paid "to the shifting boundaries of normative sexuality," since "the production and regulation of queer life has always been intimately linked to the production and policing of 'normal' sexuality and gender."

"I have no idea what any of that means," said Molly.

"Thank God," I said. "Neither do I."

Sitting in the back row, we watched as nearly every seat in the classroom was filled by a young woman. In front of us, a white student with dark circles under her eyes talked on her phone. "Seriously, Mom, I have to go," she said before abruptly hanging up. Her lavender and green iPhone case read THIS DEVICE RECORDS POLICE.

Chauncey's first lecture focused on sodomy ("antibuggery") laws in seventeenth-century New England. I typed notes in my MacBook to get down as much information as possible.

"We're committing a common error of historical thought if we think of sodomy as a strictly homosexual behavior," Chauncey said. "Not because it didn't describe men having sex with men, like it does today, but because there was no concept of homosexuality back then."

"Homosexuality" and "heterosexuality" are distinctly modern ideas, Chauncey explained. As recently as the nineteenth century, sex between men (or sex between women) was just something people engaged in—just another form of sin that anyone could be tempted to commit—like blasphemy, thievery, or drunkenness, though it was a far direr vice, since any sex outside the marriage bed was born of unfettered lust and therefore fostered societal disorder. Many considered sodomy akin to bestiality, as just another type of "wild sex" that threatened to shatter the boundary between man and beast.

Until the mid-twentieth century—and this would turn out to be the overarching thesis of Chauncey's class—it was their gender-nonconformity that distinguished this minority of people, rather than what came to be called their "sexual orientation." In this way, what we now think of as a stereotypical gay man, who is effeminate and exclusively attracted to men, or a stereotypical lesbian, who is butch and attracted to women, was back then considered something akin to a third gender, or a "gender invert." Some cynically argue that the shift from a gender-based concept of difference to one concerned with the object of desire undermined our inherent bisexuality and entrenched rigid gender norms, coercing people to avoid gender-nonconforming behavior for fear of being labeled "gay."

Others, like me, believe it helped gay people to organize politically and produce material results.

Over time, other words would be used to describe gender inverts, such as "fairies," "degenerates," "pansies," and "faggots." Some or even many of these inverts would cross-dress—the males often for fun and even public entertainment, and the women in an effort to temporarily secure some of the same rights and privileges as men. Later, in order to restabilize a society that had been upended by two world wars, a new pressure would be put on American men and women to not only pair up and procreate but also to quickly resume traditional sex roles and behaviors. Women, soft and sensitive, belonged in the home; men, strong and stoic, were the providers. Those who failed to conform were seen as disloyal to the cause. Then, during the Red Scare, when gays were purged from the US government on suspicion of anti-Americanism and vulnerability to blackmail by communists, the pressure for everyone, "normal" and "queer"—or "heterosexual" and "homosexual"—to conform to gender stereotypes would exponentially increase in order to avoid suspicion of deviance.

Contemplating the concept of the "gender invert," I recalled my own history of gender nonconformity. *So*, I thought, *perhaps there's not much of a difference between a transwoman and me after all.*

Later in the semester, said Chauncey, we would learn about Christine Jorgensen, born George William Jorgensen Jr., the US military veteran who, in 1952, was the first American to receive what was called a "sex reassignment surgery."

More than once during his lecture, Chauncey emphasized viewing the gay movement through an intersectional lens. He stressed that gay rights, transgender rights, and black civil rights were all part of one, singular fight—an argument that, I have come to think, incorrectly presupposes everyone within these populations is in staunch agreement about our priorities and what our collective goals should be. In other words, it presupposes political homogeneity. In reality, gays are ideologically diverse, as are trans and black people. And today, when trans radicals argue that sex is a spectrum, that males belong in women's sports, that gender-nonconforming children should be medically transitioned, and that lesbians who refuse the sexual advances of males are "bigots" and "genital fetishists," then no, we are not in the same fight. I would say we are fighting each other.

Toward the end of class, Chauncey launched into a lengthy aside about primary historical documents and research. He explained that scholarship about the homosexual practices of people of color is limited, since historiography privileges white people. He would try to include as much as possible about black, brown, and Asian gay history, but the vast majority of existing scholarship was about white gay people, white gay men in particular. He strongly encouraged the class to rectify this and said he would be thrilled if we left the class inspired to help unearth the history of gay people of color.

As Molly and I descended the western stairwell of Hamilton Hall, we overheard other students discuss Chauncey's class.

"So apparently he's just going to talk about gay white men the whole time," one said.

"Yeah, as if black queer people don't exist?" said another.

Molly whispered to me, "Didn't Chauncey literally just explain the reason for this like five seconds ago?"

I nodded wearily. Nine months into my tenure at Columbia, I was growing tired of this bullshit.

Chauncey's class quickly paid off. Among the first assigned readings was by the prominent queer theorist (and Foucault sycophant) David Halperin, whose work helped me begin to understand the political project at the core of queer theory as well as what "queer" in this context actually means. The lesson would prove invaluable, for it showed me exactly what I was not and never wanted to be.

"Queer is by definition whatever is at odds with the normal, the legitimate, the dominant," Halperin wrote in *Saint Foucault: Towards a Gay Hagiography*, one of his many influential publications. "It is an identity without an essence" and "available to anyone who is or feels marginalized because of his or her sexual practices." In other words, one didn't have to be gay to be queer. Halperin continued, "One can't become homosexual, strictly speaking: either one is or one isn't. But one can marginalize oneself; one can transform oneself; one can become queer."

In *The History of Sexuality, Volume 1*, Foucault claimed that the state's pathologizing and criminalization of homosexual acts are what resulted in the construction of the heterosexual/homosexual binary. As Chauncey explained in his first lecture, by the beginning of the twentieth century, homosexual acts were no longer deviant acts which people, for one reason or another, partook in; rather, they were now partaken by a distinct *type* of deviant person: a *homosexual*. The invention of the word thus invented the individual. "The sodomite was a temporary aberration; the homosexual is now a species," wrote Foucault.

In *Saint Foucault*, Halperin argues that Foucault's concept of the homosexual as a product of nineteenth century discourse provided a radical opportunity for social transformation and sparked the beginning of the anti-assimilationist, queer project. According to Halperin, this was the task that Foucault had assigned us: to "become queer."

"Queerness," then, is not a sexual orientation, but rather a radical political project and a form of revolutionary activism.

Foucault's philosophy is perhaps best explained by the *panopticon*. The panopticon is a circular prison design. In the center is a guard tower, and all around it are the prison cells. From the tower, the guard can see inside every cell, but none of the prisoners can see inside the tower. The idea is that, because the inmates never know when they're being watched, they'll self-regulate to avoid punishment for misbehaving. The panopticon's designer, the eighteenth-century English philosopher Jeremy Bentham, thought it could serve as a model for how a democratic society should operate if it wants to maintain order. Citizens who believe they're being surveilled will end up policing themselves.

To Foucault, Bentham's design had become our reality. Western society is a prison. All around us are invisible power structures that coerce and control. To attack these power structures, Foucault proselytized, we must rethink what we've been told is right and true.

The only reason we think insane people are insane is because the powerful told us what constitutes sanity.

The only reason we think success is good is because the powerful insist we must not fail.

The only reason we think a child can't consent is because the powerful deny children their agency.

Therefore, we must rethink sanity.

Rethink happiness.

Rethink decency.

To free ourselves, we must "queer" our reality.

Academics, who treat Foucault's work like scripture, constantly debate his intended meaning, much as theologians debate the Bible. I anticipate many didactic lectures from sophisticated theorists, who will insist that I have gotten him all wrong. Some of their points might be valid. But, in the end, what exactly Foucault meant by his words is largely irrelevant. What matters is the profound impact his work has had on the academy's approach to "knowledge."

In a 1978 interview, Foucault himself said that his purpose was "to find out where are the weak points of power, from which we can attack it." Foucault's priority was to undermine existing knowledge and Western faith in modernity in order to thwart the capitalist state. Some would call Foucault a Marxist, and much of his writing suggests that he was. But his vocal opposition to capitalism would wane after he realized how much it had benefitted his other great cause of sexual liberation. Ultimately it is unclear what sort of society Foucault preferred over the current one; his priority was the subversion of power, wherever it existed.

Over time, the more I learned about Foucault, the more I would come to resent him. For, ultimately, I don't think he was concerned with social justice at all. I only think he was concerned with himself. I believe he wanted us to rethink morals and ethics and what constitutes a sane and rational mind in order to make society more amenable to his transgressiveness. I have come to believe that Foucault longed for a world of radical libertinism, one in which state repression of any desire, sexual or otherwise, was taboo.

After all, the Marquis de Sade was a moral hero of Foucault's. And in 1978, Foucault himself said of sex with minors that assuming "that a child is incapable of explaining what happened and was incapable of giving his consent are two abuses that are intolerable, quite unacceptable." These attitudes pervade the discipline of queer theory. And why wouldn't they? Its aim is to rethink everything we know to be good and true, so that we might be free to behave in whatever perverse way we choose.

"It is harder for most people to sympathize with actual boy-lovers," wrote the University of Michigan gender studies professor, Gayle Rubin, in "Thinking Sex: Notes for a Radical Theory of the Politics of Sexuality," which is widely considered to be the founding document of queer theory. "Like communists and homosexuals in the 1950s, boy-lovers are so stigmatized that it is difficult to find defenders for their civil liberties, let alone for their erotic orientation." Pat Califia, a transman who worked as a marriage and family counselor in California, wrote in *Public Sex: The Culture of Radical Sex*, "Age-of-consent laws don't make sense even if you believe that the desire and ability to have sex don't develop fully until puberty. These laws are completely arbitrary and do not take into account the varying degrees of physical and emotional maturity possessed by young people or the fact that puberty is occurring at earlier and earlier ages." Califia continued, "Boy-lovers (and girl-lovers, though they are less visible) are the new communists, the new niggers, the new witches." (Interestingly, in the same essay, Califia referenced Anita Bryant's crusade in 1977, which ultimately "allowed the police to mount a terrorist campaign against gay youth and their adult lovers." I'm sure this essay, written in 1980, did a lot to quell Bryant's concerns.) And of course we can't leave out the high priest of queer theory, UC Berkeley professor Judith Butler, who wrote in *Undoing Gender* that "not all forms on incest are necessarily traumatic (brother/sister incest in eighteenth century literature for example sometimes appears as idyllic.)"

A more recent example of queer theory's intersection with child sexual abuse can be found in a social media post written by the media personality Alok Vaid-Menon, a "transfeminine" man with they/them pronouns who graduated from Stanford with a BA in feminist, gender, and sexuality studies and comparative studies in race and ethnicity.

"These days the narrative is that freaky transgender people (or as they say 'crossdressers') will come into your bathrooms and abuse innocent little girls," Alok wrote. "This type of legal/carceral culture relies on two things: the construction of morally abhorrent perpetrators/scapegoats AND the production of pure, innocent victims. In this case, as in so many cases in the past, those victims are archetypical (white) (cis) innocent little girls."

Alok, who has 1.5 million followers on Instagram, continued, "I believe in the radical notion that little girls, like the rest of us, are complicated people. There are no fairy tales and no princesses here. Little girls are also queer, trans, kinky, deviant, kind, mean, beautiful, ugly, tremendous, and peculiar. Your kids aren't as straight and narrow as you think they are."

Anita Bryant died in December 2024 at the age of eighty-four. Reports say the cause of death was cancer, although I wonder if it was Alok's diatribe that did it.

Jack (Judith) Halberstam, one of the professors Columbia hired along with Chauncey as part of its "LGBTQ faculty-diversity initiative," is now a professor in the department of English and Comparative Literature and the Institute for Research on Women, Gender, and Sexuality. Though Chauncey did not assign Halberstam's work, I eventually came across it myself, as I began to stumble down the queer theory rabbit hole. In her 2011 book, *The Queer Art of Failure*, now considered to be a part of the queer theoretical canon, Halberstam actually *promoted* failure—that is, unemployment, slacking off, ignorance, stupidity, even self-cutting—as an expression of queerness. "Failure allows us to escape the punishing norms that discipline behavior and manage human development with the goal of delivering us from unruly childhoods to orderly and predictable adulthoods," she wrote. The "disappointment, disillusionment, and despair" that are sure to result from failure might suck, but we can "use these negative affects to poke holes in the toxic positivity of contemporary life." Apparently, to Halberstam, the very benefits of personal success are "toxic."

Thinking back to the information session for LGBT student groups that I attended during my first semester, I wondered if Halberstam's book was not considered gospel among those fragile, PJ-clad "queer" kids.

Halberstam wrote that the worship of success should be left "to the Republicans, to the corporate managers of the world, to the winners of reality TV shows, to married couples, to SUV drivers." Easy for Halberstam to say. Something tells me the kids who follow her advice—the "queer" kids who thrive on nihilism, the kids who rebel and self-mutilate—might not find failure quite as enjoyable as being a published author and a well-paid Ivy League professor.

To be queer, then, is to marginalize oneself, to rebel against the existing order, even if that order benefits the many over the few. To be queer is to revel in victimhood. It is to reject Western epistemology. It is to act on one's base instincts and desires. It is to fail, even when success is within reach, if only to prove that failure is inevitable in the current system for anyone who is not cisheteronormative and white.

I wanted no part of it. I did not want to be queer; I knew the difference between right and wrong. And I did not want to "queer" reality; I had tried to do that for years with opiates, cocaine, and LSD, and it had landed me in the psych ward. Today, I wanted to live in reality. I wanted to be part of the world. And if there were aspects of the world that I thought might need changing, then I would work within the bounds of shared empirical reality to try and bring that change about, rather than demanding everyone else bend reality to my whims. I had faced homophobia and discrimination head on by advocating for my rights and for acceptance and equality. I didn't need to undermine the reality of who I was—let alone everyone else's—in order to escape oppression. I had stood up to oppression, like so many other activists before me, by appealing to others through our common humanity. I had formed relationships with people who were different from me, people who saw that I was a human being just like they were, but who happened to be attracted to other men.

LIKE CONTEMPORARY ISLAMIC Civilization, one of Chauncey's class requirements was to attend a weekly TA-led recitation section. There were a few different sections to choose from, so Molly and I made sure to sign up for the same one.

During one of our first meetings, we discussed an assigned reading, Karen V. Hansen's *'No Kisses is Like Youres'[sic]: An Erotic Friendship between Two African-American Women during the Mid-Nineteenth Century.* When it came my turn, I said, "It fascinated me to read how socially acceptable it was for black women in the 1800s to behave so romantically with one another. My gay black friends often talk about how taboo homosexuality can be in the black community."

I was thinking specifically of Shaun, who often discussed this issue with me. It was also a topic I'd recently seen explored by the black actress and writer Lena Waithe in the Emmy-winning show *Master of None.* In one episode, a black lesbian comes out to her family at Thanksgiving. The family members' mixed responses illustrate common attitudes within black society. Further, when I worked on Maryland's marriage-equality campaign, I learned that one of our biggest challenges would be in Prince George's County—one of the wealthiest majority-black counties in the country—where black church leaders and activists had rallied against gay marriage.

Three white women sitting across from me immediately signaled their discomfort. One spoke up forcefully, saying that the reason black women who behaved romantically with each other were more accepted back then was because black communities couldn't afford to alienate their own people. "They needed solidarity to fight oppression," she said.

"Right," I said unthinkingly, not so much agreeing with her as cowed by her open hostility. Her friends continued to glare at me.

"What the hell was that about?" Molly whispered, apparently as surprised as I was.

I shrugged, genuinely confused, although I was becoming accustomed to this sort of bad-faith response from my classmates. Perhaps they thought that, by merely mentioning homophobia among the black population, I was implying there was something morally wrong with black people in general, or that homophobia didn't exist in the white population.

Regardless, any possibility of a fruitful discussion about race and homosexuality was immediately squashed. The TA, probably noticing the palpable tension in the room, quickly moved on to the next reading.

The following week, Molly didn't show up for the discussion session, so I texted her.

"Switched to another section—weird vibes in that one," she wrote.

Molly was younger than me, much closer to the age of traditional students, and some of the women in the class were potential dating prospects. I couldn't help but suspect that she didn't want to be seen associating with me. If so, I didn't blame her.

I HAD CERTAINLY felt alienated during my summer internship at GLAAD, but it was during Chauncey's class that it became clear just how out of step I was with prevailing queer orthodoxy on campus. To these radicals, I was a traitor to the cause of razing the West and creating in its place some sort of radically libertine utopia. Though I should say that, in retrospect, I'm sure that a lot of my "queer" peers didn't truly believe, or even understand, the dogma they were parroting. They just wanted to belong.

To be fair, Chauncey took a fairly nuanced stance toward the material throughout the semester. Over all, I saw him as a deep well of knowledge about gay history, and he was always kind and supportive of my work in the class. In retrospect my only real complaint was his decision to omit from his lectures any details about the widespread objection among various scholars and writers to queer theory's absorption of the field of lesbian and gay studies in general. I would have to discover these thinkers on my own.

One of those thinkers is Bruce Bawer, a fiercely independent cultural critic and author of the 1993 book, *A Place at the Table: The Gay Individual in American Society*. In his 2012 book *The Victims' Revolution*, Bawer explained that Gay Studies in the United States began as a discipline, which, like other academic departments, would use reason, evidence, logic, and the nature of knowledge to inch closer to the truth. That is, it was to be a continuation of the Enlightenment project. *Per scientiam ad justitiam*—"Through science to justice"—was the motto of Berlin's Scientific-Humanitarian Committee, founded in 1897 by the sexologist Magnus Hirschfeld and considered to be the first organization of its kind.

But New Left academics, who ridiculed early founders of Gay Studies as "assimilationist," were determined to "break with the existing edifice of knowledge" à la Foucault. Soon, even hypothesizing about, say, the scientific cause of homosexuality was problematic, for this presupposed something wrong with it—something that needed to be "figured out" and possibly corrected. Further, what if there turned out to be no scientific explanation for homosexuality? Or worse, what if its cause *was* determined and, via eugenics, gays were erased from the gene pool? Neither of these outcomes would aid our cause, so best to leave it alone.

By the early 1990s, Gay Studies had been totally transformed by the social-constructionist view of sexual orientation. Social constructionists argue that homosexuality is not inherent or biological, but rather strictly the product of social and cultural norms. Like Foucault, they are often preoccupied with language, the production of knowledge, and power. In the preceding decade, queer theorists like Judith Butler made waves by applying constructionist theory to bodily sex, suggesting it is not just "gender" (norms, behaviors and roles typically associated with being a man or a woman) that is socially constructed, but biological sex as well. This speculative theory metastasized into an actual belief system, spreading through Western institutions like wildfire, which is why, today, we have otherwise intelligent people stating, in all sincerity, that sex is irrelevant to what makes one male or female. Rather, it is the feminine or masculine behaviors and social role an individual performs, or that society projects upon an individual, that defines one's sex.

Butler, I should add, has also said that the terrorist groups Hamas and Hezbollah should be understood "as social movements that are progressive, that are on the Left, that are part of a global left." In practice, of course, the effort to construct a global left (if such a thing even exists) requires the suppression of difference and dissent within its ranks.

To garner support for these radical ideas, critical theorists frequently attach them to the project of antiracism, implying that they're one and the same. In her latest book, *Who's Afraid of Gender?*, Butler reiterates the popular woke claim that "dimorphism serves the reproduction of the normative white family in the United States." (As if sexual dimorphism, rather than being an aspect of material reality, is a simple theory one can negotiate with.) She supports this argument by mentioning the experimental gynecological surgeries performed on black women in the time of slavery, when white women were held up as the ideal against which black women were measured. To Butler, this proves that the "bodies" of black women were the "foundation" upon which "sexed culture or civilization was built."

Butler is right that black women were seen as subhuman during slavery, but beyond that this ridiculous argument fails to make any sense. African and indigenous cultures around the world might have different sex roles and gender categories, but sex is the same across all of them. Sex is *universal.* And frankly, I don't know how anyone could fail to see that claiming otherwise is inherently primitivist and racist. They might use different words for it, but all humans instinctively know the difference between a male and a female. It is a knowledge the human species has possessed for hundreds of thousands of years, and it is the reason we're still here.

It would be nice if we could just laugh off these nonsensical claims. Unfortunately, they're taken seriously in the anti-Western academy. And their proliferation in universities and activist organizations has opened up a space in the US for the adoption of harmful practices and policies based on regressive notions of sex and sexuality. If sex as we know it is a fiction—just a figment of the "racist," "colonialist" imagination—then sex is divorced from the human body, and the definitions of male and female are up for grabs.

This "decolonization" of sex has created a vacuum, and something called "gender identity ideology" has stepped in to fill the void. Women are no longer adult human females who can choose to procreate or not procreate, stay home or go to work, wear dresses or pants, keep their hair long or short, and sleep with men or women. Rather, a woman is now the female stereotype, and any male who fits this stereotype, even by half measures, can call himself female—*and the rest of society must acknowledge him as such.* Even worse, girly little boys and butch little girls are no longer sissies or tomboys who may (or may not) grow up to be gay, but rather "trans kids" who've been born in the wrong body and need to be "fixed" via a medical regimen that causes sterility and anorgasmia and enslaves them to the medical industry for the rest of their lives, condemning them to fight tooth-and-nail against nature, forever.

Opposite social constructionists are the so-called essentialists who respect the biological reality of sex and sexuality. Sex, of course, is determined by the type of gamete an individual's reproductive system is organized to produce: Males produce small gametes (sperm) and females produce large gametes (ova). Approximately 0.02 percent of humans (1 in 5000) are born with what are called disorders of sexual development (DSD). Historically people with DSDs have been erroneously referred to as intersex, although every individual with a DSD can still be technically classified as male or female. Importantly, DSDs have nothing to do with transgenderism, and people with DSDs do not constitute a third sex, since there is no third type of gamete. *Sex is binary.*

Homosexuality is exclusive sexual attraction to the same sex and is likely the result of biological, hormonal, physiological, and genetic factors. It is fixed, not fluid. Social conditioning, of course, can't entirely be ruled out as a causal factor of homosexuality. And yes, cultural conditions have always affected the way homosexuals have defined themselves and lived their lives. But historical records show that exclusively same-sex-attracted people have existed across time and cultures, from the Hellenistic and Roman worlds to Renaissance Florence to eighteenth-century England and France.

The gay historian Rictor Norton explained the political root of the constructionist ideology in his 2010 essay, "F*ck Foucault: How Eighteenth-Century Homosexual History Validates the Essentialist Model." To constructionists, the state's purpose of creating a distinction between "homosexuals" and "heterosexuals" was twofold: First, to establish a *norm* (in modern parlance, "cisheteronormativity") against which all non-normative acts (and people) would be judged, pathologized, and criminalized; and second, to further the capitalist project. How would this aid capitalism? Well, within this Marxist framework, one of the state's priorities is to control the working classes' reproductive capacity to boost capitalist production. If the state can distinguish between procreative and therefore productive individuals and non-procreative, unproductive individuals, then it can determine which individuals are essentially useless, justifying discrimination and, in this case, homophobia. Straight people produce more workers and also more consumers; homosexuals produce neither.

It's a cynical and conspiratorial perspective. But it has a distinct purpose: It radicalizes the homosexual by politicizing his identity. This new consciousness encourages the homosexual to then question the validity of all things related to normative gender and sexuality. It coerces the homosexual to throw off this oppressive label so that he is no longer an object that the state can oppress. After all, you can't oppress homosexuals if there aren't any.

"To support the key claim that homophobia actually constructs homosexuality," wrote Norton, "it has been deemed necessary to throw the homosexual baby out with the homophobic bathwater. The effect of this has been to erase the homosexual from history."

But it goes far beyond eradicating homophobia (and consequently, "homosexuals"). It is also an attempt to undermine the foundations of a prosperous and stable democratic-capitalist society, such as marriage and bourgeois morality. It is thus part and parcel of the larger Marxist revolutionary project within American universities. As Norton explained, "Many pioneering theorists of the history of homosexuality were members of Socialist groups committed to the use of Marxist theory to oppose gay oppression." He continued, "The ambition of socialist 'critical theory'...is not to find an accurate historical model, but to foster social change."

In other words, critical theorists aren't after the truth. They want to reengineer society in their image by configuring a proper narrative. Kind of like GLAAD, which aims to "shape the narrative" about LGBT issues and "provoke dialogue" that leads to "cultural change." The parallels between the goal of critical theorists and the goal of an activist organization are, of course, not coincidental. Critical theorists are activists before they are educators.

Until I learned that there was an opposing view to social constructionism, I struggled to figure out why it perturbed me, particularly the notion that gay people didn't really exist prior to the introduction of the word "homosexual." My own attraction to the same sex had always felt as innate to me as my right-handedness; as much as I tried to summon physical attraction to girls, my body always failed to respond. Coming to understand and accept myself as a gay person is what made me feel whole. So to be told that my "homosexual" identity was merely a consequence of changing societal norms, rather than something innate and immutable—God-given, if you will—made me feel vulnerable and depressed. It too closely resembled the messaging about homosexuality that I had heard growing up—that my same-sex attraction was unnatural, a defect, but also something I could change, a malady from which I might be healed.

Once I familiarized myself with the other side of the argument, I was relieved to know there were other people who thought and felt like me. But I was frustrated to see academics framing the constructionist view, the "queer" view, as the morally acceptable one. I soon realized that, if you advocate for science, for facts, and for truth, you're working against critical theory's moral mission. In short, you are a heretic.

Learning this history would also be pivotal in helping me to understand the perplexing alliance between the trans/queer and postcolonial movements, best exemplified by the activist group "Queers for Palestine." Today, befuddled critics question why a group of "queer" people would side with the Hamas-controlled Palestinian territory of Gaza—where homosexuals are executed—over Israel, where same-sex marriages are legally recognized, gay people live in peace, and gays fleeing the Palestinian territories actively seek asylum. But these queers do not think of themselves as homosexual, for "homosexual"—and sex itself—is a Western, capitalist construct. To them, former Iranian president Mahmoud Ahmadinejad's 2007 claim that there are "no homosexuals" in Iran makes perfect sense. I imagine that, if he were to make this same claim on Columbia's campus today, most students, now indoctrinated in critical theory, would just nod along.

Today's queers are antinormative, anti-Western, and anticapitalist. To put it bluntly, they *hate* America and its Middle Eastern ally, Israel. "Fuck gay marriage," they say. Even more, "fuck gay rights," which are just about assimilating into Western society. Sure, Hamas militants might toss homosexuals from rooftops and oppress women, but they're fighting Western imperialism, settler colonialism, and capitalism. They must prevail, and the capitalist order must fall. We can worry about all the pesky details—like human rights—later.

Today, these queer radicals, these disciples of Foucault, want to undermine the state. Resist it. Dismantle it in order to "liberate" humanity in some final utopian sense. I want to work within it to achieve basic rights and protections for people like me. And because I would object to their radical project—because I would insist on remaining in reality, where sex is binary, a male is not a woman just because he says he is, and homosexuality is real—I would come to pay the price.

CHAPTER 12

At the end of my first year at Columbia, I already felt worlds away from the person I was when it began. Thanks to the assigned readings, I was finally getting answers to so many of the questions I had about the world, about gay history, and about myself. But a pivotal moment in this process came in January 2018, when, just as the spring semester was kicking off, I happened across a reading on my own: a *Washington Post* article titled, "When kids come in saying they are transgender (or no gender), these doctors try to help." My visceral objection to the so-called treatments being touted in the piece—an objection that would only become stronger, as I learned more about the topic—would eventually put me in direct opposition to the modern LGBT movement.

The article, written by a reporter named Sara Solovitch, told the story of a young girl named Samantha, who at thirteen had come out to her mother as transgender. Two years later, Samantha, now "Jacob," was attending her second visit to an "adolescent gender clinic," where she "was being medically evaluated to begin taking testosterone." At *fifteen*.

The gender clinic "Jacob" was attending, the Child and Adolescent Gender Center at UCSF, was founded in 2012 and was now "one of 40 or so such clinics around the country, seeing patients as young as 3 and as old as 25." The clinic's director of mental health, a woman named

Diane Ehrensaft, told Solovitch, "It's the children who are now leading us. They're coming in and telling us, 'I'm no gender.' Or they're saying, 'I identify as gender nonbinary.' Or 'I'm a little bit of this and a little bit of that. I'm a unique gender, I'm transgender. I'm a rainbow kid, I'm boy-girl, I'm everything.'"

Ehrensaft, wrote Solovitch, now counsels the kids "on their future fertility options, encouraging them to bank their sperm or eggs in case they ever want to have a genetically related baby."

It's the children who are "leading us."

Children who are "nonbinary" or "no gender" or "everything."

Children who are taking cross-sex hormones.

Children who are being counseled on their fertility options.

And yet I hadn't even gotten to the most disturbing part of the article. That part came about halfway through, where Solovitch wrote that pubescent "transgender youth" were being given something called "puberty blockers," which endocrinologists said would "buy teenagers some precious time, allowing them to put off a final decision and prevent future and unnecessary surgeries."

That is, the blockers would prevent a child's body from sexually maturing, all so that he or she could more convincingly "pass" as the opposite sex in adulthood.

And if a kid changes his mind, wrote Solovitch, "no harm done; their puberty has simply been delayed a year or two."

No harm done?!

As I read this article, something in me switched. I think the easiest way to explain it is this: When I learned that doctors were medically transitioning kids, and that this process included *giving them drugs that would stunt their natural development*, I instantly knew it was the most insane fucking thing I had ever heard. And just as insane was the way it was being framed in the *Post*'s reporting. As if this were *normal*. As if it were *progressive*.

I looked back on my own adolescence—how my schoolmates tormented me for my femininity and tauntingly questioned my sex, and how evil I felt for liking other boys—and couldn't help but think that, had these interventions been widespread in the 1990s, I may have been the first in line for them. Seeing my gender nonconformity as a medical problem to be fixed, rather than something inherently evil about me, might've sounded too good to pass up.

I'm not a faggot after all. I'm just a straight girl trapped in a boy's body.

I could admit that there were kids whose gender dysphoria would persist into adulthood, at which time they might decide to modify their sex traits with synthetic hormones and cosmetic surgeries. But the idea that a child was capable of making that kind of decision seemed outrageous. Besides, I just couldn't understand how any clinician could declare, with absolute certainty, whether a child's discomfort with his sex would persist to the point where he'd find it necessary to transition.

Moreover, I thought, shouldn't we be making more space in society for inherent gender-nonconformity, rather than medicalizing it? It was the exact opposite of what I thought might be the solution to the type of trauma I had endured as a kid. With all the talk among liberals and progressives about the evils of gay conversion therapy, how could these people not see that by medicalizing these kids, they were likely performing a new and insidious form of conversion therapy—only now, instead of "praying away the gay," they were *transing* it away?

The puberty blocker most commonly used in North America, I learned, was a drug called Lupron. Another use for this drug was the chemical castration of adult male sex offenders. I recalled the story of Alan Turing, the British mathematician who helped the allies defeat Germany in World War II by breaking the Nazis' Enigma codes. Turing a gay man was convicted in 1952 of gross indecency for homosexual acts. As his punishment, he was chemically castrated with a synthetic form of estrogen that would eliminate his drive and also act as a cerebral depressant. Turing died, most likely of suicide, two years later.

And we're giving these drugs to gender-confused kids and teenagers? We're actually *chemically castrating* little boys? Boys who might otherwise grow up to be gay?

It wasn't difficult to discover that my concerns about these practices were warranted. After some online research, I learned that, in total, there had been eleven cohort studies showing outcomes for children with gender identity disorder or gender dysphoria. In some of the studies, the subjects were either all male or all female; otherwise, it was a mixed-sex group. The cohorts came from a variety of countries and labs, and a variety of methods were used to conduct the studies, across four decades. The children in these eleven studies had mental health support during the study period, and, importantly, *did not socially transition*. That is, they were not "affirmed" as the opposite sex.

All of the studies came to the same conclusion: The majority of gender-distressed children desist by the end of puberty. That is, *they cease to express an opposite-sex identity*. Across the large prospective studies, the desistance rate was between 62 and 88 percent. And, just as I had imagined, the vast majority of those desisters grow up to identify as gay or lesbian.

This data alone showed how consequential it was, not only to give these drugs to children but to "affirm" them in a transgender identity to begin with. It was only logical: If a child is told by all of the adults in his life that he was "born in the wrong body" and that he is actually the opposite sex, then *of course* he will begin to feel distress about his body when puberty arrives. The reality of his masculinizing body will contradict everything he has been told about himself—and about reality! One didn't have to be an MD to know that.

Besides, I thought, even if gender clinicians *could* predict the future, even if they *could* determine beyond a shadow of a doubt that a child's gender dysphoria will persist to such a severe extreme that he'll want to undergo cosmetic surgeries as an adult—is blocking a child's natural development and medically engineering them to "pass" as the opposite sex really the best solution?

What about helping people to be comfortable in their bodies? What about creating a world where gender-nonconforming people aren't relentlessly shamed for their differences? No one would ever suggest liposuction for anorexic young people, who have distorted perceptions of themselves.

And what about the adults whose gender dysphoria persists but who decide *not* to undergo surgery, but instead find other ways to accept themselves for the way they are?

Over the months that followed as all of these questions bounced around in my head, I saw more mainstream news outlets—and even the leaders of GLAAD and HRC, organizations that were *founded by and for gay people*—reporting only favorably about these interventions, and I felt like I was going crazy. Soon, it would become the ACLU's raison d'être.

"Blockers just give kids time to think," journalists insisted.

But what were the long-term consequences of this type of intervention on a child's development? The *Washington Post* article had mentioned the potential effects blockers could have on bone development, which sounded serious. But what else? Every graduate of middle school science class knows that the onset of puberty impacts basically every part of a human being, from his reproductive organs to his bones to his brain. Their cavalier attitude about this obviously very serious intervention was bizarre.

Also, how long were kids expected to stay on these blockers? A year? Two years? Three? Let's say a male child starts blockers at thirteen, and it takes him three years to "figure out" his gender. And say, in the end, he accepts the reality of his sex and no longer wishes to try to live his life as a female. Now, at sixteen years of age, he's just supposed to begin puberty, years behind his peers? Is that even possible? And apart from his physical development, what sort of effect would this have on a young person's psychosocial development? This question in particular nagged at me, until I finally learned the actual statistics: Nearly all children prescribed puberty blockers go on to receive cross-sex hormones. In other words, blockers don't give a kid "time to think." They solidify him in a trans identity and sentence him to a lifetime of high-risk medicalization.

"Puberty blockers are perfectly safe; we've been giving them to 'cisgender' kids with precocious puberty for years!" proponents of this mad science insisted, referring to those rare children whose puberty begins as early as age seven or eight.

Okay, sure, I thought. *But the difference is that those kids are eventually taken off the blockers and* go through puberty. These kids, if they go on to cross-sex hormones and surgery, will *never* commence puberty. And no, you absolute lunatics, those feminizing hormones don't cause "the right kind" of puberty for him—since obviously there's no such thing as medically engineering a female puberty in a male body!

Soon, I reached a point where I could no longer bear to hear what the mainstream media and LGBT rights organizations were telling me about what they were euphemistically calling "gender-affirming care." None of them were nullifying any of my concerns. In fact, no one even seemed to be *expressing these concerns*, especially as they pertained to kids who would otherwise grow up to be gay. And after learning the dark truth about queer theory, I couldn't help but think that this seemed like part of the same plan to transgress boundaries and bend reality to satisfy the perverse whims of radical adults.

I knew I needed to summon the courage to state my concerns out loud. I'm not proud to admit, though, that at the time I was too afraid of exile.

As the debate about "trans kids" intensified over the years that followed, stuffing down my true thoughts and feelings would become torture. But at least I was beginning to think for myself.

Part 3

HERETIC

CHAPTER 13

Every June, revelers commemorate the 1969 uprising at Manhattan's Stonewall Inn, when gay men and women finally fought back against police harassment. During Pride Month, across the US, rainbow flags fly everywhere.

In Pride Month 2018, a new "Progress Pride Flag" debuted on social media. A pink and blue trans flag in a chevron shape now occupied the left side of the rainbow flag, along with a black and brown stripe to represent "LGBTQ+ people of color." (Because apparently even a literal rainbow isn't inclusive enough.) The flag was designed by Daniel Quasar, a "nonbinary" artist from Portland whose pronouns are "xe/xem." The chevron shape, "xe" had said, represented forward movement and our need to "shift focus and emphasis to what is important in our current community climate."

A year later, on the fiftieth anniversary of the Stonewall rebellion, the "progress" flag would be everywhere—and gay history would be rewritten.

"Fifty years ago today when Stonewall Inn was raided, brave LGBTQ+ New Yorkers—led by trans women of color—stood up and fought back," tweeted Vice President Kamala Harris on June 28, 2019.

This lie, that "trans women of color" had led the Stonewall riot, would be repeated ad nauseum by journalists and politicians until it had become a religious mantra.

James Kirchick, author of *Secret City: The Hidden History of Gay Washington*, wrote in *Tablet* that this claim rests largely on the purported participation in the riots of a black man named Marsha P. Johnson and a Hispanic transsexual named Sylvia Rivera. And yet, Johnson, who variously identified as a gay man and a drag queen, said himself in an interview that he didn't arrive at Stonewall until well after the rioting began. And no credible witnesses even saw Rivera there that night. Rather, Rivera had reportedly fallen asleep in Bryant Park after taking heroin. The late historian David Carter concluded in his book *Stonewall*, which Kirchick calls "the definitive account of the uprising," that "the group most responsible for the success of the riots" were "the young, homeless homosexuals, and, contrary to the usual characterizations of those on the rebellion's front lines, most were Caucasian; few were Latino; and almost none were transvestites or transsexuals."

As hideous as I thought the new "Progress Pride Flag" was, it perfectly captured our current moment. The trans/queer cult was swallowing the gay rights movement.

In early September 2018, I was privileged to be one of ten students selected nationwide to participate in the CONNECT Student Journalism Training Project, led by the Association of LGBTQ Journalists. For a week in Palm Springs, CA—under the mentorship of established journalists from the *New York Times*, the Associated Press, and elsewhere—we covered NLGJA's annual convention and local LGBT news. It was a tremendous opportunity, and I was thrilled to meet so many accomplished members of my future profession. I would learn a lot from my mentors, but in the end, the experience would be more proof of how out of step I was with the prevailing orthodoxy.

At the beginning of the week, the organizers had each of the CONNECT students pitch a topic to report on. Once our mentors approved our topics, under their guidance we would write and edit the stories, and at the end of the week, they would be published on NLGJA's website. Thus far, what I had loved most about writing for *The Eye* was learning people's stories; it harkened back to what I always thought was the best part about my job as a hairstylist. I chose to write a profile of the former AP journalist Karen Hawkins, who had recently founded the feminist online magazine, *Rebellious*, and was attending the convention. At the end of our hour-long interview, Karen complimented me on how comfortable I had made her feel, saying that it encouraged her to open up even more. It was nice to know that a skillset I had acquired in my former profession was going to benefit my new one.

Once again, I was over a decade older than the other students, though by this time I had gotten used to it. On our second night, we walked into town to grab dinner at a Mexican restaurant. Sitting outside at a picnic table, we learned more about each other—where we were from, what we were studying, and the professional lives we planned.

At one point, a black lesbian student asked a transman about his sexual orientation. "Are you typically attracted to men or women?" she asked her.

I don't know how far along the transman was in her process, but she was still visibly very female. Her eyes grew wide. "That's, like, a really uncomfortable question," she said. She started to explain but then stopped. She was clearly distressed, and for the rest of the evening, she remained mostly silent.

Later, I talked about this tense exchange with another student, a gay (or "queer") man who would go on to write for a progressive publication in New York. I'll call him Matt.

"I felt kind of bad for him," I said, being sure to use male pronouns. "I hope I didn't say anything to upset him."

"I wouldn't worry about it," he said. "That's clearly his problem."

Matt was right, of course. Although his flippancy surprised me, especially since he had so far been talking such a big game about "queer and trans allyship."

"My pronouns are whatever—he, she, they—it all works," he had said during our first group meeting.

Matt's casual response made me wonder how many of the people I had encountered over the previous two years, who had professed such a devotion to "fighting oppression" and spreading love and kindness, had basically been putting on an act. Maybe that's all it was—a performance, an elaborate Kabuki dance.

But even performances can turn ugly and violent, as subsequent events on Columbia's campus would show.

Later I told Matt a little about my experience at Columbia and tentatively expressed my misgivings about the way race and gender were talked about on campus; that in the end, I didn't really think it was all that progressive.

Matt, who is white, said he had been raised in the South and had grown up really racist against black and brown people. After he moved to a more liberal area, he realized he needed to change his perception and had "trained" himself to be more attracted to black and brown men.

"Now," he said, "black and brown men are the only people I want to sleep with."

I had no idea how to respond. "That's…interesting," I finally said.

Did he think this was something to be proud of—that he was now fetishizing men of color instead of harboring racial prejudice against them?

What was with progressive white people being so weird about race? To them, black people were all helpless victims, but they were also wiser and holier—and now they were a fetish?

And what the hell did "training" oneself to be attracted to people of color even look like? I imagined Matt sitting in front of a massive wall of television screens, all broadcasting black and Hispanic gay porn.

This idea of retraining or "reprogramming" one's sexuality—considered a moral anathema when cis white Christians proposed it for gays—would soon become commonplace among the trans and queer crowd. Gay men and lesbians who refuse the advances of trans-identified females or males are now routinely accused of "transphobia," "bigotry," or "genital fetishism." Homosexuality, they now say, isn't about sex—it's about gender, which is simply a matter of how someone identifies. Therefore, if a female identifies as a man, and I don't want to have sex with her, then I'm a bigot. "But I'm exclusively attracted to males," I might argue, only to be told, "Transmen are male, asshole."

It seems like only yesterday when it was right-wing conservatives who said that "a gay man just hasn't met the right woman yet."

ON THE LAST night of the convention, we attended a reception where the year's top journalists were honored with NLGJA achievement awards. The convention's emcees, Chicago news anchor Sean Lewis and Columbus meteorologist Marshall McPeek, took the stage around 8:00 p.m.

"Ladies and gentlemen," said Lewis, whose on-stage persona resembled Bob Barker's.

The boisterous crowd continued to converse with each other.

"Ladies and gentlemen?" he repeated, and McPeek said, "Laaaadies?"

The din lowered, but only slightly. Everyone was imbibing, and some had just discovered the shrimp station.

"Ladies and gentlemen and everyone in between," said Lewis to the crowd.

McPeek went even further: "Ladies and gentlemen, things and its."

"*Yikes*," I uttered to myself. I could tell McPeek had been trying to play off Lewis's words, rather than aiming to dehumanize anyone who didn't identify as a man or woman. I braced myself for the inevitable backlash. But I heard none, and the night continued without incident.

That is, until shortly before 11:00 p.m. I had just introduced myself to Carolyn Ryan, the gay managing editor of the *New York Times*, when suddenly the DJ switched off the dance music and the lights went up. Everyone looked toward the stage, where McPeek stood alone, gripping a microphone. He timidly announced to the crowd that he was terribly sorry for what he had said, that it had not been his intention to harm anyone, and that he hoped he could be forgiven. After a smattering of confused applause, McPeek plodded offstage, the lights dimmed, and the music continued.

McPeek, I would discover, had been an openly gay on-air personality since the early 1990s, when programs like *Will & Grace* and *Ellen* were years away from development. He had organized NLGJA conventions, founded chapters, served on the board, and was among the earliest advocates of adding the word "transgender" to NLGJA's mission statement.

But none of this would matter after a tweet by *Them* reporter Mary Emily O'Hara went viral the next day, and major news outlets picked up the story. O'Hara had been sure to mention that Fox News had sponsored the NLGJA event, which really set her followers' ire ablaze, even though McPeek was a volunteer emcee and had not been hired by the conservative network.

"The monster known as [former FOX CEO Roger] Ailes is gone, but his shitty shadow looms," wrote one Twitter user.

"Republicans are purely bigots," expounded another, who had evidently concluded that McPeek was a member of the GOP. "How much evidence do you need at this point?"

Few minced their words: "What a disgrace he is. There is no apology genuine enough to erase the vile things that came from his face."

At 10:24 a.m., the transwoman and activist Jennifer Finney Boylan, who is a professor at Columbia's Barnard College, tweeted to NLGJA, "If you fail to make any kind of statement on this, THAT will be a pretty loud statement."

The night before, as the reception was winding down, I learned that *Axios* Chief Technology Correspondent Ina Fried, who is transgender, had pulled aside NLGJA board members immediately after McPeek's blunder, which led to a behind-the-scenes confrontation with the emcee. Months earlier, I had interviewed Boylan profile for *The Eye*, so I decided to respond.

At 12:35 p.m., I wrote: "I was there. @inafried from Axios and @ nlgja members were on it immediately after it happened."

Even though I strongly believed that McPeek had meant no harm, I was too timid at the time to write that on Twitter.

Boylan liked my tweet.

At 2:11 p.m., Libby Walters, whose Twitter profile identifies her (I am uncertain of Libby's preferred pronouns) as "the first transgender conductress in the 183-year history of the Long Island Railroad," and whose Twitter followers include Boylan, GLAAD and the NOH8 Campaign, responded: "And I guess you didn't walk out? Nice."

It hadn't occurred to me—or most other people in attendance—to walk out in protest of these innocuous comments. Evidently our failure to do so was evidence of some moral defect. Now, I wasn't just supposed to interrogate my actions, but also the things I had failed to do.

Walters's was the first confrontational response I had ever received from a trans activist on the social media platform. (Since then, I have received many, including polite requests for me to kill myself.) While I can't equate Walters's sarcastic tweet to McPeek's public shaming, it triggered my scrupulosity. My mouth went dry and the blood drained from my face. I was paralyzed with fear. Any joy I had felt about spending a week in the company of established gay journalists promptly dissipated. It was the same cold, isolated feeling that I had years ago, when a girl I ran into on vacation in Delaware told me the kids back home were saying I was gay.

I desperately wanted to explain that I thought McPeek's words derived from a desire to be clever rather than a deep-seated hatred of transgender people. But I was afraid it would sound like I was making excuses for him. I wanted to say that I was on Walters's side, that I had lobbied for transgender rights in Maryland and had interned at GLAAD, where I supported efforts to fight "bathroom bills," "religious freedom" legislation, and the transgender military ban. But I was afraid of sounding like a condescending white savior. I considered forwarding the fawning profile I had written about Boylan, or an essay I had written for Columbia's literary magazine *Quarto* about my traumatic childhood experience with gender nonconformity. But I was afraid of sounding like a narcissistic, mansplaining ignoramus.

I felt helpless, and at the same time had an overwhelming urge to properly atone for my transgression. In this, I knew I wasn't alone. I frequently recognized this impulse—this need to be absolved of one's sins—in other people's response to being shamed on social media. Now it had happened to me, as when I had misbehaved in the Lamb of God, I felt desperate to get back in the community's good graces.

Finally, succumbing to the futility of the situation, I responded to Walters, "You are right, I should have." By which I meant, *I should have virtue-signaled by storming out of the hotel ballroom.* But my response felt craven and like I had somehow missed an opportunity to engage in fruitful dialogue.

NLGJA later issued an official apology, stating that McPeek had voluntarily resigned his membership. McPeek himself posted a long apology on his Facebook page which, as public apologies go, couldn't have been more sincere:

"I plan to seek out meaningful ways in which I can use this experience to learn from and listen to transgender, nonbinary, and gender-nonconforming people in our community who often face violence and marginalization, in hopes of fostering greater understanding and acceptance. I hope that you can find it in your hearts to understand my humanness, accept my heartfelt apology, and allow me to earn your forgiveness."

Many didn't buy it: "SHAME ON YOU AND YOUR NEWS STATION YOU 'PRANCE' AROUND ON," read one response.

Behold, the naked homophobia of the trans/queer cult.

By the time I made it back to New York, I had realized that, within LGBT activism and media—or what had fast become trans activism and media—there was no longer a place for gay men like me.

For the first time, my indignation toward this backward ideology that had consumed what I had thought was my "community" was beginning to outweigh my fear of transgressing. If I continued to stay quiet about it, I was going to bust.

CIS WHITE GAY

THE FALL 2018 semester began as soon as I got back from Palm Springs. That semester, I took a seminar on writing art and cultural criticism led by Margo Jefferson, a black *New York Times* reporter who wrote the acclaimed memoir *Negroland.* Jefferson was a good instructor, and she had a lot of insightful things to say about writing and criticism. She wrote me one of my recommendation letters for the MFA program to which I was later accepted.

However, I grew frustrated by how much time we spent in class judging the authors of the assigned readings and even the people written about. Many of my classmates seemed eager to find something "problematic" about the readings. It was yet another class where the primary objective seemed to be alienating those who didn't agree with the prescribed dogma.

One essay we read, a profile of a male artist who openly admitted to his interlocutor how wrongly he had treated his mother, was, I thought, especially touching for its honesty, humility, and self-awareness. The man was unafraid to admit how flawed he was, how *human*.

My classmates thought differently. "What a terrible person," someone said.

Suddenly I didn't feel so far from a Lamb of God classroom. Except there, at least, was the possibility of redemption through prayer and atonement. Here, it seemed there was nothing a sinner could do to earn grace or mercy.

Jefferson's class was one of the first in which I found the courage to speak up, to gently push back against the constant moralizing.

"I thought the man had a lot of self-awareness," I heard myself saying. "He doesn't try to deny the mistakes he's made. It's strange that people are saying he's a terrible person."

"No one said that," said Jefferson.

But at least one classmate had, in fact, said that. For a moment, I was tempted to feign agreement and stay quiet. But for some reason I felt compelled to continue.

"I feel like we all have thoughts like this man," I said, with growing confidence. "We've all behaved badly. Hell, if you guys knew half the thoughts that ran through my head, you'd be horrified."

Jefferson looked uncomfortable but said nothing.

One student sitting to my right nodded her head. "I actually agree with you," she said. "I empathized with the man."

Rather than pursuing the discussion, Jefferson introduced a new topic, and the class moved on.

I felt nervous for admitting that I had "bad thoughts" and, at the same time, flabbergasted that this should be a controversial thing to admit. That I wasn't pure. I wasn't perfect.

Years earlier, not long after I got sober, I read Anchee Min's novel *Becoming Madame Mao*, a fictionalized account of Jiang Qing, who, along with Chairman Mao Zedong, led China's Cultural Revolution. Min, a Chinese-American born in Shanghai, was a child when she joined Mao's Red Guard. *Becoming Madame Mao* as well as Min's memoir, *Red Azalea*, about her time in a worker's camp would become two of my all-time favorite books. Not only was Min an excellent writer, but that fraught period in China's history seemed to fascinate me unlike any other. No doubt because of my own experience growing up in a cult, stories about masses of people—young people in particular—who had been coerced into policing the thoughts and behaviors of others, all in the name of attaining some kind of moral purity, left me spellbound.

In Jefferson's class, as in previous ones, I found myself recalling Min's work. Everyone seemed so eager to convey that all of their thoughts were grounded in the values of diversity, equity, inclusion, and little else. Everyone was a (Maoist) Care Bear. Not unlike during Mao's Cultural Revolution, it was our collective duty to rid, first ourselves, then the campus, the city, the country, and finally the earth, of the "four olds"—traditional customs, culture, habits, and ideas that propped up capitalism and countered Communist ideology. Now, we were to rid America of old *Western* customs, culture, habits, and ideas, for what seemed like the exact same ends.

In short, everyone in this new religion was required to take responsibility for the behavior of everyone around them. They were at the same time acolytes of the ideology, and its enforcers. On the surface, it looks empowering, especially when these enforcers are gathered together, feeding off each other's zealotry and rage. But in truth this responsibility of universal priesthood is a terrible burden.

It was around that time that I began to wonder if the disorder of scrupulosity was more widespread than I thought. Whether perhaps Columbia's lockstep campus culture was actually a *breeding ground* for the disorder. If so, its effect on student mental health was clear. There was a lot of talk on campus about "stress culture," about caring for our mental health, and about "practicing self-care."

"It's okay to not be okay," students frequently cooed to one another.

The year before, in February 2017, mental health issues at Columbia had made national headlines when the *New York Post* reported that there had already been seven student deaths during the 2016–2017 school year, at least four of them suicides. That January, an exchange student from Japan leapt to her death from her dorm window.

And it wasn't just at Columbia. This was a trend that seemed be occurring on college campuses across the United States. Surveys revealed that college students were experiencing all-time high rates of anxiety, depression, and even suicidality. Suicide, I learned, is the second leading cause of death for US college students.

At Columbia, nearly every day, I heard students speak about being anxious, depressed, or not sleeping. A lot of this was undoubtedly due to the workload. Hundreds of pages of reading were assigned every week. Paper after paper. Exams. And the competition was stiff.

But I also suspected that the anxiety and the depression and the insomnia were from the terror students had of messing up, of saying something wrong, or even *thinking* it, since everyone made it so clear that they never had bad thoughts—and if anyone did, that person was *bad*. The stakes were impossibly high. If they messed up, if they misspoke about a topic, misgendered a fellow student, or if what they wrote or shared in class wasn't properly progressive—by which I mean radically anti-Western, anticapitalist, and antiwhite—they could become known as a Nazi/racist/transphobe/Islamophobe.

Even worse, someone could post about it on social media and then the whole world would know. And from that kind of shame, they knew they would never recover.

I was paranoid myself. In the middle of the night, while Drew slept soundly beside me, I'd be tempted to shake him awake, so he could reassure me *just one more time* that whatever innocuous thing I had said or done in class that week wouldn't lead to my ruin.

Recalling what I had learned about scrupulosity's origins in the epidemic of anxiety that occurred after Renaissance theologians increased the list of potentially unforgiveable sins, I realized that it was the same on campus. There were endless ways one could transgress. Although now, it might actually be worse. Students today can never be sure of what's acceptable and what's not, since the rules are always changing. What may have been fine yesterday is verboten today.

"It's not Latin*o*, it's Latin*x*," you're told.

"You can't say *autistic person*, you have to say *person with autism*."

Later, alone in your room, you read online that, according to polling, the majority of Latino people reject Latinx—in fact they prefer "Hispanic." "People with autism"? You're actually supposed to say "autistic person," since autism is not something someone has, but is rather a fundamental part of a person's "identity."

Then comes confusion, when one hears another student say with impunity the exact same thing he had said, and for which he was lambasted. Why is it okay for this other student to say it, but not me? It's not always known. Since critical social justice discourse is based on the distorting of reality and the "queering" of what's true, it will often be incoherent and contradictory. Once again, the point of critical theory isn't to establish new truths and morals by which everyone must abide, but to disrupt current ideas about what is moral and true.

Occasionally, though, the reason for the double standard is clear: It is about identity. That is, what is acceptable for a black or brown person is not acceptable for a white or Asian person. Unless of course that white or Asian person is trans. Or disabled. This makes them marginalized, which makes them somehow purer in spirit, closer to the truth, and hence immune to criticism. Hence the reason we see droves of young people scrambling to put transgender flag emojis and obscure health disorders in their social media profiles. Their trans identities and their disabilities are their redemptive lamb's blood. The shadow of the new Red Guard passes over, leaving them unharmed.

Other behaviors at Columbia also looked like symptoms of scrupulosity. Take the traditional rite of confession, which for many Christians becomes a compulsion. The modern sins of privilege and of whiteness likewise require continual repentance. People need to "do the work." They need to admit (confess) their racism, even if they don't think they are racist. In fact, the more they insist they aren't racist, the more it's clear they are. At Columbia, if a student shared in class, they would often preface their statement with an acknowledgement of their privilege, as if to say, "I understand that my privilege might distort my perception, and that perhaps I really have no right to speak at all, about anything—ever."

Land acknowledgments are similar. Ostensibly, they're meant to honor indigenous people, but in fact they serve more as a form of public repentance. "I am standing on Lenape land," means, "We should all be ashamed of ourselves for the genocides our ancestors committed—even if they were not my actual ancestors." And then it becomes religious custom. If one doesn't begin with a land acknowledgement, the absence of it is notable. And that person should be judged for what they *didn't* say. Clearly, this terrible person should repent immediately.

Then there are the public demands for apology. "Confess! Confess! Confess!" the cult leaders in the HBO series *Game of Thrones* screamed at the highborn woman they have imprisoned and brought low for her hubris. When she finally does confess, she has to complete a public walk of shame, totally naked, while being spat on and pelted with filth. "Shame! Shame! Shame!" they shriek at her.

These tendencies on the identitarian left would be brought to a boiling point in 2020, when the George Floyd protests led to a total institutional takeover of a new and very regressive antiracist orthodoxy, one that sanctions racial discrimination so long as the target is white, Jewish, or Asian—and that is now being rolled back with great difficulty. That year, Minneapolis mayor Jacob Frey had to submit to his own walk of shame after he confessed during a struggle session that he wouldn't commit to defunding the police. "Shame!" the mob of thousands screamed at Frey as he walked, head down, through the crowd. At least he got to keep his clothes on.

CHAPTER 14

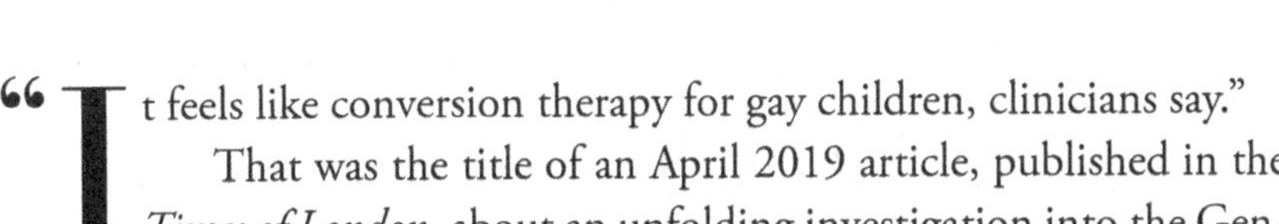

"It feels like conversion therapy for gay children, clinicians say."

That was the title of an April 2019 article, published in the *Times of London*, about an unfolding investigation into the Gender Identity Development Service at London's Tavistock clinic. I discovered the article on Twitter, where I had clandestinely begun to follow people who were objecting to pediatric sex trait modification.

"Ex-NHS staff fear that homophobia is driving a surge in 'transgender' young people," read the subtitle.

The article, written by Lucy Bannerman, was the result of interviews with five gender specialists who had recently resigned from GIDS. "So many potentially gay children were being sent down the pathway to change gender," wrote Bannerman, "[that] two of the clinicians said there was a dark joke among staff that 'there would be no gay people left.'"

One clinician told Bannerman, "It feels like conversion therapy for gay children. I frequently had cases where people started identifying as trans after months of horrendous bullying for being gay. Young lesbians considered at the bottom of the heap suddenly found they were really popular when they said they were trans."

Said another, "We heard a lot of homophobia which we felt nobody was challenging. A lot of the girls would come in and say, 'I'm not a lesbian. I fell in love with my best girlfriend but then I went online and realized I'm not a lesbian, I'm a boy. Phew."

A third clinician said, "I would ask who they wanted to have relationships with, but I was told by senior management that gender is completely separate from sex. I couldn't get on board with that, because it isn't. Some people were transitioning to match their sexuality." The clinician continued, "For some families, it was easier to say, this is a medical problem, 'here's my child, please fix them!' than dealing with a young, gay kid."

After devouring Bannerman's article, I read it a second time. And then a third.

So I wasn't crazy. This was really happening.

How had this madness even started? And how long had it been going on?

Not long, it turned out. The treatment pathway of puberty blockers followed by cross-sex hormones and surgery, I learned from online research, was developed in Amsterdam in the 1990s and early 2000s. It was originally known as the Dutch protocol.

In previous decades, Dutch clinicians had observed high rates of depression and even suicide in adult trans-identified males, and they speculated that it was their inability to "pass" as women that eroded their mental health more than anything else. Thus, they thought, why not prevent these males from masculinizing at all by suppressing their puberty and feeding them only estrogen? No, this obviously wouldn't change their sex (an impossibility), but it *may* prevent them from having to go through quite so many surgeries later in life. And they'll be happy!

Yes, this meant clinicians would have to perform the difficult task of weeding out the actual "trans kids," so that they didn't accidentally castrate the wrong people. But they were confident they could do it.

The Dutch Protocol was officially published as a "successful" treatment regimen in 2006, in an article funded by Ferring Pharmaceuticals, the manufacturer of the puberty blocker, triptorelin. Of the first seventy adolescents in Amsterdam given puberty blockers from 2000 to 2008, sixty-two were homosexual and only one was heterosexual.

One of the participants died at age eighteen from complications following vaginoplasty. An adult male's genital tissue is what is traditionally used to construct a neovagina, but in this case, suppression of the boy's puberty prevented his genitals from fully developing. The surgeons chose to use part of his intestine, which became infected with E-coli. He developed septic shock and multiple organ failure.

The practice began in the US in 2007, when Boston Children's Hospital opened the nation's first hospital-based pediatric gender clinic. In a matter of years, the number of pediatric gender clinics would be in the hundreds.

In the US, the Dutch protocol became "gender-affirming care." The same drugs would be used, but, unlike the Dutch, American doctors and clinicians, under pressure from radical activists, would be discouraged from even trying to filter out the kids they thought were more likely to grow up identifying as trans. Instead, every child and adolescent must be affirmed and allowed to commence medicalization.

Once I learned all of this, any vindication I felt was immediately replaced by indignation. Not just because of how antigay these practices were, but also because of the complicity of LGBT organizations, which had become so quick to frame any objection to the practice as "transphobic," as an "attack on transgender and nonbinary children," or as a "right-wing dog whistle."

In the US, the issue had become a political one, which meant that the truth no longer mattered, only fealty to one's tribe. Good liberal Democrats heard "right-wing dog whistle" and, ironically, like Pavlov's dogs, immediately knew how to think and behave.

"Gender-affirming care," good.

"Protecting gender-nonconforming kids," bad.

That May, Ellen Kahn, the foundation director of HRC's Children, Youth & Families Program, called those who objected "frauds promoting alarming lies and fake science that will end up harming LGBTQ children."

What the hell was "fake" about gender clinicians raising the alarm on the medical harm being done to gay young people?

And what the hell was an "LGBTQ child"? That acronym included lesbian, gay, bisexual, transgender, and "queer" people. All gay people weren't trans. And all "queer" people weren't lesbians. It made no sense.

Besides, if they were trying to prevent others from "harming" these demographics, then what about the L, G, and B? The ones who were being erased in this dystopian nightmare?

THAT SEMESTER, I enrolled in a course called "Muslim Masculinities." The instructor was a Middle Eastern Studies scholar named Derek Mancini-Lander, who had earned his PhD at the University of Michigan. The class was designed to introduce us "to the complexities of gender studies in Islam" and to "complement the predominant focus on Muslim women by exploring and problematizing the social and cultural construction of masculinity in the Islamic world." Readings included Dror Ze'evi's *Producing Desire: Changing Sexual Discourse in the Ottoman Middle East* and Khaled El-Rouayheb's *Before Homosexuality in the Arab-Islamic World* as well as Jack (Judith) Halberstam's *Female Masculinity* and feminist sociologist Raewyn Connell's *Masculinities.*

I liked Derek. His approach to the material was steeped in queer theory, but he was kind, and he seemed to welcome freethinking. His neatly groomed mustache, tweed jackets, and fitted vests made him look like the quintessential Ivy League professor.

Derek's TA Ilona was also very friendly. However, in the class's required weekly discussion section, which Ilona led, I ran into more of same moral relativism that I had been encountering at Columbia since my first semester. It was starting to feel like my instructors had been hired as PR reps for Islam.

Ilona, a straight Jewish woman who was perhaps a few years younger than me, came from a family of first-generation immigrants from the former Soviet Union. After earning her master's degree in Islamic Theology from Harvard, Ilona continued her studies in Qatar and Morocco before traveling to Israel, where she was a Comparative Religions fellow at the Hebrew University in Jerusalem. She had come to Columbia to earn her PhD in the university's Islamic Studies program. Today, Ilona teaches AP World History at a private high school in Florida.

During one memorable discussion section, Ilona lectured the class on the controversial Quranic verse of An-Nisa 4:34, which states: "Men are the managers of the affairs of women for that God has preferred in bounty one of them over another, and for that they have expended of their property. Righteous women are therefore obedient, guarding the secret for God's guarding. And those you fear may be rebellious admonish; banish them to their couches, and beat them. If they then obey you, look not for any way against them; God is All-high, All-great." (The Quran, trans. Arthur John Arberry [1955].)

Ilona explained that critics of Islam cite this verse as evidence that Muslims are inherently violent and misogynist. But, she said, one way to interpret it is to think about the context in which it was written. At the time, every man's duty was to sustain the health of the Muslim community (*ummah*), and that included keeping the peace in his home. This verse was merely instructing men to discipline women who were causing unrest, which threatened the larger community.

I remain confident that Ilona wasn't condoning spousal abuse or the abuse of women in general. However, because she never brought the discussion back to its appropriate conclusion—which is that at least some criticism of this verse is warranted since men beating their wives in order to control their behavior is pretty much the definition of patriarchal violence and misogyny—I remember leaving the class thinking, *It kind of sounded like she was saying it's okay for Muslim men to hit their wives.*

Sometime during that semester, the government of Brunei announced the implementation of a new penal code that would punish men convicted of homosexual sex with death by stoning. It would be the final phase of the implementation of sharia law, which began in 2014, when Brunei became the first southeast Asian country to implement the Islamic penal code.

One day, Ilona spoke about the recent developments in Brunei. "Western media is of course spreading the narrative that they're going to immediately start executing gay people," she lamented. "As if the requirements to reach a guilty conviction aren't extremely difficult to satisfy."

In this case, I knew Ilona was right. To obtain a conviction, the law required no fewer than four witnesses. Still, her dismissive attitude alarmed me. Gays were already being hanged from cranes and thrown off rooftops in places that practiced sharia law, like Iran and Gaza. Thus, even if the draconian law wouldn't immediately result in the execution of homosexuals, it certainly didn't leave one optimistic about life for gay people in Brunei.

Ilona's comment inadvertently clarified for me some of the readings that Professor Dabashi had assigned for Contemporary Islamic Civilization. In his books *Islam in Liberalism* and *Desiring Arabs*, Joseph Massad wrote about the "Gay International." By this he meant "Western male white-dominated" LGBT-rights organizations which, in their purported efforts to liberate gays and lesbians from oppressive authoritarian regimes, end up imposing Western configurations of sexual identity onto non-Western cultures. To Massad, the work of the Gay International is just another iteration of Western "human rights imperialism," in which Westerners insert themselves in foreign cultures and spread Western homogeneity under the altruistic guise of furthering "human rights."

Though I kept these thoughts to myself at the time, when I read Massad's work, I couldn't help but think that he was leaving out a very important detail: Gay men and women live their lives with impunity in the West. They actually flee their native Arab and Muslim countries to seek asylum in the Western world—and also, it should be noted, *in Israel.*

By the spring of 2019, I was more confident of my footing as a gay rights activist and more willing to voice my objections. "I understand what you're saying," I said to Ilona. "But I do think people need to be held accountable for enacting laws that will create a really dangerous environment for gay people to live in." I noticed a student sitting across the table from me nod in agreement.

"Absolutely," said Ilona. "And I didn't mean to suggest otherwise."

I was glad to hear it. But her consistently defensive approach to the material was starting to wear thin. In class, while Derek lectured, Ilona sometimes interjected, "Is there a way for us to look at this differently? To 'queer' it a little bit?"

As we have already seen, "queerness" had become an all-purpose academic tool for subverting conventional meanings. "Queering" a topic meant peeling away or "deconstructing" what we already knew (or thought we knew) about it, a practice that sometimes included peeling away empirical truths, ultimately rendering the subject meaningless.

In practice, it might go something like this:

Me: "The Iranian regime executes gay men."

Queer theorist: "Ah, but what is it to be 'executed'? Does the one who is thrown off the rooftop to his death not have agency? Is he not, in a way, *performing a radical act of liberation*? Is he not now, in death, liberated from a life lived under an oppressive regime? Further, what is a 'gay' man? Sounds to me like you're applying Western constructs of sexuality. Are there actually 'gay' people in Iran? Perhaps this man—this man who was flung to his death from a rooftop—did not exist as you perceived him to exist. Perhaps he did not exist at all. And what, really, is a 'man'?"

This might read as satire. But it's an accurate depiction of a mind in thrall to an abstract theory that has nothing to do with reality. Every year, queer theorists put forth unethical and inhumane ideas disguised by verbose jargon to sound progressive and liberating. These theorists often publish their work in academic journals that go largely unread and unnoticed. In 2007, Jasbir Puar, the graduate director of Rutgers' Women's and Gender Studies department, suggested in her book *Terrorist Assemblages: Homonationalism in Queer Times* that suicide bombing is merely "a modality of expression and communication for the subaltern." To Puar, suicide bombing can be compared to "queerness" insofar as the queer person, like the suicide bomber, rebels against the white, Western hegemonic order: "The dynamite strapped onto the body of a suicide bomber is not merely an appendage or prosthetic; the intimacy of weapon with body reorients the assumed spatial integrity (coherence and concreteness) and individuality of the body that is the mandate of intersectional identities."

Suicide bombers. They're here, they're queer, get used to it!

Amid this blizzard of abstractions substituting for reality, academics' efforts to undo "Orientalist" views of the Muslim world seemed to be blinding them—and their impressionable students—to the exceedingly harsh conditions for women and gays in Muslim-majority nations. Such extreme cultural relativism was clearly just creating excuses for non-Western people to behave inhumanely, either because of their geopolitical and economic circumstances or because messaging and optics were more important than preserving the ideal of universal human rights. Progressives routinely embrace this concept of human rights—which is arguably Western liberalism's most important contribution to the world—and yet they discount it as colonialist "white supremacy" when applied abroad. Universal human rights had been entirely reinterpreted as nothing more than a tool of Western imperialism. Unfortunately, with the deconstruction of the concept goes any concept of individual rights. Which, come to think of it, is the point of the multiculturalist agenda: to replace individualism with racial group identity.

By emphasizing "other ways of knowing" and constantly denigrating the West as a corrosive evil, the university was training students to dismiss and deconstruct Western values before they had fully understood the magnitude of Western liberal achievements—including the rule of law, the separation of church and state, freedom of the press, the abolition of slavery, and the political enfranchisement of women and other minorities, none of which have been obtained in Muslim-majority nations. Basically, they were being taught about the West through the lens of its illiberal, authoritarian enemies.

THAT SEMESTER, DEREK assigned the work of Afsaneh Najmabadi, an Iranian-American Harvard professor of women, gender, and sexuality, who has written extensively on transexuality in Iran. In her book,

Professing Selves: Transsexuality and Same-Sex Desire in Contemporary Iran, Najmabadi quoted an Iranian lesbian woman whom the state had approved for gender-reassignment. "Once I was diagnosed as TS [transsexual]," the woman said, "I started having sex with my girlfriend without feeling sinful." In other words, now that she understood her same-sex attraction to be a byproduct of a medical defect rather than indicative of the sin of homosexuality, she was relieved. She was just "a straight man born in a woman's body."

The statement disturbed me, and not just because of what I had learned about the medical harm being done to young people who might grow up to be gay. Over the previous two years, in the US, I had seen more and more gay or lesbian adults opting for a trans or nonbinary identity. The labels themselves wouldn't bother me so much if it weren't for what identifying as trans or nonbinary seemed to entail, which, more often than not, turned out to be cross-sex hormones and surgery—including, for males, castration. By that time, I was learning about some of the severe health consequences of ingesting unusually high levels of masculinizing or feminizing hormones and of the high complication rates and risks of transgender surgeries. Was it possible that even adult gays and lesbians were identifying out of their sex in order to combat homophobia?

I thought back to my days in the Lamb of God, and of the one openly homosexual man in the community that I knew of. His name was Blair. For a while he lived a couple streets over with the Schaeffers, who tried to get him back on the straight and narrow. Blair loved God and wanted to be good.

Blair, a hairdresser, would come to our house and cut my family's hair in the kitchen. After we left the Lamb of God, my mom continued to get her hair done by Blair. Soon, she told me, he was identifying as transexual and eventually underwent vaginoplasty. Within a few years, he regretted his transition. I never learned what happened to Blair after that, since it was around that time that my mom stopped seeing Blair. Not because she judged him, but because she feared he would get distracted by everything going on in his personal life and fuck up her hair.

I decided to google Blair. The very first search result was a 2018 *Daily Signal* article titled, "This Man Received 167 Sex-Change Surgeries. He Lives in a World of Regret." The author was a man named Walt Heyer, who received gender-reassignment surgery in 1983 and has since detransitioned. According to Heyer, between 1987 and 2005, Blair underwent so many gender-reassignment surgeries—167, to be exact, at the cost of $220,000—that he wound up in the Guinness Book of World Records. Blair, Heyer wrote, "has since found his true male self in following Jesus Christ."

I was stunned. I opened Facebook to search for Blair's name. It turned out we had one mutual friend, which made him easy to find.

Blair's posts were haunting. There was picture after picture of Blair, swollen and bruised after yet another "gender-affirming" surgery. One photo caption reads, "Biting the bait of Satan. Sadly there [are] many others like me who have been rejected by biological parents [and] have traveled on this sick road [of] self-mutilation to be loved." Other photos are captioned with Bible verses.

One picture is of Blair in high school. "They said, 'why don't you smile,'" Blair wrote. "They didn't know I was called faggot, queer, sissy, a girl. I guess my heart had become hardened."

On February 25, 2015, Blair posted a picture of himself and a woman with permed hair. "1989, me happy being ex gay." This would have been when I knew him. I assume the woman in the picture is a girlfriend he found in the Lamb of God.

Besides old pictures of himself, there were photographs Blair had taken of his bible. The pages were covered with various shapes and icons—circles, flames, and stick figures—drawn in red ink. Some passages were underlined: "Now therefore ye are cursed."

Is this all that transgenderism is? I wondered. *Gay people trying to escape self-hatred?*

It's a big part of it. In his 2016 book *Sex Science Self*, the gay UC Davis professor Bob Ostertag documents the history of sex hormone research. Ostertag, a gay man living in San Francisco, wrote in the introduction that he became curious about the topic when "more and more people in my own social circles began taking them to 'transition' their gender." But when he asked someone in his community to educate him on the hormones, either they seemed to know as much as he did or they became hostile. "This was especially striking," Ostertag wrote, "since so much of the intellectual energy fueling transgender activism comes from that part of academia that takes pride in deconstructing ideas scientists take as given. Why were hormones getting a free pass?"

Perhaps because among their earliest uses were attempts to "cure" homosexuals and also to punish homosexuals for acting on their proclivities. Beginning in the 1940s, men arrested for homosexuality—including the WWII hero Alan Turing—were sentenced to chemical castration with estrogen. Widespread knowledge of this history wouldn't exactly be good PR for today's trans movement. What's more, Magnus Hirschfield, the early twentieth century German doctor considered a pioneer by modern-day trans activists, may have organized the first documented "sex reassignment" surgeries. But, "at the same time," Ostertag wrote, "Hirschfield was also arranging the first surgeries to 'cure' male homosexuals."

In his book, which he dedicated "to my people, the freaks and the queers," Ostertag, who was himself a young "freak" in the 1960s and 1970s, wrote that the gay rights movement began in part as a demand for doctors to leave them the hell alone. He quotes the disco icon Sylvester, who described "gay liberation" as meaning, "I could be the queen that I really was without having a sex change or being on hormones." Now, with the same fervor, activists are demanding "the right to receive medical treatment," wrote Ostertag.

Even psychiatrists at institutions where "sex reassignment" surgeries first took place in the US were outraged by the practice. They argued that the patients were "self-hating homosexuals who needed counseling more than surgery," wrote Ostertag. And many of the surgeons felt the same way. Even Christine Jorgensen, the American GI who made headlines in the 1950s after undergoing reassignment surgery, once stated, "I identified myself as female and consequently my interests in men were normal." Jorgensen called homosexuality "deeply alien to my religious attitudes." And yet, in 2019, during the fiftieth anniversary celebration of the Stonewall riots—known to be one of the most pivotal events in gay rights history—Jorgensen was listed on the Stonewall National Monument's Wall of Honor as one of America's fifty "pioneers, trailblazers, and heroes."

In *Sex Science Self*, Ostertag compared Jorgensen's statements about homosexuality to a 1980s ruling in Iran, in which Ayatollah Khomeini declared that homosexuals who undergo "sex reassignment" are acceptable in the eyes of Allah.

Curious to learn more, after class one day I asked Derek about transgenderism in Iran. He pointed me to some more literature. And down the rabbit hole I went.

Ostertag was right: Khomeini issued his fatwa in 1987. As I've already written, in Iran, homosexual acts between men are punishable by death. Gay Iranians, who, like in other cultures, are often innately gender-nonconforming, are frequently harassed by Iran's Morality Police. For decades this harassment, along with the mental anguish they experience as a result of the teachings of the state religion of Islam—which, like Christianity, derives its antigay religious beliefs from the story of Lot (*luti* is the Arabic term for men who have anal sex [*liwat*] with other men)—has forced homosexuals into a dark corner: transition or live under the threat of violence, in shame.

There is no accurate data on how many sex-reassignment surgeries are performed in Iran. However, over the last decade it has been reported that the state performs more than any other country in the word, besides

Thailand. (With the astronomical rise in trans-identification in the West in recent years, this may no longer be true.)

Writing for the BBC in 2014, the journalist Ali Hamedani interviewed a lesbian woman named Donya, whose story sounded similar to that of the young woman Najmabadi quoted in her book. As a butch young girl, Donya kept her hair short and wore caps instead of headscarves. Police officers often harassed her in the street. "Why are you like this?" they'd say. "Go and change your gender." So Donya did. She received hormone therapy for seven years, grew facial hair, and even contemplated surgery. But some of her friends had terrible post-surgical complications. Thankfully, after connecting with some supportive international friends online, she was able to accept herself as a lesbian. She escaped Iran and eventually claimed asylum in Canada.

Continuing my research, I soon came across the 2008 documentary *Be Like Others*. Directed by Tanaz Eshaghian, the film follows the stories of gay men in Iran who undergo gender reassignment. In one scene, filmed in the waiting room of the surgeon's office, a young man named Farhad speaks with a local journalist. He asks her, "But what if I want to stay the way I am? What if the operation damages my body?" The journalist answers, "Are you saying you shouldn't have to have a sex change, but go ahead and wear women's clothing?" Farhad says, "I'm saying that the fact that I have to do this takes away my right to any sort of choice. I am forced to undergo surgery."

In another scene, a man named Askar lies in a hospital bed. It's the day before his castration. "I don't know what it's like in those Western countries," he says, "but I hear two men can just marry each other. And you know, it is a big sin to do it from behind."

Eshaghian asks him, "If you weren't living in Iran, would you have this operation?"

"No," he says. "If I didn't have to operate, I wouldn't do it. I wouldn't touch God's work."

At the end of the film, Farhad has changed his mind and decided not to have surgery. After he met people who had gotten the operation, he said, "I saw their lives and saw that many were suicidal because they couldn't be sexually satisfied. They lose a lot. They have complications from the operation after a while. I want to have a decent life. Be like others."

When Eshaghian catches up with Askar, it has been twelve months since his surgery. He is now a prostitute. Islamic law allows for temporary marriages. Since transsexuals can't get pregnant, Askar says he "can get married once an hour or so."

"I thought I would finally find my place in society," he tells Eshaghian. "But I didn't."

I was immediately reminded of Blair's story. The film, I thought, perfectly illustrated the homophobia that appeared to be at the heart of transgender medicine. And yet, I was surprised to learn, in 2010, it was nominated for a GLAAD Media Award for "Outstanding Documentary." How far that organization had fallen in less than ten years.

I continued to wonder how the situation in Iran compared to what I saw occurring today in the West. It would be outrageous to think it was the same, considering that we live in a liberal democratic society, where gays and lesbians are allowed to get married and openly serve in the military. And yet, just because we had made legislative gains and public opinion about these issues had changed, didn't mean that everyone was now simply okay with homosexuality and gender-nonconformity in general. Often, people were allowed to be gay, so long as they didn't act *too* gay. I, for one, was intimately familiar with the pressure to conform to traditional notions of masculinity. And I knew many gay people still suffered from severe shame and guilt about their sexuality, either due to societal stigma, religious indoctrination, or both.

Over time, I would learn more about this issue, and just as importantly about some of the other reasons why people identify as the opposite sex. And as the strange alliance between the radical left and Islam came into clearer focus, I would see how queer and postcolonial theory had created a space for regressive ideas about gender to once again proliferate in the West. Perhaps today, radicalized gays and lesbians in the West have more compelling reasons than ever to identify as trans and to medically transition. With one stone, they can destroy two birds: their internalized homophobia, and "western hegemony." Cutting up their bodies is a liberating expression of "queerness," not unlike the suicide bomber who blows himself up.

CHAPTER 15

Max and I met at a birthday picnic for Molly in Central Park. Born and raised in rural Connecticut, Max was also in GS, a semester or two behind me. He was twenty-nine, studying the arts, and like me, in recovery for drug and alcohol addiction. Max reverberated with a keen intellectual curiosity, humility, and warmth. We agreed it would be cool to grab coffee sometime.

One afternoon during the Fall 2018 semester, I ran into Max as I was exiting Butler Library. We sat down on a nearby bench and chatted for a while.

"How do you like Columbia?" I asked him.

Max was quiet for a moment. "I've started having panic attacks in class," he said. His face, which normally displayed a tranquil stoicism, turned a distressing shade of gray. He continued, unprompted, to describe an experience he recently had in a screenwriting workshop. During a discussion about the film industry, a young black woman shared honestly about her insecurities. She was afraid she wouldn't project enough confidence, and asked the professor how she could assert herself without coming across as overbearing. She was typically quite reserved, she said, and mostly kept her thoughts to herself.

Max empathized. He said, "I think part of that is that you're young and you're learning how to find your voice. When I was twenty-one or twenty-two, I was a little bit reserved in how I presented myself. I thought my voice didn't necessarily matter, and I hadn't really learned to speak what I believed in."

Another student, a black male, was quick to police Max's contribution. "I don't understand why you think you get to tell her what it's like to be a black girl in the workplace," he said in a typical passive-aggressive construction that shames its object while conferring moral superiority on the speaker.

Max was shocked. He turned to the young woman. "Is that how you interpreted my comment?"

She said yes. And perhaps she had interpreted it that way. Or maybe she too was afraid of being shamed for having the wrong opinion.

Everyone else in the class was quiet as Max attempted to explain. He said he just wanted to share his personal experience, and he apologized.

Max told me, "They made it about race. It turned into me saying something wrong when I was only trying to be encouraging."

The experience unnerved him. He felt humiliated and ashamed. Later that day, Max wrote to his professor, with whom he had formed a friendship, saying he felt weird about the interaction. The professor, who was black, assured Max that he hadn't done anything wrong, and that some people were just edgy and looking to fight.

I told Max that I had had similar experiences, and we agreed that it would be good to talk about this more. I left the conversation feeling relieved but also paranoid, like I had just joined a dangerous conspiracy.

Two weeks later, Max and I met at Joe's. After getting our coffees, we wandered onto the campus quad. It was the first blustery day in November, so the typical throngs of students that peppered the lawns in front of Butler Library were sparse. Nevertheless, I found myself lowering my voice whenever another student walked by.

As I described my own experience at Columbia—including my depression and resurfaced OCD—Max's face seemed to brighten. It relieved the pressure in my heart to be able to speak honestly about this. Max divulged a few more anecdotes, which he, too, seemed relieved to get off his chest.

One such incident had occurred in the same screenwriting workshop. The class, which comprised mostly students of color, was discussing one of the assigned readings. A student said, "The only reason we're reading this is because it was written by a generic white guy with a mediocre white guy opinion and that's what sells now." Max remembered thinking, "What does that mean?" A few more comments were made by other students, and the environment in the classroom became "racially tense." Later that night, his professor emailed to apologize. "I hope you didn't feel uncomfortable or singled out by the 'mediocre white guy' comment. It's something to be said about Columbia, if anyone were to have made a 'mediocre black girl' or 'mediocre black guy' comment, I would've been furious."

It was a kind gesture, although it would have meant a lot more if he had shared these thoughts in class. But apparently even black professors at Columbia know when to keep their thoughts to themselves.

I know there are some readers who will think this anecdote innocuous, or even an example of black female courage. You might be thinking that a white man who has been sheltered all of his life by the dual privileges of his race and his sex can surely handle a little goading from a class full of women and minorities. What such readers fail to understand is that these kinds of remarks, which are so commonplace in Columbia's classrooms, alienate white men and can either make them angry and resentful, or so depressed that they become suicidal. Further, these remarks—which would otherwise be condemned as microaggressions—exemplify precisely what the students claim to be against: racial and sex discrimination, condoned by the university itself.

But that, I suppose, is the point of the new antiracism. It is what "decolonization" in education looks like. This is just part of our induction into the topsy turvy world of the Maoist intersectional revolution.

As Max spoke, I felt angry in his defense. His classmates couldn't know his history or what struggles he had had to overcome. They didn't know his mind, his feelings, or the sacrifices he might have had to make. Reducing an individual to their immutable characteristics is the opposite of empathy. *Besides,* I thought, *there's nothing uplifting or empowering in putting other people down. All it does is communicate weakness.*

Max said that his anxiety attacks had gotten pretty bad. In class, "I would want to say what I thought, but I was so concerned with how it would be perceived, that it became almost impossible to share what I was thinking. If I say something stupid or unclear, I'm going to be confronted in some way. It became better to just not say anything at all."

I was all too familiar with the level of self-censorship on campus. What I didn't know was how rampant it would become in high schools and colleges elsewhere, especially after the 2020 George Floyd riots.

Max appreciated how opinionated the students were. But what concerned him was that there seemed to be a "correct opinion" and an "incorrect opinion." When a student shared a thought that bordered on heretical, Max said, inevitably another would pointedly ask, "What do you mean by that?"

"It was always said in an antagonistic and suspicious way," he said.

Max's fears extended even to asking simple questions. "I had to make sure the question didn't position my identity in a place of power above others. I needed to make sure it didn't seem like I'm speaking down to whatever the subject is." The atmosphere was stifling.

The results of this kind of suppression, and the unfortunate consequences of a white person speaking his mind out of turn, would soon be vividly on display.

In the early morning hours of Sunday, December 9, 2018, a sophomore physics major named Julian von Abele unleashed what Columbia officials and many in the news media called a "white supremacist" tirade on students of color outside of Butler Library. The incident was captured on camera by Columbia student Aala Nasir who posted it on Twitter with the caption: "Disappointed, but not surprised. Twitter, do your thing #ColumbiaWhiteExcellence."

"We built the modern world!" cries Von Abele in the video. He's a skinny, bespectacled white guy.

"Who?" says a man off camera. It's dark outside. The windows in Butler Library glow.

"Europeans built the modern world!"

"Europeans?!"

The camera pans toward the throng of students confronting him. A black female student says something like, "The modern world took up slavery, but go off, sis. Go off, sis!" There are a lot of voices yelling at the same time.

"We invented science and industry, and you wanna tell us to stop because, *Oh my god, we're so bad!*" Von Abele says, in a mocking tone. "We invented the modern world!"

A man yells, "You fucking degenerate!"

"We saved billions of people from starvation!" says Von Abele.

"Are you joking?!" says a woman.

"We built modern civilization!" cries Von Abele. "White people are the best thing that ever happened to the world."

A man goads him, "Say that one more time! Say that one more time!"

Von Abele jumps up and down with his hands in the air. "We are so amazing! I love myself! And I love white people! Fuck yeah, white people! Fuck yeah, white men! We did everything!" Then he says, "I don't hate other people. I just love white men."

Needless to say, the video quickly went viral. Twitter "did its thing" in spades.

Later that day, the deans of all three of Columbia's undergraduate schools sent a joint email to the Columbia community. "We write to you to unequivocally denounce a deeply disturbing racially charged incident involving Columbia undergraduates that took place…this morning," they wrote, adding that an investigation by the Office of Student Conduct and Community Standards was underway. "We are alarmed at the rise of incidents of racism and hate speech in our world today… At Columbia, we stand firmly against white supremacist language and violence." Since the deans knew this might be a "difficult time" for students, their "on-call team began to provide individual support as soon as we learned of the incident." They wrote that an "open reflection space," hosted by Multicultural Affairs, would be held the following night in Lerner Hall, so students could "be in community with each other."

"Students of color harassed outside Butler by Columbia sophomore spewing racist, white supremacist rhetoric," *Columbia Daily Spectator* headlined its article about the incident. University Senator Alfredo Dominguez (CC'19) told *Spectator*, "[Von Abele has] been here for a year and a half and [he is] still thinking about people this way. It's clear that the University needs to take a further stance about better educating its students more holistically."

Von Abele, it appeared, was in desperate need of reeducation.

By this time, I had been at Columbia for nearly two years. Not for the first time, I immediately thought of Isaac Newton's third law of motion—that for every action, there is an equal and opposite reaction. It's quite simple: If you create a campus culture in which white men are demonized inside and outside of the classroom every day of the week, a culture in which administrators, faculty, and students alike seem to *endorse* this kind of racial discrimination, then *of course* the Julian Von Abeles of the world are going to react this way, eventually. When you tell white male students again and again that this is an "inclusive space" in which "everyone is welcomed and valued equally," and then proceed to treat those men like they're the devil—eventually, someone's going to snap.

For Von Abele, it was an unhinged tirade in the middle of the night. For Max, it was panic attacks. For me, it was a despair I hadn't felt since my family left the Lamb of God, when I feared I was evil incarnate.

In one of my darkest moments at Columbia, I imagined sitting in the middle of the quad with a small placard that read, CIS WHITE GAY, and lighting myself on fire. Maybe that sounds dramatic and far-fetched. But only five years later, two different white men would self-immolate in public. One of them, Aaron Bushnell, a US Air Force member who screamed "Free Palestine" as he set himself on fire outside of DC's Israeli embassy, would be seen by many leftists as a martyr. "Self-immolation is a nonviolent act of despair," wrote the trans/nonbinary writer Masha Gessen in the *New Yorker*, casting this appalling act of mental illness as a legitimate political statement. In *Left Voice*, socialist Samuel Karlin expressed his hope that Bushnell's horrifying suicide would inspire "the type of revolutionary movement that can actually succeed at freeing Palestine and do it as part of a larger fight to end the whole system of imperialism which creates the conditions where it's normal for people to burn."

People seemed to believe that "white male privilege" cloaked white men in some impenetrable armor, as if their tolerance for incessant criticism, judgment, and shame about their immutable characteristics is infinite. Some maintain that white men deserve this treatment for inflicting the same type of criticism, judgment, and shame upon women and people of color for centuries. This is certainly arguable. But should a certain group of people be forced to repent and pay for the supposed sins of their ancestors forever? Was that really the solution to racism? *More* racism? Hadn't we already learned where that leads?

Five months later, another race-related campus controversy made national news.

On April 11, 2019, Alexander McNab, a black student who was in his last year at Columbia—and whom I had met during that first staff meeting for *The Eye* in early 2017—was approached by public safety officers at Barnard's Milstein Center and quickly pinned down after he refused to show his student ID.

The rule at Barnard, located across Broadway from Columbia's main campus, is that students are required to show ID when entering the campus after 11:00 p.m. The incident occurred around 11:30 p.m. McNab, who later told the *New York Times* that he knew about the rule, had heard a voice repeatedly calling out "Hello, sir" when he walked through the gates. He said he figured it was a public safety officer asking to see his ID, but he chose to keep walking. McNab said that on a previous occasion he had been approached by security officers in a hallway at Barnard. Barefoot at the time (he was taking a break from his Afrobeats dance practice), officers asked to see his ID and mentioned that they had been having issues with homeless people sleeping on campus. McNab told the *Times* that he intended his refusal to show his ID "to be a communicative act," one that would highlight a problem with racial profiling on campus. "What I realized is every time I show my ID when I'm asked, the conversation about this remains silent," he said.

According to the *Times*, when McNab didn't respond and kept walking, the officer called for assistance. A group of public safety officers caught up with him in the Barnard building. When they asked him to show his ID, he refused. "Mr. McNab said he raised his voice so the other students could hear, and then said no, telling them this was the third time he had been asked recently," the *Times* reported.

What followed was partly captured on video by a Barnard student. Six security officers (four men of color and two white men) surround him, asking for his ID. A black officer grabs McNab's arm. McNab jerks it away and yells for them to take their hands off. The white officer suggests they go outside and talk about the issue. McNab keeps yelling. The black officer briefly pins McNab down on a counter. Finally, McNab removes his ID from his pocket to show the officers.

"This is the third time Barnard public safety has chased me down!" McNab yells. "And you put your hands on me! I didn't touch any of you! You ought to be ashamed of yourselves!"

The white officer tells him to walk outside with them; McNab refuses. The officer takes his ID; McNab demands his ID back. The officer says he's going to hold on to it until he makes sure McNab is an active student. The officers head for the exit and the video ends.

Caroline Cutlip, the white Barnard student who recorded the video, told the *Washington Post*, "The moment I saw him pinned back…it was so reminiscent of police brutality things I've seen online. I need to say something. I feel like I am someone who can use my privilege to say something here."

The next day, *Columbia Daily Spectator* published an article about the incident: "Black Columbia student physically restrained on countertop by Barnard Public Safety requesting to see CUID."

The editors were sure to include a "content warning": "This piece includes graphic description and a video of a physical encounter between Public Safety officers and a student." I tried to imagine the intended reaction to this. Are there seriously college-aged students who cannot handle "graphic description" and a video of this type of encounter? Who is this hypothetical student, and what the hell are they doing on a college campus, so far from the safety and comfort of their childhood bedrooms? One cannot have a reasonable conversation about a heated topic that deserves nuance and fact-based evidence with people who require trigger warnings. Nor can reasonable conversations be had with those who think it's necessary to add them.

The *Spectator* reported that, according to witnesses, the Public Safety officers "responded negatively" to students who tried to "correct" the officers' "view of McNab's actions." (The *Washington Post*, in its reporting on the incident, said that several students were crying when it happened.) "When I corrected them, they started screaming at me," Barnard student Norah Hassan told *Spectator*. She was shocked that "the people supposed to serve and protect me were pointing at me and screaming."

What appeared to be lost on Hassan is that the officers were trying to do exactly that: serve and protect her. They were following the campus rules—asking for students to show ID and approaching any who didn't comply. McNab was the one who was putting her at risk by refusing to identify himself. While he was throwing his tantrum, the officers could have been giving their attention elsewhere, possibly to students who needed it. The whole thing, which McNab admitted he orchestrated, was a huge distraction. A protest performance.

Like clockwork, student groups and professors circulated a petition that condemned "the racial profiling of and use of force against a Black student on Barnard's campus." The petition, originally created by the Columbia University Women of Color Pre-Law Society, called the

McNab incident "indicative of the harassment (including sexual harassment) and policing students of color, and particularly Black students, face from public safety officers on Columbia's and Barnard's campuses everyday [sic]." The petition called upon both schools "to reform the training of public safety officers." The petition was signed by all four Columbia undergraduate governing bodies, sixty-seven student groups, and seventeen faculty members.

Apparently, no one seemed concerned about homeless people sleeping in university buildings or local residents harassing or victimizing students—a problem that, as everyone knows, has been endemic at Columbia's urban campus for decades, leading to constant demands for stepped up security.

The day after the incident, Barnard placed the five officers and their supervisor on paid administrative leave while T&M Protection Resources, an independent firm, investigated whether race had been a factor in the encounter. Meanwhile Barnard president Sian Beilock informed students in an email that the college would host a "listening session" at which students could provide feedback to the college deans, representatives from Public Safety, the counseling center, and the Office of Title IX and Equity. On Columbia's campus, a "reflection session" would also be held that evening, according to a separate email from a Columbia dean.

That night, Barnard students held a demonstration. "Fuck you, Public Safety!" the group of young women shouted, ignoring the fact that it was they who the campus guards had been protecting.

The following Sunday, Beilock sent out another public letter in which she apologized to McNab and stated that there was "a pervasive sense that racial bias remains pernicious on our campus." The *Times* reported that she had since apologized to McNab in person.

Four months later, T&M issued its official report, which stated, "T&M did not find evidence to support a determination that race was a factor in the confrontation between BCPS and the Columbia University Student." T&M did find, however, that the safety officers' response intensified the encounter "and was inconsistent with best practices for a campus security department." The report also noted that T&M had made numerous requests to arrange a meeting with McNab. But he continued to state that he was unavailable. One month after the incident, McNab sent an email which stated, "After some more consideration with my family and lawyers, I have decided that it would be in my best interest to decline your offer to participate in your investigation."

One might think that McNab, who had provoked the incident as a "communicative act" to highlight racial profiling on campus, would want to help investigators get to the bottom of this serious issue. Wouldn't he want to be part of the solution? Instead, T&M had to rely on "the numerous and differing accounts he gave to various media outlets."

These accounts take up three of the report's twenty-five pages. In a video uploaded to Facebook on April 12, McNab said he was "unaware" that he was required to show ID at the gate. In an interview published by *Columbia Daily Spectator* the same day, he said he was aware of the rule but was frustrated because he didn't think white students were asked to show their ID as often as he was. On a podcast on April 18, McNab said he was "pretty sure" the safety officer was calling for him to show his ID, but decided he wasn't going to cooperate. The report also cites McNab's conflicting statements to *CNN*, the *Washington Post*, *Inside Edition*, and *Amsterdam News*.

On August 15, 2019, Beilock issued a statement about the company's findings. She never states directly that the investigation found no evidence that race had played a role, nor does she note that McNab had refused to participate. Instead, she wrote (misleadingly, I believe) that T&M "reported on community perceptions of racial bias" and about "flawed policies and training that *may* lead to biased enforcement" (emphasis mine). Nevertheless, Antonio Gonzalez, who had been the Executive Director of Public Safety at Barnard for twelve years, would be replaced by Barnard's former Associate Dean for Equity, Amy Zavadil. Zavadil, along with a new safety group cochaired by the Vice President for Diversity, Equity and Inclusion and the Executive Director of Equity, would "review current policies (making sure they are transparent and equitably enforced) and help in Barnard's assessment of campus openness and security more broadly."

It is not clear if the findings of the report and the public safety changes that were implemented at Barnard did any good.

What we do know is that, four months later, a first-semester freshman at Barnard was murdered just off-campus.

On a Tuesday evening in December 2019, I attended Traditions in Nonfiction, a weekly creative writing seminar held in Hamilton Hall. The class was taught by Elianna Kan, a thirty-something writer and translator who had taught my Structure and Style seminar two years earlier.

During the class, we workshopped the first draft of a student's essay about the history of a Cuban restaurant chain in West Harlem. The student, I believe, was Hispanic, and the man she interviewed, the restaurant's owner and the nephew of its founder, is a Cuban immigrant.

After the author read her piece aloud, a white student raised her hand. "I have an issue with the way you portrayed the Harlem community," she said, referring to the opening paragraph in which the author had written that back in the seventies, prostitutes leaned against "grimy" walls, smiling at passersby, while loitering teens smoked cigarettes and made "lewd gestures" at cops.

"It's kind of like a trope," the white student said. "And you make the people sound like props."

I raised my hand and asked the author, "Is this the language the owner used when you interviewed him?"

She nodded.

Undeterred, the white student continued. Apparently, the author's choice to use the label "crackheads" for the drug addicts who would break into the restaurant, assault the female employees, and steal their money was insensitive. And what, exactly, was the point of including the story about the cook's intellectually disabled, nonverbal son, whose quality of life dramatically improved when he began hanging out in the restaurant instead of staying at home watching TV?

It's not like I didn't understand these criticisms. When a journalist bases a story on someone else's account, they need to provide appropriate context. In this case, the author could have clarified that the owner's description of 1970s Harlem might not be shared by all who lived there at the time, or that the crack epidemic led to a slew of antidrug legislation that disproportionately criminalized people of color. She could also have cut the story about the owner's disabled son. Yes, it was uplifting, but clearly the only way for a properly woke reporter to write about retarded people is in the context of their systematic oppression by the white male capitalist power structure.

The author explained that the finished piece was going to be much longer and would ultimately focus on the effects that Columbia's ever-expanding campus has had on local restaurants and businesses. Then she turned to the white student who had criticized her essay and asked, "Do you think I should just delete the whole thing?"

No! I wanted to scream. You should not just delete your words—and the words of the Cuban immigrant you interviewed—because they fail to adequately represent a white woke person's agenda. Is some editing required? Absolutely. Could we have taken a few minutes to discuss the complex nuances of local discourse regarding race relations in Harlem? Perhaps, although we already knew how that conversation would go. But you should never, ever censor yourself just because somebody with a moral superiority complex told you to.

There's something next-level racist about a white person who has lived in Manhattan for all of five minutes criticizing a Hispanic woman for not writing the "right" kind of story based on a Cuban immigrant's firsthand account.

Instead of saying—or mansplaining—any of this, I simply said, "I don't think there's anything problematic about her piece if it's based on a firsthand account," a comment that somehow managed to send a ripple of tension around the room. "Besides," I added, "I would be kind of disappointed if this turned out to be another think piece about the 'Evils of Columbia.' If you want to read one of those stories, you can just open the pages of *Columbia Spectator*." Indeed, *Spectator*'s website has an entire "Housing and Land Use" section, where student-journalists report on Columbia's decades-long encroachment into Harlem.

The other students looked at each other. One student said, "I don't think it has to be one or the other. She can still keep the material even if it ends up being about gentrification."

I nodded. I hadn't meant to suggest she should abandon her original idea. I was just trying to say that I didn't want the immigrant's story and that of his nephew to be lost.

In wrapping up the discussion, Elianna tried to distill the students' critiques into something more palatable. "There's just something a little voyeuristic about your piece," she told the author. "I don't hear *your* voice in it. For example, you say that the restaurant is just as bustling at 2:00 a.m. as it is at 2:00 p.m., but I can tell you haven't been there at 2:00 a.m. Maybe you should go and see what it's like."

Again, I wanted to object. Did Elianna really think it was a good idea for this nineteen-year-old girl to venture into Harlem in the middle of the night? Did she want to be responsible for any mishap that might result?

This time, I stayed silent. God knows that I, a cisgender white man, would be chased off campus with pitchforks for suggesting that a Harlem restaurant at two in the morning is anything but safe. Since Harlem is predominantly black and Hispanic, it was absolutely verboten to suggest that the surrounding neighborhood was dangerous, even though everyone knew that it was.

The very next day, I took the B train to West Harlem to get a haircut. Afterward, I decided to go to campus to get some schoolwork done. Typically, I'd walk through Morningside Park, which sits on a steep incline between Harlem and Columbia's campus. But it was bitter cold that December day, and given its longstanding reputation of being unsafe, I felt leery of walking through the park by myself. I decided to call an Uber.

My driver dropped me on Amsterdam Avenue, just outside the campus gates at Saint Paul's Chapel. From there I walked to Avery Hall, where I had lunch in the basement café. After that I walked to Lewisohn Hall, which has a lounge reserved for GS students.

Shortly after that, I got an email from Columbia's campus alert system saying there had been a robbery and stabbing in Morningside Park. That night an email went out from Columbia's Public Safety office. Attached was a crime alert announcing that an eighteen-year-old Barnard freshman named Tessa Majors, the victim of the robbery and stabbing, was dead. The attack occurred at 6:45 p.m. just inside the park near West 116th Street.

According to the report, Tessa was jumped by three teenagers who demanded her wallet and phone. There was a struggle, and one of the teens reportedly held Majors in a headlock while another stabbed her multiple times. The boys then fled. Tessa, severely wounded, climbed the steep stairwell to Morningside Drive, where she collapsed mere yards away from Columbia President Lee Bollinger's front door. A campus security guard found her unconscious, and she was taken to Mount Sinai Saint Luke's Hospital, where she was pronounced dead.

Two of Majors' assailants were fourteen years old. The third was only thirteen.

The day after the murder, Columbia students downplayed the incident to the *New York Times*. Orenna Brand, a twenty-year-old junior, said she was "trying to remind" her younger classmates "that they can still be courageous and go out in the city and go about their lives." Amanda Ong, a twenty-one-year-old senior, said that her peers' warnings to avoid the park were "racially coded." She told the *Times*, "Nothing like this has ever happened while I've been here. It seems like an isolated incident."

Ong could not have been more wrong. There had in fact been a steep increase in robberies and muggings in Morningside Park that year. But she can't be entirely blamed for her ignorance: As far as I know, not once did the university alert students about the increase in violence. According to the *Times*, "there had been twenty robberies reported inside Morningside Park or on its perimeter this year, compared to seven in the same period last year." On May 8, the *West Side Rag*, an online news outlet, reported that in the previous two weeks, three robberies had been committed by children between the ages of twelve and fifteen. Captain Aneudy Castillo of the twenty-sixth precinct said that none of the victims could identify the perpetrators "because they snuck up and attacked them." He added that in total there were five or six assaults for which he believed the same teens were responsible.

One assault had occurred in April. Bob Lederer, a long-time AIDS activist and cohost of the progressive radio show *Out-FM*, had suffered traumatic brain injury after being beaten and kicked in the head about one block south from where Tessa's murder occurred. Lederer survived and has recovered.

In 2019, Columbia issued twenty-eight crime alerts to students and faculty via an email and text messaging system. None were about the slew of assaults and robberies in Morningside Park. Mind you, none of this was news to residents who had considered the park dangerous—especially at night—for many decades.

Two days after the murder, the NYPD had two of the suspects in custody. Columbia students and faculty were quick to voice their concerns about the rights and wellbeing of the alleged killers. The lead paragraph in a *Spectator* article mentioned the "community members and city officials" who feared the case would repeat that of the infamous Central Park Five, referring to the wrongful conviction of five black and Latino teenagers for the rape of Trisha Meili, a white woman who was attacked while jogging in Central Park in April 1989.

Katherine Franke, a professor of law, gender, and sexuality studies at Columbia Law School, wrote on Facebook (and later in an expanded piece for *Spectator*), "[T]his whole thing just reeks of Columbia's uncomfortable relationship with Harlem and our failure to address urban violence with anything other than policing." Instead, she called for "a restorative, not retributive, response."

For those who are unfamiliar with these fashionable progressive approaches, "retributive" justice focuses on assigning consequences to the perpetrator of a crime, while "restorative" justice is about repairing harm and healing the perpetrator's relationship with the victim and society. Although I'm not sure what restorative justice would look like in this case, since the victim is dead.

White supremacy, colonialism—these are the high priests' explanation for every unfortunate development, even in instances where a white woman is murdered by black teens. They are the woke dog whistles that tell their disciples, "One must not look too closely at this, for to do so would reveal inconvenient truths."

In January 2025, Franke would resign from her job after independent investigators retained by Columbia found that comments she had made during an interview with *Democracy Now!* had violated Columbia's policies. During the interview, Franke had stated, without evidence, "So many of those Israeli students who come to the Columbia campus are coming right out of their military service and have been known to harass Palestinian and other students on our campus." She also blamed Israeli students for a "toxic chemical" attack at a pro-Palestinian rally that had caused "significant injuries" and led to "several students" being "hospitalized." The investigators found that her comments had adversely impacted Israeli students—a protected class under Title VI—and contributed to a "hostile learning environment."

In her statement of resignation, Franke would repeat the claims about the "toxic chemical" attack, even though by that time it was well-known that it was actually a prank spray called "Liquid Ass," which Columbia's Department of Public Safety determined was nontoxic, legal, and could be easily purchased online. The spray was released not by multiple Israeli students but by one single Jewish student who, yes, had previously served in the IDF, as all Israeli citizens are required to do. Some students, distressed by the foul smell, did seek medical attention, but none were hospitalized.

As more information about Tessa's murder trickled out, I thought back to my decision to take an Uber from the hair salon. What if I had walked? I might've arrived on the scene right when it occurred. The stairs Majors climbed were the same ones I'd have taken. What if those teenagers jumped me? I'm a big guy—six-foot-two. But after learning about Lederer's assault, I realized I wasn't immune to being victimized that way. My vulnerability sunk in even more after I read the testimony of the thirteen-year-old boy who had been arrested. He told the NYPD that he and his friends had been following a man, until they saw Majors.

Some students were brave enough to tell a *Gothamist* reporter about the university's failure to warn them about the park's dangers. They stated that students had to take it upon themselves to advise each other to steer clear of the park. Meanwhile Barnard's Director of Media Relations, Kathryn Gerlach, "declined to answer multiple questions about whether the school cautioned students about entering the notoriously dangerous park *before* Majors was fatally stabbed" (emphasis in original).

Three years earlier, I had begun my tenure at Columbia with a highly romanticized view of its rich history of radical activism. Now, it was safe to say, that view had been demolished. I felt like I was living in an Orwell novel. Seeing these bizarre events unfold, I was compelled to do a closer reading of Columbia's activist history, mainly to find out if the media's depiction of it had been accurate—or just agitprop. For weeks, I spent countless hours in Butler's stacks, tearing through books, and also online, combing through the archives of *Columbia Daily Spectator*. Ultimately, none of what I learned surprised me. It only brought everything I had witnessed into clearer focus.

The German critical theorist, Herbert Marcuse, who some have called the "Father of the New Left," was a leading figure at Germany's Institute for Social Research, which later became known as the Frankfurt School of Critical Theory. In 1934, after the rise of Hitler, the institute's founders moved the institute to New York, where it became affiliated with Columbia University. It would eventually return to Germany after the fall of the Nazi regime, but its legacy at Columbia would persist. The university soon became the fountainhead of an illiberal social justice ideology grounded in critical theory.

In 1966, at an antiwar conference in Frankfurt, Marcuse was joined by Rudi Dutschke, a leading figure in West Germany's Socialist Students Union. Later, Dutschke would write to Marcuse that violence and rioting weren't accomplishing what they had hoped, and that it was time for the New Left to infiltrate the institutions of academia and media. In order to extend the base of the student movement and subvert capitalist domination of society, Dutschke explained, they must begin a "long march through the institutions."

The "long march" was an allusion to Mao Zedong, who became chairman of the Chinese Communist Party after leading a famous year-long retreat (a "long march") to evade advancing Nationalist forces before his ultimate victory in 1949.

In 1968—the same year the Red Guards were abolished in China—massive left-wing protests erupted on American university campuses, perhaps the most memorable and consequential of them occurring at Columbia. It was the beginning of America's New Left—an anticapitalist, antimilitarist political movement led by student radicals and Black Power activists. There began the American Red Guard's "long march" through Western institutions, which has culminated in the illiberal chaos we see today.

Students for a Democratic Society (SDS) sat at the center of the radical Marxist political movement. Unlike the Old Left, whose revolutionaries were working-class laborers fighting capitalist exploitation, the New Left's revolutionaries were young, mostly white intellectuals on elite college campuses. In the 1960s, SDS had over three hundred campus chapters and thirty thousand supporters. Its manifesto, known as the Port Huron Statement, proposed the university as a "base" for SDS action, where students could "look outward to the less exotic but more lasting struggles for justice." It declared that a "new left of young people and an awakening community of allies" would bring political power and revolution.

On March 27, 1968, the SDS organized a peaceful demonstration in Columbia's Low Library, demanding the university break ties with the Institute for Defense Analysis, a weapons-research think tank affiliated with the Department of Defense. Six antiwar student activists, who would come to be known as the "IDA Six," were suspended for violating Columbia's ban on indoor demonstrations.

Meanwhile, Columbia had plans to construct a new gymnasium in Morningside Park. The gym, to be built on the park's steep incline, would have an entrance and facilities for Columbia students at the top, and a separate entrance and facilities at the bottom for Harlem's mostly black and Hispanic residents.

Radicalized students and Harlem residents alike saw the blueprint as a form of racial segregation and a potential violation of the Civil Rights Act of 1964. Student activists, already dismayed by the expansion of Columbia's campus that had led to the displacement of local residents in Harlem, began protesting "Gym Crow," as they called it, along with Columbia's purported involvement in the Vietnam War and its punishment of the IDA Six. A month after the demonstration at Low Library, the protests overflowed into Morningside Park, where construction on the gym was underway. Soon, protesters had occupied six university buildings, essentially bringing the campus to a halt. Interestingly, there was a split along racial lines within the protests. Black students and locals were concerned with stopping the construction of the gym, while white students mainly hoped to radicalize more white people.

The protests were partly successful. Construction on the Morningside Park gym permanently ceased. Instead, the park would become a criminal's playground.

Six years later, in 1974, a nineteen-year-old Barnard student was walking through Morningside Park when she was attacked and gang-raped. She spoke to the *Columbia Daily Spectator* a day after the attack, telling them that three twenty-something men had raped her at knifepoint while a group of children quietly watched. After the three men fled, one of the youths who was watching also raped her. The *Spectator* reported that the student "bore no bitterness toward her attackers, whom she identified as being black." She told the *Spectator*, "At first, I thought that they ought to bomb Harlem. Then I thought that maybe we all ought to be Communists, so that no one would be raised to do something like this."

When I read that quote in *Spectator*'s online archives, I was astonished by the victim's willingness to minimize the brutality of her own sexual assault, all in the name of the prevailing orthodoxy. Five decades later, this orthodoxy persists. At the expense of student's safety, Columbia remains reluctant to frame the park and the area around campus as dangerous because of its racial demographics. This reluctance permeates the student body. One must distrust what they can see with their own eyes. One must let down their guard and allow others to transgress their boundaries. One must prioritize social justice ideology over one's own personal safety.

This ideology is the cancer that pervades Columbia, I realized, *but perhaps it is also the administration's convenient excuse, the cloud of squid ink it emits to distract people from its own rapacity.* Columbia is an invisible empire in New York City—the largest property owner in northern Manhattan. If the crime is blamed on the perpetrators, then the Marxist argument, expressed in *Spectator*'s pages by that Barnard student in 1974, that Columbia's capitalist encroachment into Harlem would lead to poverty for its inhabitants and therefore more crime, would be proven correct. Thus, blaming the "white supremacist power structure" thwarts responsibility.

If this was the case, the university could even keep its hands clean in the process. Useful idiots like Katherine Franke were obviously more than willing to do its dirty work.

CHAPTER 16

When I enrolled at Columbia, I had planned on applying to the university's renowned journalism school. But as my tenure at the university wound to a close, I had begun to think that a graduate nonfiction writing program was the better way to go. Columbia's MFA program was one of the most reputable in the nation, and I knew that if I landed a spot there, I might have a better chance of making it as a writer professionally. When I learned that current MFA students taught free creative writing classes to Columbia students and staff, I decided to enroll in a six-week course called Writing to Make a Difference, which was (naturally) geared toward writers passionate about social justice. The course was being led by an MFA student named Marcelle Shehwaro, a Syrian refugee and journalist who had already won an award for her reporting from war-torn Aleppo. She was writing her thesis about her mother, who had been shot and killed at a checkpoint by the Syrian regime. According to her LinkedIn profile, Shehwaro is now the digital content coordinator for the New York City Department of Education, where she implements strategies to enhance the DoE's online presence.

About fifteen other people showed up to the first meeting: a mix of undergrads and PhD candidates of various ethnicities, none of whom I recognized. We sat around a large table in a fourth-floor classroom in Dodge Hall, the home of the MFA program. For our first exercise, Shehwaro—a woman in her mid-thirties with dark eyes and long, dark hair—arbitrarily split the class into groups of three and told us to share with our partners a specific social justice issue that we were hoping to tackle.

I was put in a group with two other men—a soft-spoken Asian immigrant and a Jewish student majoring in philosophy. "I've been really concerned about 'shame culture,'" I told my little group. "I see it online, of course, but also on campus—people being publicly shamed for their ideas. Even if the ideas are problematic, I think it's counterproductive."

The Asian student said something I couldn't quite hear. When I asked him to repeat himself, he said, "I think that's a really good idea." He proceeded to stare at the floor.

The Jewish student agreed. During his freshman year, he said, he had been dumped by all his closest friends for using an "ableist slur." Specifically, he'd called a music band "lame." His story didn't surprise me at all, and I told my peers as much.

After class, as I made my way down the long corridor, the Asian student caught up with me. A few weeks earlier, he told me, another student had publicly scolded him for using the term "cross-dressing."

"I didn't know it was bad," he said.

I don't remember the exact context in which the student had used the term. If he had used it to describe a transgender person, I could understand how he had, in fact, transgressed: One must always communicate the belief that a trans person is *actually the opposite sex*, despite all evidence to the contrary. Trans people are not "cross-dressing" as the opposite sex. Rather, they are dressing as their *true sex*.

Regardless of the context, however, this topic is nearly impossible for anyone—*including trans-identified people*—to navigate, since definitions are constantly changing, and what is acceptable to say one day is often unacceptable the next. For example, the term "transvestism," which describes the practice of dressing in a way that is typically associated with the opposite sex and is often sexually driven (fetishistic) is now verboten and has actually been replaced by "cross-dressing." Further, transvestite/cross-dresser is now included under the broad definition of "transgender," which has replaced "transsexual." To make matters even more complicated, many drag queens—males who caricature women by donning fake breasts, hip pads, cartoonish wigs and makeup in a way that used to be celebrated as a legitimate subculture—have been coming out in droves as transgender. They are no longer men who impersonate women; they are transwomen. And since "transwomen are women"—as we are required to believe—then these drag queens *are* women.

I will have more to say about this in a later chapter. For now, I will leave you with two caveats: First, "transgender" today has no single, coherent definition; and second, most males who identify as transwomen are either "autogynephilic" or "homosexual transexuals." That is, they are either nonhomosexual males who are sexually aroused by the thought of themselves as female and therefore identify as women to satisfy their paraphilia, or they are effeminate gay males who live and sometimes even pass as the opposite sex, since it is what feels natural and comfortable to them. Further, passing as "normal" straight women helps these effeminate gay males to thwart antigay discrimination. The former category, the autogynephiles, who, it might be said, are not inherently feminine and rarely "pass" as female, comprise the overwhelming majority of trans-identified males.

One early-November morning in 2019, I found an empty seat in Butler Library to read the text Shehwaro had assigned that week—a 2016 *New Yorker* profile of black actress Viola Davis, which detailed her childhood of extreme poverty and the havoc her abusive, alcoholic father wreaked at home. I had long been a fan of her acting, but my admiration deepened on reading the article. Rather than a victim, Davis was a survivor. She had risen above her early struggles and built a life of success. I immediately wanted to go out and watch all her movies.

My reading was also influenced by the course I took that semester on African American Literature taught by Robert O'Meally, the director and founder of Columbia's Center for Jazz Studies. The course included seminal texts by major black figures—autobiographies and essays about unfathomable oppression and fierce determination. Over the summer, I had reread Toni Morrison's *Beloved*, and for the first time, *Song of Solomon*, after her death that August.

After jotting some notes on the Davis profile, I grabbed a coffee from Butler's cafe and made the short walk to Hamilton Hall to attend O'Meally's class. Once the class had settled in, our professor announced that Morrison's memorial would be held later that day at St. John the Divine, two blocks away from campus. When class ended, I packed up my things, hurried down the street, and waited in line with the throng of other mourners. St. John's is one of the largest cathedrals in the world. Attendance was in the thousands. Prominent figures including Angela Davis, Oprah Winfrey, Ta-Nehisi Coates, Fran Lebowitz, David Remnick, Kevin Young, Jesmyn Ward, Edwidge Danticat, and Michael Ondaatje delivered eulogies. I felt a warm sense of inclusion. I couldn't quite believe I had the privilege of attending this memorial in such distinguished company.

But there were also darker thoughts. Over the previous three years, ideas about white male supremacy and my supposed complicity in it had been hammered into my head. It was not unlike the lessons about the evils of homosexuality (another immutable aspect of my identity) that I'd been taught by my religious mentors—painful memories of which I was often reminded whenever I entered a church.

As the service progressed, I couldn't ignore the feeling that I was some kind of malevolent interloper. That I didn't belong among this group either. I wasn't good enough, moral enough.

Intrusive thoughts rattled my brain: *You racist piece of shit. Toni Morrison would spit on your face. You don't belong here. Get out.*

When the service ended, I left hurriedly, convinced on some level that this white male evil coursing through my body was visible to others.

CIS WHITE GAY

"What did you all think about the *New Yorker* piece?" Shehwaro asked us the following week. When I replied enthusiastically, she asked me for specifics, which I provided. She said she was glad I'd gotten so much out of it, but added that it was vital to consider some major missteps that the author had made.

Shehwaro turned toward the dry-erase board and uncapped a black marker. The first misstep, she told the class, was the author's decision to open the piece by mentioning Meryl Streep, a white actress. This was a profile of Davis, not Streep.

Her marker squeaked across the board.

The second was the author's reliance on well-worn tropes about black women—such as that they are all victims of violent childhoods. Why hadn't the author centered Davis's success more—like the production company that she and her husband had started together?

Speaking of the husband, why did the author include so many quotes from him? This was *her* story to tell. We didn't need the intrusion of a man's perspective.

Lastly, Shehwaro took issue with a section in which the author converses with Davis in her kitchen while she cooks collard greens, a stereotypically black Southern dish.

As she listed her grievances on the board, I realized with embarrassment why she had assigned the piece: It was an example of exactly what *not* to do if we wanted to "make a difference" with our writing—the *right kind* of difference, that is.

I suddenly realized that by praising the piece, I had made myself look like a tone-deaf cis white male.

On the other hand, I wasn't so ready to abandon my own judgment.

"I guess I can see your point about Meryl Streep," I offered, "but it didn't affect my reading, only because Davis has talked in the past about how close she and Streep are."

Shehwaro gave an unconvincing nod.

While another student spoke, I took the article out of my backpack, realizing that I had somehow neglected to notice who had written it. The author turned out to be theater critic John Lahr. I picked up my phone and googled him. A white man in his seventies appeared on my screen.

"What if Davis *liked* the profile?" I asked.

"That doesn't matter," came the curt reply.

I looked around the room. No one spoke. I kept going.

"So much of the article consists of quotes given by Davis—about her past," I said. "And it's not like this guy *made* her cook collard greens. Davis says that it's her specialty. If that was a part of their interaction, why shouldn't he include it?"

"These are the things that the author chose to include," Shehwaro replied, seeming flustered. "Just think how much other material he probably left out."

It appeared that Shehwaro was operating under two major assumptions: one, that Lahr's creative choices had been born of his maleness and whiteness; and two, that it was his maleness and whiteness that made the profile not only problematic, but possibly *harmful* to black women.

Why, I wondered, would we be encouraged to obscure the truth about a person's story, just because it might reinforce stereotypes about that person's identity or group? What was wrong with highlighting Davis's determination to overcome hardship? What was wrong with the fact that she, like a lot of black Americans, enjoyed eating collard greens? Or that she had a supportive husband—himself an accomplished black actor?

Instead of saying any of this, I acquiesced. "Okay," I said, letting it drop.

Next it was time for an in-class exercise. This time we split up into pairs. My partner was a female undergrad with whom I had yet to interact.

We were instructed to reread the profile together and make a list of all the problematic choices Lahr had made. My partner tore a piece of paper from her notebook and began to number it.

"So the first one would be the inclusion of Streep, I guess," I said.

She wrote it down and then offered another example. Meanwhile I continued scanning the article—a profile of a powerful and successful black woman whose story, just a day earlier, had affected me, a white man, so deeply—for problems.

I looked up at Shehwaro, who sat nearby.

"I object to this assignment," I suddenly said, more loudly than I had intended.

My classmates stopped working and looked up.

"Why?" Shehwaro asked.

"Because I would just be making things up." My heart raced as I fumbled for some wokespeak. "Besides," I quickly added, "I don't think it's right for me, a white man, to try and prescribe the 'correct' ways that black women should or should not be written about."

I wasn't exactly proud of myself for cloaking my objection in unassailably woke terms. Nonetheless, an internal pressure to assert my own perspective had been building for some time. There was so much more that I wanted to say—mainly that this type of identity-focused instruction was counterproductive, alienating, and discriminatory—but I couldn't find the words.

Shehwaro nodded. A young woman sitting to my left said earnestly, "I get what you're saying." Apparently, my stratagem had worked. I exchanged a glance with the Asian student, who watched silently from the opposite end of the room. He smiled knowingly.

I didn't attend the last two sessions of Writing to Make a Difference. I had planned to, but when the next Wednesday evening rolled around, my legs refused to carry me inside the building. Apparently, they had arrived at the same conclusion as my brain: Shehwaro and I had very different ideas about what it meant to "make a difference" as a writer.

In February 2020, I was accepted to the creative nonfiction writing program at an esteemed Midwestern university—including complete tuition remission, plus a generous annual stipend. I had also been accepted to Columbia's MFA program and its journalism school. However, the cost to attend either program would have added another seventy grand to my already-exorbitant school loan tab. After talking it over with Drew, we decided that if I chose the MFA program in the Midwest, I would temporarily move out of state while he would stay behind in New York. It would be difficult to do long distance for a couple years, but we both knew that the opportunity was too good to pass up. I gladly accepted the university's offer and planned to move to the Midwest in August.

I couldn't believe my luck. It meant I'd have two whole years to do nothing but write. Maybe I'd even be able to put together a manuscript about my childhood in the Lamb of God. Plus, I'd graduate with the credentials to teach creative writing at the university level. I shuddered at the thought of teaching the type of students with whom I'd been stuck in class for the previous three years. But maybe the culture at Columbia was an anomaly. Maybe other universities hadn't been captured by this cultlike ideology.

Meanwhile, that semester, I enrolled in a Senior Nonfiction Workshop; a course in Masterpieces of Western Art (in fulfillment of a Core requirement); a basic course in mid-twentieth century American history; and a survey course on the history of Christianity, taught by Robert Somerville, Columbia's Tremaine Professor Emeritus of Religion.

After only a few weeks in Somerville's course, I couldn't believe how little I actually knew about the subject. As immersed as I had been in prayer and worship as a kid, all that had been impressed upon me was that God was to be feared and obeyed, and that it was my job to be perfect in his eyes—or else. As many times as I had heard "Praise the Lord!" and "Thank you, Jesus!" growing up—and uttered those words myself, between fervent prayers of repentance—I'd somehow never absorbed the Christian belief that Jesus actually *forgave* us, or that he granted mercy and grace to those who asked for it.

What fascinated me most was learning what attracted the apostles to Jesus's teachings in the beginning, in particular Paul, who had never even met him. The fact that Jesus had died for his sins, that he had redeemed his wrongdoings, meant that Paul didn't have to agonize over his own imperfections. He could just be human. Perfection was, after all, impossible. It was for God alone. Therefore, Paul could finally let go. God's love was available to him through Jesus. Through Jesus, God accepted him just as he was.

As I studied Paul's epistles, I was surprised to discover how desperate I was for the grace and forgiveness that he had discovered. Columbia was barren. There was no grace or mercy here. Critical social justice ideology wrought nothing but shame and resentment. It was my job to repent for the original sins of my whiteness, my maleness, my privilege, forever and ever. What's more, these sins were inexpungable. Beyond redemption. The work of repentance would never be done and in the end, I'd be no closer to salvation than I was at the beginning.

To be confronted by Christianity in this way was oddly comforting. I couldn't bring myself to believe that Jesus had literally risen from the dead, or that he was the offspring of a virgin birth. And I still couldn't separate Christianity from the antigay teachings of the Christian church.

But I could believe in the idea of forgiveness and grace. I could believe, or at least entertain the belief, that that forgiveness and grace was available to me, no matter how imperfect I was. And I could believe that I could extend it to other people. People who, I knew, desperately needed it.

That March, the COVID-19 pandemic hit New York, and all my classes went online. I couldn't help but feel relieved. The campus was not a hospitable environment for independent thinkers. I finished out the rest of my final semester from the wingback chair in my living room. Every evening at 7:00 p.m., Drew and I listened as thousands of New Yorkers opened up their windows and banged their pots and pans in support of all the first responders.

In May, we watched Columbia's online commencement ceremony on my computer screen. I graduated summa cum laude.

CHAPTER 17

After graduation, I was hopeful that the MFA program would be different from my experience at Columbia. It was, after all, at a Midwestern university, and although it had a strong national reputation, it wasn't in the ultraprogressive Ivy League. Then, in late May, George Floyd was killed by a white cop in Milwaukee. The entire country, cooped up and glued to their social media feeds, went out into the streets, sparking a long summer of protests as well as riots and looting. In that climate, free thinking became difficult, not just on college campuses, but *everywhere.*

None of what I saw surprised me, since I had just spent three and a half years in an ideological reeducation camp. Still, I will never forget the images I saw projected on my television and my Twitter feed: white people washing the feet of black people, just as Jesus washed the feet of the Apostles; baptisms and prayer circles at the newly consecrated George Floyd Square; the call-and-response sermons of the Black Lives Matter activists as hundreds of white onlookers raised their hands to the sky; and—most vividly—the struggle session of Mayor Jacob Frey, conducted in Maoist fashion by BLM activists, which ended with him walking, head down, through a crowd of thousands, as they screamed, "Shame! Shame! Shame!" after he'd refused to publicly commit to defunding the Minneapolis police department.

A new religious movement had swept the country. Intersectionality, one of many lenses through which to study, and hopefully improve, a pluralistic society, had seemingly overnight become a nationally sanctioned, fundamentalist dogma. One's morality was no longer judged on the basis of words and deeds, but rather was intrinsic to one's racial and gender identities. It was officially a race to the bottom of the privilege pyramid—a contest to claim the most oppressed identity in a bid to claim more power.

It felt surreal, watching the critical theories with which I had been inundated at Columbia come to life across the country. Things got more insane by the day.

Really? You want to *abolish the police*?

Really? *All* white people are racist?

Seriously? The *only remedy* for racial discrimination against black people is state-sanctioned racial discrimination against whites and Asians?

Do you *really* want to be saying that "self-reliance" and "objective, rational linear thinking" are specific to "white culture"?

What kind of ass-backward world were we living in? It seemed the more ridiculous the idea, the more eager the masses were to go along with it. And the more willing wealthy white progressives were to open their checkbooks.

THAT JUNE, AMIDST the chaos, the writer J.K. Rowling, who had recently begun speaking out about gender ideology's erosion of women's rights, tweeted: "If sex isn't real, there's no same-sex attraction. If sex isn't real, the lived reality of women globally is erased. I know and love trans people, but erasing the concept of sex removes the ability of many to meaningfully discuss their lives. It isn't hate to speak the truth."

Like pretty much every other human, I was an enormous fan of Rowling's *Harry Potter* series, and I have no shame in stating that I have devoured the entire series more than once. (I may or may not have also attended meet-up groups in New York for Potterheads—but I'll keep those details to myself.) Seeing such a world-renowned figure speaking in defense of gay and lesbian people in a way that was sure to land her in trouble—no matter how reasonable it was—made me admire Rowling and her work even more.

Days later, Rowling put out a full statement on her website. Her 3,600-word, nuanced essay detailed her many reasons for speaking out about this issue, including her own experience of surviving domestic abuse and sexual assault. Rowling wrote, "I refuse to bow down to a movement that I believe is doing demonstrable harm in seeking to erode 'woman' as a political and biological class and offering cover to predators like few before it. I stand alongside the brave women and men, gay, straight and trans, who're standing up for freedom of speech and thought, and for the rights and safety of some of the most vulnerable in our society: young gay kids, fragile teenagers, and women who're reliant on and wish to retain their single sex spaces."

I was bowled over by her words. Again, I felt vindicated.

I'm not crazy. Other people see this happening too. Even J.K. fucking Rowling.

Once again, that vindication was immediately replaced by indignation, when I saw the response of LGBT organizations. The following month, after Rowling expressed on social media her belief that "we are watching a new kind of conversion therapy for young gay people, who are being set on a lifelong path of medicalisation that may result in the loss of their fertility and/or full sexual function," GLAAD attacked her on Twitter. Rowling, they wrote, was using her platform to "target trans people." And her comparison of "medically necessary hormone therapy to dangerous 'conversion therapy'" was "reckless," they said. HRC called her comments "transphobic," "unacceptable," and "flat-out dangerous."

Five years later, the anger I felt as I read the words of these organizations that purport to advocate for the health and wellbeing of gay people remains so strong, I find it difficult to type these words.

IN THE LATE spring, I was notified by administrators in the MFA program that the graduate school would be hosting a virtual seminar for "white allies." I decided to sign on, figuring that this, more than anything, would give me an idea of the campus culture that awaited me.

The facilitator was a white German graduate student representative on the university's Board of Trustees and a "change agent" for the Office of Diversity, Equity, and Inclusion. After viewing the viral *How Can We Win?* video (in which author Kimberly L. Jones gave an impassioned defense of looting), we were asked to share our reactions with the group. Some of the participants said they felt guilty and sad. One wondered how whites could "empower" black people instead of "saving" them. The facilitator said that, as an "empath," it was hard for her not to cry while watching the video, but she knew that if she did, she'd only be "centering my whiteness." She advised the group not to unload their emotions on their black friends. "It's not about you, but it *is* about you," she stated, using the paradoxical language that is characteristic of this sort of antiracist teaching.

During the Zoom session, we learned about "performative white allyship," as when white women go on mission trips to Africa and pose in pictures with black babies. We also learned how to become "coconspirators," with a willingness to risk our social standing and accept whatever consequences might come from "dismantling white supremacy."

We learned how to "correct" the speech of others, what media to consume, and how to spend our money. "Do I support Louis C.K. even though he's sexually assaulted women?" asked the facilitator. "Does my Chick-fil-A sandwich support the murder of LGBTQIA people abroad?" We learned how to interrogate places of work, study, and worship, how to talk to fellow whites, and the proper way to protest. We also learned the various roles that are available to us in effecting social change (e.g., "healers," "disruptors," "caregivers").

I signed off, genuinely horrified. This was not about "social justice." It was religious indoctrination. And I knew how this stuff worked. Even if I was just as opposed to racism and injustice as these zealots, to object to their methods and dispute their dogma would mean exile.

LATER THAT SUMMER, I received notice from the MFA program's director that, due to the pandemic, my first semester (and likely the second one) would have to be conducted online. For the time being at least, Drew and I wouldn't have to figure out a long-distance relationship after all.

Around the same time, I learned about an open letter that members of the graduate student body had written to the university's English department. It included a list of demands: "Hire and Retain Black Faculty," specifically those who are "actively antiracist in their pedagogy and scholarship," and "Recruit and Retain Black Graduate Students," a process, they insisted, that "will lead to greater and much needed diversity of thought," although, to be safe, they asked that current PhD students be able to review incoming applications and "offer recommendations regarding admission decisions."

Other demands included a requirement for "all students to become conversant in critical race studies" and for the university to "Address and Combat Microaggressions"—including "microassaults," "microinsults," and "microinvalidation"—by training department faculty, adjuncts, and graduate students to "interrogate our own unexamined racist biases" and "engage in 'microinterventions.'"

A few days later, I emailed one of the professors who had accepted me into the MFA program (I'll call her Professor Shelton), asking to talk privately with her. Over the phone, I described the oppressive culture I'd encountered at Columbia and explained how fearful I was of running into the same thing there. She replied that she, too, was concerned about this new culture of censorship, as were many of her colleagues.

By way of illustration, she described an incident two years earlier, when a white nonfiction writing fellow read aloud a personal essay about the night he visited a Washington, DC strip club. There, as fate would have it, he met a black exotic dancer who turned out to be from the same African village in which he had lived as a Peace Corps volunteer. According to Shelton, the essay was sensitive and thoughtful. The students, however, were outraged, claiming that the author had appropriated a black woman's story and exploited her sexuality. A petition was issued calling for the university to condemn the student. The backlash was awful, Shelton said. She assured me that, if I ran into any trouble, I could count on her support.

I wouldn't be at the university long enough to test her promise.

THAT FALL, AS soon as the (virtual) semester began, I found myself either swallowing my words or walking on eggshells every time I opened my mouth.

The other fellows in the nonfiction program were Sarah, a Jewish lesbian from LA who grew up in a leftist communal household and edited a far left magazine; maya, a biracial woman who used they/them pronouns and insisted her name be spelled lowercase; Janeane, Lisa and Megan, three white women with baby bangs; Brianna, a black woman who had cofounded a consulting business that provided organizations with antiracism training; Jamie, a white woman from Chicago who had worked in finance; and Lucy, a twenty-three-year-old white woman who had majored in marine biology.

Then there was me, the only male and evidently the virtual embodiment of everything wrong with the world.

I knew instantly that maya was going to be a problem, not only because of the social justice dogma she spouted but because of her avowed "queer" identity and plural pronouns. I was well-aware that being queer had little to do with sexuality but rather signaled adherence to a rigid political ideology; and I had come to see that demands for other people to use weird pronouns and improper grammar was less about validating a person's identity than exercising power over others. It was coercion, plain and simple.

I also knew that the only way to assure myself safe passage in this kind of milieu was to stick to an apologetic, self-effacing stance. The problem was that, by this time, I'd learned how diminishing that state of mind was—not to mention debilitating and depressing. I could simply no longer self-censor, even if speaking my mind was often terrifying.

Like typical writing workshop instructors, Professor Shelton assigned a diverse array of memoirs and essays to read and also tasked us with writing pieces to submit for criticism. During our workshops, the criticism my classmates provided was mostly constructive. But as at Columbia, nearly everything was sifted through a politically correct moral filter. That mode of criticism was so ingrained that my refusal to employ it seemed to confound the other students.

For example, when we discussed a journalist's book about miners, at one point I criticized the author's use of a specific rhetorical device. That is, my comment was about the author's craft and not about the content. Nevertheless, Sarah quickly launched into a sermon.

"Well, Ben, you have to realize that, under capitalism, these miners were being exploited by a corporation...."

"Yes, I'm aware," I responded, perhaps a little too sharply. "I wasn't talking about that."

"Oh, okay," she said, although she still seemed confused. Then the class moved on.

Early in the semester, Sarah, who identified as "genderqueer," submitted an essay about her uncle who had died of AIDS in the early 1990s. (If "genderqueer" seems unfamiliar or confusing, just picture a butch lesbian with a shaved head.) I thought it was excellent—thought-provoking, informative, elegiac. But there was one section that bothered me. Sarah said she sometimes wondered whether her uncle might have turned out to be the kind of older white gay man who is "casually misogynist," "full of racial microaggressions," and practices the kind of politics that marginalizes women, trans people, people of color, and immigrants. She speculated that, had he lived, he might have turned out to be a totally different kind of "queer" than she. The paragraph dangled on its own in the essay, for no apparent reason other than to signal that Sarah held the correct political views and was therefore morally pure.

During our workshop session, I noted that this section seemed to present an unnecessary digression. If she really wanted to go there, I suggested she lean into it more. Give us some examples, expound upon them, and connect it all back to her uncle. Otherwise, this short section could alienate potential readers, particularly gay white men who had survived the AIDS crisis. I added that these broad-brush claims about "cis white gays" were already made ad nauseam on progressive social media and had started to feel like clichés.

As I spoke, Sarah nodded politely. Encouraged, I said that my skin had prickled when she implied there were different kinds of queers—a "good" kind and a "bad" kind. I explained that during my own time working for LGBT rights, and as a student at Columbia, I was frequently on the receiving end of thinly veiled hostility from other LGBT people merely because I am "cis" and exhibit a traditionally masculine form of gender expression. I told the class that as a child I was gender-nonconforming but was bullied so badly in middle school that I obsessively de-feminized myself. So to now be ridiculed by my own people for being gender-*conforming* was disorienting, to say the least. I added that I couldn't help but detect a similar note of hostility in Sarah's otherwise deeply moving essay.

In retrospect, I realize that I was imposing my own sensitivity on the class by rattling off a list of things that had offended me, which is what I judged others for doing. But I had grown tired of hearing my hard-won identity as a gay man casually ridiculed, while others' were handled with kid gloves. I was tired of trying to thrive in a culture in which speaking or writing insensitively about certain kinds of people was considered the gravest of sins, but degrading people like me was perfectly acceptable, even celebrated. I had spent decades hating myself and trying to conform to what other people wanted me to be. I obsessed over being "good" and "kind," and felt deeply ashamed if I inadvertently offended someone else. "I, too, have suffered!" I wanted to shout. "I, too, have experienced oppression!" But that didn't seem to matter. I was, by virtue of my race and male identity, the categorical Oppressor.

When I finished, my mouth was dry and I was trembling. I knew I had taken a risk and made myself vulnerable to correction and criticism. Thankfully, Lucy commented that she had had a similar reaction to that section. My heart rate slowed.

Then maya spoke up. Her arms were crossed, and she was scowling. She said, "Well, I for one *appreciated* what the writer had to say here. All of the forty-plus gay white men I know are full of racial microaggressions."

Deflated, I sunk in my chair. That frozen feeling returned—a cruel mixture of terror and dread. The other students were mostly quiet as we ran out the clock and the class ended.

After I signed off the Zoom call, my living room was unnervingly silent. Not for the first time, I imagined exiting my seventh-floor apartment and ascending the single flight of stairs to the rooftop. I imagined what my body would look like, sailing past my living room window.

A minute later, Jamie, with whom I had become friendly, called me. "What the hell was that?" she said. "Talk about microaggressions! That was just *aggressive*." I replied that I was used to it; that sort of thing had occurred all the time at Columbia. Jamie, who, before the MFA program, hadn't been in academia for many years, seemed dumbfounded.

Used to it or not, for the next hour I was consumed by familiar feelings of paranoia. I texted Sarah that I hoped I hadn't said anything offensive and wished I had expressed myself better. Mercifully, she replied that she appreciated what I had to say.

This would not be my last run in with maya. A second incident occurred in a class on literary criticism, in which we were discussing Maggie Nelson's unconventional memoir, *The Argonauts*, which is about motherhood, marriage, and queerness. The book begins with an explicit reference to the dildo-assisted anal sex that the author has with her spouse, a transman. (The passage implies that her spouse dons a strap-on to penetrate her.) Lucy remarked that from the first page, she suspected that Nelson was intentionally trying to provoke her readers.

maya interjected, opining that perhaps Lucy thought it was provocative because she was straight and therefore not used to reading or thinking about the kind of sex queer people have. Sarah, nodding in agreement, added that when you're perusing books at Barnes & Noble, any references to sex in a book you happen to pick up will typically refer to heteronormative sex, and that queer people don't often get to see their sexual lives reflected in art.

I didn't think they were entirely wrong—obviously, the majority of existing literature depicted sex and romance between males and females. But wasn't that mostly because straight people are the vast majority of the population? Anyway, wasn't it considered sinful—a form of "appropriation"—for a straight writer to depict "queer" sex if it wasn't a part of that writer's "lived experience"? It was really just simple math. Besides, gay and lesbian sections have been found in major bookstores for decades.

I summoned the courage to push back a little. "I have a lot of straight friends," I said, "and many of them have anal sex. So I don't know if one can label anal sex as strictly 'queer.'" My delivery was casual, jocular even, so my classmates chuckled.

For the rest of class, my queer classmates were mostly congenial, but I sensed the familiar hostility lurking. I knew that academics really don't like it when cisgender white men interrogate their reductive narratives and make interesting points about gender and sexuality. They seem to need to own that conversation. I started to feel the same sort of paranoia that I had felt after workshop. Had I said something that indicated I was exclusionary of trans or nonbinary people? Did I say something inappropriate about anal sex? Hours would pass before a more rationally conceived question would smack me in the brain: Why the hell am *I* the one who's paranoid about saying something inappropriate? How was it that in a classroom mostly populated by people who identified as "queer," a gay man should be afraid to comment on anal sex in literature?

At one point the conversation landed on self-censorship. I sat quietly as maya and Sarah spoke about their fear of writing honestly. Sarah had been commissioned to write a review of a book by a queer writer. She had a lot of criticism about it, she said, but she didn't want to publish the piece because she and the author ran in the same literary circles. She was afraid how it might affect her professional relationships, so she thought perhaps it was best to keep her true thoughts to herself. "I know exactly what you mean," maya said. "Whenever I'm writing, I'm always thinking to myself, 'What would Black Twitter have to say about this?' I end up second-guessing myself because I'm afraid I've gotten something wrong."

No one was benefitting from this illiberal culture of censorship, I realized. Not even the people who rigidly enforced it.

"It bums me out to hear this," I said to my classmates. "I want to hear what you have to say. I wish you would write what you actually think." I brought up the writer Meghan Daum, who I had once heard say in an interview, "As a writer, nobody can love you until somebody hates you," meaning that a writer's job is first and foremost to write honestly, and if they're writing honestly, they are doubtless going to piss somebody off. "The only writing that pleases everyone," she said, "is bad writing."

Sarah shook her head, and I thought I detected a shudder, as if the thought was too frightening to contemplate.

Throughout the rest of the semester, many other incidents followed, ranging from eye rolls and icy silences to full-on sanctimonious social-justice lectures. When the next semester began (still virtually), I tried to find a class where I could be anonymous and invisible. At one point, I considered taking a poetry class about grief. But on the first day, the professor (they/them) spent most of the class talking about the breakdown she suffered after her transgender partner died, the weeping fits she had in the shower, and her queerness—and I knew it would just be a space for the professor to indulge her narcissism. As she went over the syllabus, she pointedly added that "cis-sexism will not be tolerated in this class"—a caveat that I knew from experience meant "cis" people would be belittled and not allowed to speak without constant correction. Before the session even ended, I navigated to the registration page and withdrew. I eventually settled on a literature class on "great American writers," an art history course, and my required writing workshop.

CHAPTER 18

The fateful email went out on a Wednesday afternoon in early February, a couple of weeks into my second semester. It came from Professor Shelton. The subject read, "No workshop today."

My heart sank. Instantly I knew this wasn't good. Trembling, I clicked it open.

> *Dear All,*
>
> *As many of you know, a situation has arisen concerning the workshop that requires our attention. [The faculty met] this morning to discuss an action plan that will include a mediated conversation with the workshop and a representative from the Academy for Diversity, Equity, and Inclusion.*
>
> *I will be getting back in touch with you with further information once we have that meeting scheduled, which we hope will occur at the earliest possible time. For today, we will not be holding workshop, as we feel that the involvement of the academy is necessary.*
>
> *My apologies for the short notice.*

Blood pounded in my temples. My skin prickled.

This was because of me. Because of something I had posted on my Substack—a personal essay behind a paywall that no one in the class was meant to see. But somehow, someone had.

Now I would face the consequences.

I closed my computer and stood up, intending to walk across the hall to Drew's office, where he worked diligently at his law job. Instead, I pushed my chair beneath my desk and lay on the hardwood floor.

Feel it, I told myself. *Feel the fear. Don't pray it away.*

The faces of my teachers and classmates flashed across my mind, each one looking more disdainful than the last. "How could you?" they all seemed to be saying.

I concentrated on my breath. My heart rate slowed. The fear, mighty enough to snuff me out, slowly subsided. It became a dull ache, until finally, it was nothing.

THE OFFENDING ESSAY had actually been written at the suggestion of an old friend, whom I had recently gone to visit near my hometown of Baltimore. Late into the night, I had confided some of the madness I'd encountered at Columbia, and now in the MFA program. For an aspiring writer, the opportunity should have been a dream come true. But a regressive and cruel ideology, operating under the guise of "social justice," had captured our universities. Even worse, it had been explicitly formulated to leave people like me in its wake.

"You need to write about this," my friend said.

"How? I'll be crucified."

"All I know is, you *have* to."

Easy for her to say.

That night I lay awake devising a way to share my "lived experience" without summoning an angry mob of self-righteous ideologues who would accuse me of outrageous thought crimes. I had just started a Substack and accumulated a handful of readers, including some old friends and family members who generously signed up for paid subscriptions.

Maybe this was something I could write just for them, to give them their money's worth.

I sat up, opened my laptop, and began to write. What came out were the few anecdotes I shared above, including one more about a time in class when I noticed maya roll her eyes as I was talking about my lifelong interest in the Oscars red carpet fashion. As in this book, I used pseudonyms in my article.

"As a gay man, to see another person roll their eyes when I'm talking about a stereotypically gay aspect of myself is reminiscent of the type of vitriol I and many other gay men have long received from mainstream society," I wrote. "I've come a long way since I was a young person—a person who was called a faggot, who was publicly interrogated in middle school about whether he was a boy or a girl, and who nearly died of shame when he learned that his eighth-grade class had voted him 'Most Likely to Be a Fashion Designer.'

"Being an openly gay man has required bravery. It still does, in many places. Including, evidently, in predominantly LGBTQ spaces.

"Again, I can't be sure why maya rolled their eyes. But I can't help but take it personally, especially because many of the ideas she espouses in class are steeped in queer theory (and critical theory in general), whose adherents often equate biological sex with gender and who seem to want to deconstruct gender (therefore *sex*) so thoroughly that it no longer means anything. What's the harm in that, you ask? Well, for one, it means that it is becoming problematic for me, a gay man, to say, for example, how much I like dick, since, according to many 'progressives,' some men do not have dicks, therefore my statement is trans-exclusionary and transphobic."

I concluded by posing a few rhetorical questions.

"Isn't it strange how, suddenly, in the year 2021, for a gay man to say he likes dick can be construed as offensive by both the far right and the far left?"

"Isn't it funny how many aspects of the moralistic woke left mirror those of religious fundamentalists?"

And: "To my gay readers: Have you noticed how uncool it's become to describe yourself as gay, instead of using the much more popular—and infinitely more vague—term 'queer'?"

The essay allowed me to express myself in a way that I never felt I could in my writing class or my workshop discussions. I was stating what I truly thought without "accounting for my privilege" or atoning for my immutable identity.

I called the essay "The New Homophobia in Higher Education," with the subtitle "Why, in a progressive American university, am I afraid to say I'm gay?" Before I could think too long about it, I hit publish. It was an immediate catharsis. *Maybe now I won't feel so alone.*

Impulsively I grabbed my phone and opened Twitter, wondering whether to tweet a link to my two-hundred-odd followers.

The only other time I had dared to tweet an unorthodox take was a year earlier, in response to an article on a Columbia student-run news blog. The title said a student had "passed away," and directly underneath that was an "editor's note": "This article contains mentions of death."

When I read the trigger warning, something in me snapped. I just couldn't understand how students were expected to go out and live in the world if they couldn't handle the reality that sometimes people die. Anyway, like any other sensible person, I ranted about it on Twitter. Minutes later, a student responded that I was an "absolute piece of shit." I deleted the tweet and spent the rest of the night wondering what it would feel like to jump off the George Washington Bridge.

I didn't want to be confronted with that level of anger again. But I also knew that a few of my followers were gay people who may have had similar experiences. Anyway, if I tweeted a link to the essay, surely none of my classmates would see it.

I WAS WRONG, of course. And in retrospect, I was naïve to think that I would get away with it.

Now I realize I didn't want to. I needed to get the hell out of there—not just the MFA program but out of academia. If a writer wants to be any good, he has to write what he actually thinks. In the academy, it had become impossible to do that. Here there was only one acceptable way to think about the world, and my way was not it.

That night I received a text from Janeane, a second-year graduate student in my cohort who followed me on Twitter, letting me know she had read my Substack post. I braced for an onslaught of ridicule. But she said she was sorry to hear about my experience and that she also had known maya to be quite mean. The previous year, while they were workshopping Janeane's personal essay, maya had told her it was clear she had never suffered. When Janeane pushed back, maya doubled down. From then on, Janeane felt uncomfortable sharing her work with the class.

"I'm so sorry," I wrote. "That's awful." But secretly I was glad to find out that I wasn't alone after all.

THE DAY AFTER that first fateful email, I received a second one.

> *Dear Ben,*
>
> *By now, you might have heard that some of your workshop cohort was upset by one of your newsletters ("The New Homophobia in Higher Education"). We have only seen screenshots of parts of it (which were sent to us). [We] wondered if you would consider sending us the entire piece. As you know, we're working to hold a mediated conversation with the workshop about this.*

So someone in my cohort (I never learned who) had read my post, taken screenshots of the problematic parts, and circulated them among the other students (excepting me of course). Later I learned that, by describing maya's behavior unfavorably, she might claim that I was attacking her as an "outspoken person of color."

I sent my professor the piece in its entirety and received a follow-up email asking my permission to share it with the chair of the English department, "relevant members of the Academy for Diversity, Equity, and Inclusion," and workshop participants.

In other words, no one—not my professors, the department faculty, nor the DEI department—had actually read the essay before cancelling our workshop and publicly launching an investigation.

It was ridiculous. A total embarrassment. I couldn't believe how cowardly everyone was behaving. Not to mention that I had been made to feel like I had committed some terrible crime, all for writing something they *hadn't even read.*

Flabbergasted, I responded to my professors, granting them permission.

As I WAITED for their response, I busied myself by continuing with the assigned work for my literature course on great American writers. That week, my professor—an English scholar whom I can barely remember, being that I would only be in his class for two weeks—advised us to read Ralph Waldo Emerson's "Self-Reliance." It was the first time I had ever read this particular essay.

In his essay, Emerson relayed a conversation he once had with a friend who tried to preach church doctrine to him. Emerson asked his friend, "What have I to do with the sacredness of traditions, if I live wholly from within?"

"But these impulses may be from below, not from above," his friend warned him.

Emerson replied, "They do not seem to me to be such; but if I am the Devil's child, I will live then from the Devil."

This line frightened me. But the fear subsided, and I was left with a piercing clarity.

Why had I, for my entire life, so eagerly believed what other people said was true? Why had I trusted everyone else to tell me what was good and what was right? Why had I allowed so many people to convince me I was evil, when none of them could even agree over what constituted good and evil?

If I am to think for myself, yes, I will be in danger of transgressing.

But at least I will be free.

THERE'S NOTHING QUITE like that first shot of hope when you finally realize you're done. That you have don't have to wait for anyone's permission to free yourself from an intellectual and creative prison. That you can actually just *leave.*

The next day, as I notified the university of my intent to withdraw from the program, the hope washed over me, and, for what felt like the first time in years, my mind quieted. It was like that night in the psych ward all those years ago, when, desperate for a reprieve from the constant fear and self-hatred, I had screamed those obscenities at God, and the anguish had finally ceased.

You are good enough.

You don't have to take this anymore.

You don't deserve any of this.

The director urged me to reconsider. "I am confident that we are going to be having productive and hopefully healing conversations around this," he assured me in an email. "So one alternative to immediate withdrawal would be to participate in these conversations (as difficult as they may be) with us and the workshop group and then decide if continuing in the program—which we would very much like for you to do—seems more possible at that point or if withdrawing still feels like the right option for you. Another possibility is to take a leave of absence instead of withdrawing."

I imagined what it would be like to stay in the program and reassert myself during the DEI-mediated discussion—which, I was fairly certain, would turn into a struggle session. I knew I would be gaslit, and that it would become a forum for all the familiar intersectional clichés, in which I would be cast as the oppressor. I knew that my concerns would be invalidated, then pushed aside; that the focus would land on my crime of daring to write something that depicted my insufferable classmates in an honest light, where it would stay until I had properly confessed and atoned.

Not this time.

My response was the easiest thing I've ever had to write: "My decision is final."

For a moment, I grew anxious, wondering what I was going to do, now that I was just another unemployed college graduate. But I quickly let that go. I no longer had it in me to be scared.

Instead, my thoughts turned to my classmates and professors, both in the MFA program and at Columbia before it. I couldn't believe that this is what had become of higher education. Falsely advertised as a place of free inquiry, where adults could interrogate established narratives and confront uncomfortable truths, the academy had become a religious commune. A place where emotionally stunted, sanctimonious assholes who had never had an original thought in their lives made names for themselves by dutifully reciting scripture while policing the thoughts of others. It was a funhouse mirror image of the religious cult I grew up in.

I thought about maya, the classmate who had rolled her eyes when I spoke in class. The one who callously stated that "all white gay men are racist," as if to remind the class that the combination of my sexual orientation and the color of my skin meant that I did not deserve their empathy. The one who thrived on shaming others, and who made herself bigger by putting other people down.

I had known way too many goddamn mayas—in the MFA program, at Columbia, at GLAAD. I was done.

And what the hell is nonbinary, I thought, *besides a smokescreen for narcissism? How stupid do you have to be to not realize how* regressive *it is? How* performative*!*

My heartrate quickened.

And why should *I have to accept that racism is okay, so long as it's directed at white people?*

Why should *I grovel to straight women who dare to accuse me of being improperly gay?*

Why can't *I criticize the absolute bullshit of queer theory?*

Why can't *I think socialism is shit?*

And why would anyone…

I stopped myself from continuing down this dangerous path, just as I had done countless times over the previous four years, whenever I had begun to question a tenet of social justice ideology that everyone insisted was the key to a better future, but which I felt would drag us back into the past.

That was when I realized I had not only been self-censoring my speech, *I had been censoring my own thoughts.*

This was the state of modern academia.

Now, out of the academy, I would finally be free to think and write whatever I wanted. After four years through the looking glass, I could once again live in the real world, where up was up and down was down, where sex was real, and where people were individuals rather than the sum of their intersectional "identities." A world populated by real, complicated, imperfect people, rather than brainwashed jackboots and the cowards incapable of defying them. I didn't have to wait around to be shamed and excommunicated. *This* community, *this* church, I could leave on my own accord. Like *Alice in Wonderland*, I could simply stand up and scatter my antagonists with a wave of my hand.

Fuck all of you.

You're nothing but a pack of cards.

"Prayer is the contemplation of the facts of life from the highest point of view," Emerson wrote in "Self-Reliance." "But prayer as a means to effect a private end is meanness and theft. It supposes dualism and not unity in nature and consciousness. As soon as the man is at one with God, he will not beg."

Just as I would no longer pray in the obsessive and fruitless manner that had wasted so many precious hours, I would no longer answer to the high priests of the Church of Social Justice. I would not recite their required catechisms, pledge allegiance to their nonsensical ideology, nor flagellate myself at their altar. I would not confess to that which does not require confessing in order to earn favor that will never come. I would reject their cancerous, regressive, and false doctrine.

"I will stand here for humanity," wrote Emerson, "and though I would make it kind, I would make it true."

CHAPTER 19

It would be a massive understatement to say that my political perspective had changed since the day I first walked through Columbia's wrought iron gates. It's more like it was shattered.

Nevertheless, on Election Day in November 2020, just as I had done four years earlier, I cast my vote against Donald Trump. After Joe Biden won, I was cautiously optimistic. Then, in early 2021, Trump's refusal to accept the results and the events of January 6 confirmed my belief that America had made the right decision.

But after four years in academia, I also wondered just what, exactly, we were signing up for. The regressive ideas about race and sex that I had encountered in the classroom had made their way into the mainstream. "The only remedy to past discrimination is present discrimination," Ibram X. Kendi wrote in *How to Be an Antiracist*, which Democrats quoted like it was scripture. Had I voted for a political party or a religious sect?

In the months after I left the MFA program, while I collected myself and recalibrated, I got a part-time job as a receptionist at an acupuncture clinic in Manhattan's financial district. It was exactly what I needed at the time. There, I scheduled appointments, restocked needles, and disinfected treatment rooms between clients. On my downtime, as meditative music drifted through the clinic's surround sound, I wrote.

In July 2021, I got my first paid work as a writer. Jon Kay, an editor at *Quillette*, which publishes nonpartisan analysis and cultural commentary, accepted my pitch to write a longform essay about my experiences in academia and LGBT activism. Kay, a fantastic editor, gave me the time and the space to candidly write my story. The essay, which *Quillette* titled "As A Gay Child in a Christian Cult, I Was Taught to Hate Myself. Then I Joined the Church of Social Justice—and Nothing Changed" was published in July 2021. It would become the basis for this book.

Quillette has a global readership, so my essay made some ripples, if not waves. The response was overwhelmingly positive. Emails flooded my inbox from readers who appreciated what I had to say, from gay men to women to a staffer at, of all places, the fundamentalist Christian organization, Focus on the Family. Wrote the staffer, "You have captured the (ironic) problem and brutality of the new fundamentalism better than anyone I have read. I have really been struck recently by how the evolution of gender identity is really canceling sexual orientation. And I am honestly outraged for the lesbians that their spaces and culture are being erased by trans patriarchy. (Look at those words coming out of my mouth!)"

I was thrilled. Daring to write boldly was turning out to be worth it.

Then came an email that shocked me even more than the previous one. It was from the Lamb of God School's current headmaster. He said he had known my parents in the '80s; in fact, my father had been his pastoral leader and mentor when he was in law school. He wanted to thank me for sharing my story. He asked if I would be open to a conversation, one that could perhaps bring some reconciliation and healing. He assured me that the school had evolved since I was there, and that students are now taught to think critically about the Bible and Christian beliefs.

Some months passed before the headmaster and I finally connected over the phone. After reminiscing about the old days, I thanked him for his email. He spoke kindly as he reiterated some of the things he had written, but underneath his words I could sense a defensiveness that I hadn't detected in his email. It was as if, in the months since then, his views had hardened again. If that was the case, I didn't resent him for it. I remembered what it was like to subscribe to a fundamentalist religious dogma. I was an outsider, an infidel. He could only acquiesce so much.

After we hung up, I was surprised by my feelings, or rather, the absence of them. I felt nothing. No fear, no shame, no self-doubt, no anger. I was serene. Even the headmaster of the Lamb of God School no longer had any power over me.

Perhaps the greatest benefits of publishing the *Quillette* essay were the connections I made with other gender heretics. For years, the mainstream media had done everything it could to frame opposition to "gender ideology" as a right-wing moral panic, even though people from across the political spectrum were speaking out against the state's institutionalization of a belief system that divorced sex from material reality. Many of these heretics were kind enough to reach out to me. Before I knew it, I realized I had found a new community, only this time, it was a community that questioned dogmas instead of demanding fealty to them. There were many things my new friends and I disagreed about, but we disagreed respectfully, like adults. We didn't shame or censor one another; rather, we listened to each other's perspectives in good faith. Sometimes, so thoroughly convinced were we by a friend's argument, we even changed our minds. I had never in my life been a part of an intellectual community like this one.

Inspired by my new group of "problematic" friends, who were all, in one way or another, bravely pursuing inconvenient truths, I dug further into my research. I interviewed gender clinicians; gay Iranian refugees; detransitioners; and other gay, lesbian, and transgender people who, like me, had had it with activist organizations that falsely claimed to speak for all of us. More writing opportunities followed, which led to radio, television, and podcast interviews and even speaking engagements at local school board meetings and national conferences. I followed all of the threads that I had picked up at Columbia and in the MFA program but, within those totalitarian environments, had felt afraid to pursue.

It didn't take long for me to regret my vote for Joe Biden. Right after he was inaugurated, the president essentially dismantled Title IX by issuing an executive order that prohibited discrimination on the basis of "gender identity." This gave males the right to enter female bathrooms and to play on female sports teams. Then Biden appointed as US Assistant Secretary for Health Admiral Rachel Levine, a straight male in his sixties who, after marrying and having children, insisted he was a woman. When Levine was sworn in, the White House tweeted that he was "the first 4-star female officer in the US Public Health Service Commissioned Corps."

The first *female*.

In his new role, Levine immediately began advocating for "gender-affirming care" for young people, falsely claiming that there was medical consensus around this mad science and that, if kids were denied this "medical care," they would kill themselves.

By that time, trans identity had exploded across the Western world, in particular among teenage girls, a demographic that is especially susceptible to social influence. We had begun to hear more stories of detransitioners, including many young people who had undergone irreversible surgeries, only to realize they had been misled by therapists and doctors—and in some cases by radical activists who had groomed them online. Researchers in Finland performed a systematic review of the evidence that purported to prove the efficacy of puberty blockers and cross-sex hormones for young people, only to find that all of that evidence was either "low" or "very low" in quality. That is to say, hardly any conclusions could be confidently drawn from that evidence, therefore the risks and uncertainties of the medical protocols outweighed any known benefits. Later, Finnish researchers determined that suicide among young people seeking gender services is not only rare, but when comparing this cohort with a cohort of matched controls, there was no convincing evidence that gender-referred youth are more likely to commit suicide than the general population, after controlling for psychiatric treatment history. In 2020, Finland reversed course, prioritizing psychotherapy for gender dysphoric youth over medicalization. Soon, Sweden and the UK, after their own evidence reviews came to the same conclusions, would do the same.

Meanwhile, in the US, under the Biden Administration, it was full steam ahead. While Republican-led state legislatures, following the science, enacted bans on puberty blockers and cross-sex hormones for minors and bills that barred males from playing on women's and girls' sports teams, Democrats, snug in the pockets of ideologically captured NGOs and perhaps even of medical professionals now profiting enormously from "gender-affirming care," behaved as if "sex changes" for kids and boys in girls' locker rooms were the next frontiers in civil rights. In April 2021, during his first joint address to Congress, the president addressed trans-identified young people directly. "I want you to know your president has your back."

Meanwhile, as cults do, the gender cult became even more extreme. They continued to lie about pediatric sex-trait modification being "life-saving" and to fearmonger worry-sick parents of trans-identified kids with the suicide myth. But soon they were also arguing that access to puberty blockers and cross-sex hormones was a child's human right and denying them this right was to deny them their autonomy. The lightning-fast speed in which "nonbinary" had become a recognized identity to one that might need to be medicalized *in children* was a sight to behold.

On March 1, 2021, Jules (née Julian) Gill-Peterson, a trans-identified Johns Hopkins professor and author of the 2018 book *Histories of the Transgender Child*, tweeted to his thousands of followers: "give puberty blockers, for free, to young people—without parental consent. the end." Dr. Jack Turban, an assistant professor of child and adolescent psychiatry at the University of California, San Francisco, who had become a leading proponent of pediatric sex-trait modification, seemed to agree with Gill-Peterson's tweet. He responded: "It's done with birth control, and it's hard to argue GnRH analogs [puberty blockers] are more dangerous."

In a coincidence of sorts, less than two weeks later, the British newspaper the *Times* published an article about Guy Sorman, who had been a close acquaintance of Michel Foucault before his death from AIDS in 1984. Sorman, a prolific writer and international professor of economics, told the *Times* that, when he visited Foucault in Tunisia, where Foucault was living in 1969, he had seen Foucault offer money to local Arab boys as young as eight, telling them to meet him at the local cemetery, where he would have sex with them. "There is a colonial dimension to this," Sorman told the *Times*. "A white imperialism."

The reaction to the *Times* article was fairly quiet, save the French reporters who were quick to write articles debunking Sorman's claims. Foucault lived in Tunisia in 1968, not 1969, they said; or the boys he had sex with were teenagers, not eight or ten. However, Haythem Guesmi, a Tunisian academic and writer, did write in *Al Jazeera* that, while he didn't want reports of Foucault's "child sexual abuse to be used to attack his scholarly work and academia in general," he did think it was "important to acknowledge that Foucault's monstrosity had permanently changed the lives of many faceless and nameless Tunisian children and caused rippling traumatic effects in their lives."

Other than that, there was no organized outrage, no campaigns among students and academics to posthumously cancel Foucault and burn his books. Not that I would have preferred this fascist reaction, but I did find it hypocritical of the left, which is typically so keen to relitigate the sins of the past. It turns out that it's not about the crimes themselves but about who committed them—and who is alleging them. Sorman, according to critics of his claims about Foucault, cannot be trusted. He might've founded the global humanitarian organization Action Against Hunger, but he also at one time defended Ronald Reagan.

Today's Red Guards often talk about how "exhausted" they are having to explain issues of social justice to "ignorant people." I believe them; the mental gymnastics they have to perform to make their backward ideas make sense does sound exhausting. But what *I* find exhausting is having to pretend like we don't notice that the radical trans movement, grounded in queer theory, is fundamentally pedophilic in nature.

Two months after Gill-Peterson tweeted that every kid should be able to chemically castrate himself, the *New York Times* published his op-ed, in which he lazily argued that the possibility of social influence contributing to the surge in trans identification among young people was nothing but right-wing propaganda.

Gender ideology was now entrenched in every American institution.

In November 2021, the *Washington Post* published an op-ed titled, "The mental health establishment is failing trans kids." The authors were Drs. Laura Edwards-Leeper and Erica Anderson.

Dr. Edwards-Leeper was the founding psychologist for the Gender Management Service (GeMS) clinic at Boston Children's Hospital, which opened in 2007 and was the first hospital-based pediatric gender clinic in the US. She adapted the Dutch protocol for use in the US.

Dr. Anderson, a transwoman and the former president of the US Professional Association for Transgender Health (USPATH), is a clinical psychologist who also works with gender-diverse youth.

In their essay, the authors wrote, "The pressure by activist medical and mental health providers, along with some national LGBT organizations to silence the voices of detransitioners and sabotage the discussion around what is occurring in the field is unconscionable."

Evidence of this "unconscionable" behavior was everywhere, I noticed, especially when it came to GLAAD. In May 2021, the CBS news program *60 Minutes* aired a segment about trans medicine that included testimonies from detransitioners who had been rushed into medical treatment and later regretted it. In the weeks or months before it aired, GLAAD, I have been told, tried relentlessly to take control of the narrative. But CBS pushed forward, delivering an evenhanded segment that conveyed the truth about these practices.

GLAAD was dissatisfied. The organization tweeted that *60 Minutes* aired a "shameful segment fearmongering about trans youth." It added, "Parents of trans youth could walk away with the false belief that young people are being rushed into medical transition." GLAAD called the claims that kids' trans identities are being influenced by YouTubers and online communities as "dangerous" and "ridiculous."

It is galling that an organization that purports to advocate for gays and lesbians, who are often the victims of this medical harm, could so shamelessly tweet this misinformation. What is "ridiculous" is that anyone, in 2021, could think that social media has played little or no role in the sharp uptick in trans identification among young people.

Since then, GLAAD has refused to give up. In February 2023, a van hired by GLAAD pulled up outside the *New York Times* building in midtown Manhattan. On it was a billboard about gender-affirming care for youth that read, "The science is settled." For anyone like me who has been immersed for years in the issue of adolescent gender medicine and has seen the damage that it has reaped could not imagine a more preposterous statement. Not to mention that science, as it were, is never truly settled.

On the day GLAAD hired the van, it delivered a letter signed by a bunch of know-nothing celebrities to the *Times*. The letter included a list of demands: The *Times* must change its narrative about trans issues (timing: "immediately"), allow trans people to dictate the narrative ("hold a meeting" with "transgender community members and leaders" "within 2 months"), and hire more trans people ("two trans people on the Opinion side and at least two trans people on the news side within three months"). To justify its demands, GLAAD wrote that Republican legislatures were using *Times* reporting to argue for bans on gender-affirming care for minors.

Only totalitarians try to manipulate the free press.

Thankfully, the *New York Times*, in an exceedingly rare display of journalistic integrity, responded by saying that GLAAD and the newspaper have different goals and that they stood by their reporting.

The February 2023 debacle was a huge embarrassment for GLAAD. I had coffee with a writer for the *Times* the day before GLAAD delivered its letter. The next day, when I texted him about it, he wrote back, "That's insane. GLAAD used to be respected." He added, "A group of celebrities and activists say something is bigoted, and there can be no further discussion."

In 2023, I interviewed Dr. Edwards-Leeper (who insisted I call her Laura) for this book. During our conversation, she consistently used the word "cult" to describe the current state of pediatric trans medicine.

At one point, I told her about my childhood, and my concern that, if I were growing up today, I would have been erroneously affirmed as a transgender girl.

"I'm sure you would have," Laura replied.

CHAPTER 20

In 2021, when Admiral Levine was first sworn in as assistant health secretary, I had thought his full-throated backing of "gender-affirming care" was simply misguided. But after I learned more of the truth about transgender identity, I found his support of these antigay practices to be egregious.

As I wrote above, historically, there have been two distinct subtypes of males who identify as trans: effeminate gay men (in scientific literature, "homosexual transexuals," or HSTS) and men who are sexually aroused by the thought of themselves as women ("autogynephilic" transexuals, or AGP). AGPs represent the overwhelming majority of trans-identified males.

People who identify as transexual suffer from gender dysphoria, described in the DSM-5 as a "marked incongruence between one's experienced/expressed gender" and one's natal sex. This condition used to be known as "gender identity disorder," but in 2013, at the behest of activists, it was renamed to focus the diagnosis on the distress rather than the individual, which they believed would reduce stigma.

To alleviate this dysphoria, some decide to identify and live as the opposite sex by changing their names, hairstyles, and wardrobes; ingesting synthetic, masculinizing, or feminizing hormones that modify their secondary sex characteristics, like body hair and body fat distribution;

and undergoing various plastic surgeries—all to appear more like the opposite sex. If their transition is convincing, they are called "passing." That is, they "pass" as the opposite sex.

Because homosexual transexuals are very different from what are called autogynephilic transexuals, the common definition of gender dysphoria is lacking. Homosexual transexuals are innately gender-nonconforming—they are naturally effeminate males or butch females—and their gender-nonconformity has been evident from early childhood. They are often bullied and rejected by their peers and even by their own families. Some suffer from terrible religious guilt. Some live under the constant threat of violence. Thus, they identify as the opposite sex and transition in order to *protect* themselves—to *fix* themselves.

One homosexual transexual I met told me that "social dysphoria" is a better definition than "gender dysphoria" when it comes to this cohort. By transitioning, effeminate gay men become facsimiles of straight women, and butch lesbians become facsimiles of straight men. They blend into society, and everyone is happy.

For a while, anyway. Eventually, for some, the lack of natal sex hormones and the daily ingestion of synthetic, cross-sex hormones can create terrible physical and mental health problems. And those who undergo various "sex reassignment" surgeries often suffer severe and ongoing complications. Because it is impossible to actually change one's sex, some homosexual transexuals become exhausted by the endeavor. They will feel like they are constantly fighting nature. At this point, they might choose to detransition—to discontinue medical transition and once again identify and live as their natural sex.

But this process can be very complicated. Some male homosexual transexuals have been castrated; they no longer have their testes, which produce testosterone. Thus, besides infertility and moderate-to-severe issues with sexual function, these detransitioned gay men will have to deal with ingesting synthetic testosterone for the rest of their lives.

They also may need to undergo corrective surgeries to address lingering complications. Castration is, of course, irreversible. "Top surgeries" (implants for males and double mastectomies for females) can also be difficult to correct, especially for females. Some will no longer have enough skin and breast tissue to reconstruct a breast, even with the aid of implants. Females who undergo top surgery will not be able to breastfeed if they have children.

For autogynephilic males, on the other hand, their opposite-sex identification is sexual in nature. It is a *paraphilia*. They are *attracted to themselves as women*. They typically are not gender-nonconforming in childhood. Their propensity to become aroused by thinking of themselves as women doesn't typically occur until sexual maturity, although they may have related fantasies when they are younger. While "passing" as women can sometimes be quite easy for homosexual transexuals, since they are inherently gender-nonconforming, autogynephilic transexuals often have a more difficult time passing. Again, AGP males make up the majority of trans-identified males; historically, about 75 percent of them.

The typology of transsexualism was developed (and the term "autogynephilia" coined) by American-Canadian psychologist Ray Blanchard, which he based on his own research in the 1980s and 1990s. It applied only to males. Since then, Blanchard has written, "I do not think that this phenomenon in females is the exact counterpart of autogynephilia in males, and therefore I have called it 'autohomoeroticism' instead of 'autoandrophilia.'" Blanchard explained, "Autogynephilic (male) gender dysphorics are attracted to the idea of having a woman's body; autohomoerotic (female) gender dysphorics are attracted to the idea of participating in gay male sex." He elaborated further: "For autogynephiles, becoming a lesbian woman is a secondary goal—the logical consequence of being attracted to women and wanting to become a woman. For autohomoerotics, becoming a gay man appears to be the primary goal or very close to it."

Blanchard's typology was written about in behavioral geneticist J. Michael Bailey's 2003 book *The Man Who Would Be Queen: The Science of Gender-Bending and Transsexualism*. Sensitively written and apolitical, Bailey's book describes various case studies and explains in laymen's terms existing scientific research about transsexualism. Nevertheless, the backlash from trans activists was severe.

In a 2007 journal article for *Perspectives in Biology and Medicine*, Bailey and his coauthor, Kiira Triea, explain the reason why Blanchard's work (and Bailey's book) sparked such ire. Mainly, it is because many trans activists prefer the theory about transsexualism that competes with Blanchard's; that is, the theory that all males who identify as transexual "share the same psychological condition," which is the possession of a "female gender identity." They are desperate to believe that they have the same or similar "neural circuitry" as natal women and that this is what causes their female gender identity.

This theory about neural circuitry—what some call "having a female brain in a man's body"—is widespread. Activists who espouse this theory typically cite "brain sex" studies that suggest specific brain regions in trans-identified males more closely resemble those of natal females than other males. The problem with these studies is that they did not control for sexual orientation and prior hormone treatment. The studies that do control for these variables produce the opposite results. If anything, these "brain sex" studies suggest a biological basis to sexual orientation.

According to Bailey and Triea, it's possible AGP males prefer the "female gender identity" theory because they fear that clinicians will not approve them for medical transition if they know it's motivated by erotic desire. They also may fear that people, knowing the truth about their trans identity, "will consider them sexually deviant."

In their article, Bailey and Triea write that studies indicate a correlation between autogynephilia and a tendency to derive sexual pleasure from pain or humiliation. "[A]utogynephilic males are more likely than other males to become sexually aroused to stimuli depicting masochistic themes," they wrote.

Evidence of this correlation is everywhere. Take Julia Serano, who helped popularize the word "cisgender." Serano wrote in the 2007 book *Whipping Girl*, "While I never really believed the cliché about women being good for only one thing, I found that that sentiment kept creeping into my fantasies. I would imagine myself being sold into sex slavery and having strange men take advantage of me. It's called forced feminization, and it's not really about sex, it is about turning the humiliation you feel into pleasure, transforming the loss of male privilege into the best fuck ever."

Here, Serano equates being female to a state of humiliation, and gets off on the idea.

Then there is Andrea Long Chu (née Andy). Chu, who transitioned in 2018, has written about his obsession with "sissy porn," which is porn depicting the forced feminization of males. In his book *Females*, Chu wrote that the "barest essentials" of "femaleness" are "an open mouth, an expectant asshole, blank, blank eyes."

Chu also wrote:

"Getting fucked makes you female because fucked is what a female is."

"To be female is, in every case, to become what someone else wants. At bottom, everyone is a sissy.... The asshole [is] a universal vagina through which femaleness can always be accessed."

And: "I transitioned for gossip and compliments, lipstick and mascara, for crying at the movies, for being someone's girlfriend...for feeling hot, for getting hit on by butches, for that secret knowledge of which dykes to watch out for, for Daisy Dukes, bikini tops, and all the dresses, and, my god, for the breasts."

In 2013, years before he came out as trans, Chu wrote an essay for the Duke University student newspaper about his girlfriend: "every day I oppress her because she's a woman and because she's Chinese ... I fetishize her Chinese qualities and use them to massage my own colonial sense of multiculturalism. I relish the notion of having mixed-race children but I remind myself that I would never raise them with a backward Chinese notion of family. I objectify her. I exoticize her. I see her race and her gender before I see her."

Chu, a male who is three-fourths white, now identifies as an Asian-American woman, almost like he's trying to become the ex-girlfriend he once fetishized and oppressed. Some might even say Chu is "appropriating her lived experience."

In 2023, Chu was awarded the Pulitzer Prize for Criticism. In a March 2024 cover story for *New York* magazine, "Freedom of Sex: The moral case for letting trans kids change their bodies," Chu advanced the "castration for kids is a human right" argument. He wrote, "The anti-trans bloc has in general targeted children because Americans tend to imagine children both as a font of pure, unadulterated humanity and as ignorant dependents incapable of rational thought or political agency." Chu continued, "We will never be able to defend the rights of transgender kids until we understand them purely on their own terms: as full members of society who would like to change their sex. *It does not matter where this desire comes from*" (Chu's emphasis).

While many AGP males speak and write unabashedly about the paraphilic nature of their transgender identities, others want to debunk the theory of autogynephilia altogether. Some have gone to radical extremes, like the trans activist Andrea James.

After *The Man Who Would Be Queen* was published—which does not moralize about Blanchard's transexual typology nor do anything even close to endorsing discrimination of transexuals—James went after Bailey. He posted photos of Bailey's young daughter on the internet, labeling her—and I quote—"a cock-starved exhibitionist." James wrote online that there "are two types of children in the Bailey household," namely those "who have been sodomized by their father" and those "who have not."

James's decision to attack Bailey is odd, since in a 1998 email to Dr. Anne Lawrence, an openly autogynephilic physician and sex researcher, he wrote that Lawrence's work "backs up my own experiences…I readily admit to my own autogynephilia."

The historian and bioethicist Alice Dreger wrote a phenomenal book in 2015, titled *Galileo's Middle Finger*, which details the harassment campaign trans activists leveled against Bailey for writing his book. Dreger first wrote about this topic in a 2006 blog post, after she learned that James had been invited to speak at Northwestern University, where Dreger worked. In the post, titled, "The Blog I Write in Fear," Dreger wrote that, after witnessing what happened to Bailey, "[A]s a scholar who works on sex and politics, I found myself deeply intimidated by Ms. James's actions. Because of Ms. James's behavior, I became afraid of the ways in which I might be putting my own family at risk by the work

I do advocating for intersex rights." She was sure to add, "I am not saying Ms. James does not have the right to speak [at the university]. What I am saying is that I don't think we should be putting our university's good name near her."

In a follow-up post written a month later, Dreger wrote that James had "unfortunately lived down to my expectations by sending me obnoxious emails including threats." The university counsel, after reading James's emails to Dreger, suggested Dreger alert the police. Dreger didn't repeat the specific threats in her update, though she did mention that James wrote in one email, "Bad move, mommy," which suggested to Dreger that James was "still interested in dragging people's children (including now my own) into her intimidation tactics." James even showed up at Dreger's office when Dreger wasn't there. He sent Dreger an email with the subject line, "Mommy Knows Best," writing, "Sorry I missed you the other day. Your colleagues seem quite affable, and not as fearful as you...Bad move, Mommy...We'll chat in person soon."

I use male pronouns when referring to James, since he is male, but the mainstream media—and Dreger, in her book—use female pronouns. The use of incorrect pronouns, while "kind" and "trans-inclusive," obscures the very important fact that we are talking about a male who showed up unannounced at a female's place of work and sent her intimidating and threatening emails about herself and her child. Males are about three-and-a-half times more likely to commit crimes of violence than females, according to the US Department of Justice Statistics. Transwomen are males, in the end, and data shows that male propensity for violence tracks across this demographic.

Both Bailey's book in 2004 and Dreger's book in 2016 were nominated for Lambda Literary Awards. The Lambda Literary Foundation, founded in 1987, sought to bring attention to books written by gay and lesbian authors that were going unnoticed and unreviewed. Award categories include gay fiction, lesbian poetry, and lesbian memoir or biography. A transgender category was added in 1997.

The nominations for Bailey's and Dreger's books were soon withdrawn after activists deemed them "transphobic."

CIS WHITE GAY

Along with knowing the truth about the suicide myth, understanding the distinction between AGP and HSTS males is the key to protecting gender-nonconforming children, especially young boys, from the gender industry and its most zealous supporters, like Secretary Levine. The reason why is perhaps best explained in a March 2023 Twitter post by my friend Cori Cohn, an adult male who was "affirmed" as a teenager and underwent sex-reassignment surgery at nineteen.

"I really wish I could make everyone understand that adult males who transition have persistent fantasies that they'd transitioned as children, and that the strain of activism aimed at boys is to experience this fantasy vicariously," Cori wrote. "I wish I could make everyone understand that there are some doctors and surgeons, even trans-identified ones within [World Professional Association for Transgender Health] leadership, who are complicit in materializing adult fantasies by sexually modifying boys. Transitioning boys especially is about the sexual gratification of adult men who project their wishes and regrets onto subjects who cannot consent to the actual process of medicalization. This is a tough truth to reckon with."

When I texted Cori to make sure he didn't mind me quoting him in my book, he elaborated on his original post. He told me, "The key concept that I struggle to communicate—and I know this from having been the target of these men when I was young—is that their sexual desire is internally directed. They want boys to transition not out of desire for the boys, but to relieve their own unfulfillable fantasy of being that boy."

Secretary Levine's "lived experience" does not in any way translate to the "lived experience" of children who are confused about gender. Levine is not gender-nonconforming and lived most of his life identifying as a man. He got married and had children. He played football for his all-boys prep school, for God's sake. In a recent interview, he even stated that he couldn't imagine is life without his kids. And yet, the protocol for which he advocates—puberty blockers followed by cross-sex hormones and surgery—*guarantees infertility*, severely compromises sexual function, and increases the probability of serious and chronic health risks.

In a July 2023 appearance on *The Megyn Kelly Show*, Helen Joyce, author of *Trans: When Ideology Meets Reality*, said she thinks of AGP males as "the nuclear reactor at the heart of the [trans radical] movement." (The movement's "foot soldiers," she added, "are the young women who have grown up in queer theory in universities"—and, I must say, I agree with this assessment.) "Without this hard core of men whose dearest and sole desire in life is to force everybody to pretend that they're women," said Joyce, "this would not have got so far."

AGP males really need to believe, and they need others to believe, that they really *are*, inside, women, and that they have *always* been women—which means they had to have been *trans children*. Thus, said Joyce, "these men are the ones who want children put on sterilizing drugs to validate their [own] sexuality."

Men like Levine are nothing like the girly young boys that wrestle with deep internal shame about their same-sex attraction. That's not to say he has never known shame in relation to his sexuality. But it is not the same. *He* is not the same. And no, of course I cannot be certain that Levine is an autogynephile, though it is likely, since Levine fits the bill to a *T*. But what I can be absolutely certain of is Levine's complicity in allowing this medical scandal to persist for as long as it has.

For years, activists have claimed that a systematic review of evidence supporting the efficacy of "gender-affirming care" is impossible. Yet, as I stated above, countries like Sweden, Finland, and the UK have managed to do exactly that, and in the end have found that the efficacy of these treatments cannot be substantiated. Yet, in 2024, it was revealed in court findings out of Alabama that WPATH, an activist organization that develops the Standards of Care for trans medicine, had actually commissioned Johns Hopkins University to perform one of these "impossible" reviews. And when it showed, just like all of the other reviews before it, that the evidence was lacking, WPATH suppressed publication of the review. Not only that, but emails between WPATH and Admiral Levine's office revealed that Levine pressured WPATH to entirely remove its age guidelines from its most recent Standards of Care—standards by which gender clinicians across the US are advised to abide. Evidently Levine feared that recommending medical transition for adolescents would invite political backlash and lead to legal restrictions on the practice.

These deplorable actions should have immediately led to the end of Levine's career as assistant secretary for health and to the end of "gender-affirming care" for minors in the US. And yet, Democrats, activist organizations, and the liberal media continued to double down. It's difficult not to speculate that our for-profit healthcare system could be a factor in prolonging this medical scandal. A study published by the *Journal of General Internal Medicine*, whose authors analyzed commercial insurance claim data, showed a *700 percent increase* in medical diagnoses for gender dysphoria (from 8.1 to 64.4 per 100,000 enrollees) between 2013 and 2019. In the same period, the use of gender-affirming hormone therapy increased nearly *800 percent*. Clearly, there is *a lot* of money to be made in "gender-affirming care."

At the end of the day, homosexual men who identify as transgender are remarkably different from autogynephiles. Therefore, it's obvious that treatment protocols must take into account the motivation behind trans identification. Comprehensive mental health therapy, as opposed to immediate "affirmation," is not, despite what GLAAD might insist, "conversion therapy." It merely prevents the huge risk of infertility, sexual dysfunction, and serious health risks as well as a lifetime of medicalization.

Socially and medically transitioning kids who will likely grow up to be gay is the *real* conversion therapy.

Do I think autogynephilic males should be shamed for their paraphilia? No.

But nor do I think kids should be harmed for it.

CHAPTER 21

By early 2022, I had become desperate to reach a wider audience about the harms of modern LGBT activism. I got lucky that April, when *Newsweek* agreed to publish an op-ed I wrote about the antigay practice of "gender-affirming care."

"Sure, the religious far right remains something of a threat," I wrote, "and I, like any other gay person, can still be stung by antigay slurs and can fear the threat of violence in less-accepting spaces. But today I am equally fearful of the radical activists I once longed to emulate, activists who push a regressive, anti-liberal agenda that reifies gender stereotypes, downplays the seriousness of long-term medicalization and ultimately seeks to abolish my identity—for without biological sex, there is no homosexuality." I concluded, "It's time that LGBT rights organizations answer to the growing number of gays, lesbians and trans people sounding the alarm on the medicalization of homosexuality by radical queer activists."

The night before *Newsweek* was scheduled to publish my op-ed, titled "The New Homophobia," I was anxious. After this, there would be no going back. The "LGBT community" would officially brand me as a heretic.

The next day, my sisters visited New York with my nephews. It was a welcome distraction, although I couldn't resist checking my Twitter feed, especially after some accounts with large followings had tweeted a link to my *Newsweek* piece. Then, in the afternoon, J.K. Rowling tweeted a link to it, and it officially went viral.

I was thrilled—even more so later that evening, after I received a personal message on social media from Ms. Rowling herself. I won't share the details of her message, but suffice it to say, for the rest of the night, I couldn't stop smiling.

Sometime during the height of the COVID pandemic, I had opened Facebook to see that a friend, "Dan," who is around my age, had come out as a transwoman. After all these years of living as a gay man, of getting married and raising a kid, now, suddenly, Dan realized he had been "born in the wrong body."

In no time, Dan's social media became a living document of his many surgeries. Photo after photo after photo. Soon, he began posting diatribes that were identical to those of the radical trans activists I had seen online for the previous two years: "Cis" people are terrible, transwomen are oppressed, gender dysphoria is hell, being "misgendered" is violence, being "affirmed" is euphoric.

The day after *Newsweek* published my op-ed, Dan sent me a direct message on social media, claiming I was actively harming our community. "Who hurt you?" he asked me, as if, due some inexplicable trauma, I had gone crazy.

I didn't respond. Although I did think, immediately after I read it, *Who hurt* me*? I'm not the one who just got his balls chopped off!*

I wondered what specifically had led Dan down that path. He was very involved in social justice activism, and being very familiar with the inner workings of that world myself, I knew how one could become radicalized into making that decision. Transitioning had become the ultimate "fuck you" to Western hegemony and "cisheteronormativity."

But occasionally, when I came across another one of Dan's posts, my thoughts returned to Blair, the gay man in the Lamb of God who went on to identify as transexual and undergo a record number of "gender-affirming" surgeries. I also thought of what I had learned about gay men in Iran. Maybe, like them, Dan had transitioned to thwart homophobia and stifle shame. Maybe, whenever he went out in public with his husband and kid, he was sick of having what felt like a target for hatred on his back. Maybe, if he could convincingly pass as a woman, passersby would see him as part of a "normal" straight couple.

After I read online the stories of gay Iranian refugees, I reached out to two of them for more answers. I wanted to see if the media's reporting of the situation in Iran was accurate, and if they, too, thought that something similar might be occurring in the West.

One of them, a man named Nima, left Iran in 2017. He now lives in Australia, where he sought asylum. Like me, Nima presents like a typical if not slightly effeminate man, but growing up, he was very effeminate. However, the abuse he suffered went beyond mere bullying. Nima was raped.

"Iran is a very patriarchal country," he told me. "Males are considered the most powerful, and anyone who does not fall into the criteria of being very macho and masculine, they categorize that person as a woman. And then that starts the bullying and humiliation and all kind of things. If a [feminine] man gets raped, then that's his problem. He is the culprit. Even in the case of the criminalization of homosexuality in Iran, they usually punish the receiver, or the 'bottom,' as we call it."

In some ways, that didn't sound so different from gender ideology in the West. Here, ideologues proselytize that one's sex is determined not by the gametes his or her reproductive system is organized to produce, but by how masculinely or femininely he or she behaves, and also on what antiquated gender roles they prefer.

Nima confirmed what I had previously learned: Gay men, he said, have very few options in Iran. They can suppress their desires and marry women (typically under pressure from their families), or they can change gender from male to female. The most important part of that transition, he said, is "the removal of the penis."

"It needs to be done," he said.

Some of Nima's gay friends who remained in Iran have married women, some were forced to transition, and some willingly chose to transition. A few who have transitioned seemed happy. Others, he said, "suffer from depression and trauma after what they have gone through."

Arsham Parsi is the founder of the International Railroad for Queer Refugees, headquartered in Toronto. In March 2005, Arsham found himself in danger after authorities discovered he had been advocating for the local gay population. He first fled to Turkey, and later to Canada. Parsi's book, *Exiled for Love: The Journey of an Iranian Queer Activist*, was published in 2015.

Arsham said that a lot of effeminate gay men in Iran have been mistaken to think that transition was the solution. "They decided to have sexual reassignment surgery and after a while it was tough because it wasn't who they were, and we had a very high suicide rate among people who had transitioned," he said.

This, of course, had also been the case in the West, which was one of the reasons why clinicians had started medically transitioning young boys. The clinicians thought that if they more convincingly passed as women, then maybe they wouldn't be suicidal.

Arsham said that a psychiatrist in Iran had once told him to warn his friends about the issue. "As long as they come to my office and I'm sitting in this chair, I'm a government employee," the psychiatrist had said. "I have to give them medication, I have to put them on hormone therapy, I have to send them to shock therapy."

It wasn't just the gays and lesbians who were under pressure, Arsham said. The doctors and therapists were too.

When I spoke with Laura, she said something similar about US gender clinics, which are now hiring more trans-identified people to make the teenaged patients feel more comfortable. These new hires get placed in intake and clinical coordinator roles and are often the first line of communication with the parents who call. In theory, this is great, Laura said. The problem is people forget that these hires are not professionally trained in medicine or mental health.

"I think it sometimes taints the thought process and the logic of the professionals who have been trained to do medicine or diagnose mental health issues," Laura told me. "They're wanting to be good social justice warriors in their work, and this trans person that's working with them is telling them, 'This is what you need to do.' It probably becomes a moral or ethical dilemma for them. How do they incorporate their ethical responsibilities in medicine with what they're being told is the right thing to do?"

In the US, then, it's the radical activists playing the part of the Iranian regime.

As far as transition regret in Iran goes, Arsham said he has spoken with "several people" who told him that, if they had been born outside of Iran or if they had fled Iran prior to their transition, they never would have done it. Viewing it as the only viable option, they had convinced themselves and everyone around them that it was the right thing to do. Family members often objected, which sometimes made the gay men double down on their decision.

"[They would tell their families], 'This is who I am, you have to accept me, I'm going to do it even without your consent, I'm going to leave home,'" Arsham said. "Now, it's hard for them to go back to their families and say they were wrong, that they made a bad decision."

Arsham said he knows three Iranian men who transitioned in Canada only because they had fallen in love with men who were living in Iran and planned to go back to have relationships with them. However, a year or two after the surgery, the relationships didn't go anywhere "because they always had a sign on their forehead that they used to be a guy," he said. "Now they can't do anything about it."

Arsham knows other Iranian refugees who were "100 percent sure" that they were transgender, but after they escaped to Canada, they realized transition was unnecessary. "They said, 'I don't need to do that. I can be gay. I can be feminine. I can dress like a woman or anything, I don't need that to go through surgery. I can be who I am.'"

Like me, Arsham believes the solution to homophobia is to accept yourself for you who are and to find other people who will do the same.

"Don't put a mask on your face and lie to yourself," he said. Otherwise, one becomes a "victim of ignorance, lack of information, and government pressure."

Arsham continued, "Today, we have two societies to fight: mainstream society and our own community."

After speaking with Nima and Arsham, I began interviewing gay men in New York, LA, Colorado, England, the Netherlands, and the Czech Republic, who have detransitioned. These men are part of a growing cohort of gay detransitioners who had sought refuge from homophobia in trans identity, were blindly affirmed by professionals, and were fed the twin lies that transition would be a cure-all for their woes and that there was nothing all that complicated about medical transition, since the body—operating so separately from the brain—can be manipulated with ease. Their stories, which go entirely ignored by LGBT organizations, sound remarkably similar to the stories I learned of gay men in Iran.

Paul Garcia-Ryan, a New York psychotherapist and the executive director of Therapy First, a mental health organization that advocates for comprehensive mental healthcare for gender-distressed young people, was affirmed as transgender at fifteen.

"I would describe my first couple of years of transition as the happiest that I had felt in my whole life," he told me.

No longer an effeminate boy, he was now just a normal girl.

"I wasn't happy because I was being myself," he said. "I was happy because I got space from a hostile environment. I was no longer embodying what that hostile environment was targeting."

"Tim," affirmed at sixteen, in the Netherlands said, "For my entire life, I had such a problem admitting that I was gay, but then I found out about trans and immediately I went for that."

He continued, "With estrogen, my libido just kind of died. And it felt so great because I always viewed my sexuality as something bad and something gross and then it was gone and I felt such a relief."

Brian W., from LA, came out as trans while studying queer theory in college. "When I came out [to my] sociology department, I don't think I'd ever been so celebrated," he said. But the love-bombing was short-lived. "They ended up hating me because they found out I was somewhat conservative," he said.

Brian was "ruthlessly" bullied for being gay as a child, both at school and by his father at home. After turning to drugs and alcohol to cope, he found himself in therapy.

"I told [my therapist] I sometimes feel a little bit more feminine," Brian said, "[and that] I wasn't the most masculine little boy. And I told her I'm absolutely a drug addict. And she said, 'All your problems are because you are a straight woman.' That kind of appealed to me because my dad always hated gay people. Not that he loved trans people of course, but for some reason it appealed to me, that like, I'm not really a gay man."

Ritchie Herron, in England, had a similar childhood experience to Brian. He, too, was bullied. And he said, "I was scared of the fact that I was attracted to other boys." At the gender clinic, nobody questioned his experience, even when he told them about his homophobic upbringing and his mental health issues, which included panic attacks and OCD. They put him on goserelin, a hormone blocker typically used to treat women with breast cancer and to chemically castrate sex offenders.

Daniel Black, who now lives and works as a hairstylist in Prague, was raised as a Jehovah's Witness. When he was fifteen or sixteen, he realized he was gay. Six months later, he began identifying as transgender. By transitioning, he thought, "I will be as feminine as I want and it won't be weird, because I will be a woman who dates men. I felt like I will be normal."

When Daniel was seventeen, he was prescribed estrogen and a testosterone blocker, the same drugs "used for rapists," Daniel said sardonically. On hormones, Daniel's sex drive depleted. After his bottom surgery at eighteen, his libido was "complete zero," he said. "Just nothing."

Brian Belovitch prefers to call his detransition a "retransition." Belovitch, who lives in New York, is sixty-seven. He is the author of the 2018

memoir *Trans Figured: My Journey from Boy to Girl to Woman to Man.* When Belovitch was sixteen, he came out as gay. After his mother threw him out, he started to hang out at a downtown apartment building that was full of transwomen and drag queens. Eventually, Belovitch started dressing in drag. Because he was young and somewhat pretty, he was a convincing woman, which earned him attention and praise.

"If you grow up the way I did," he said, "in an environment where I was never regarded as anything but troublesome or difficult or wrong or faggy or queer, and all of a sudden you're getting acceptance in your community, you're celebrated for your femininity, for your beauty, whatever—it became like a drug for me."

Soon, Belovitch became addicted to heroin, crack cocaine, and alcohol. "There was always some artificial coping mechanism. Even my choice of going down the path of being trans was just a desperate attempt to not make myself gay."

In 1986, Belovitch got sober in Alcoholics Anonymous. He worked the twelve steps and went to therapy. One day, Belovitch's therapist asked him, "What do you think about gender? What are your perceptions of what is male and what is female?" Belovitch said that nobody had ever asked him those questions before. "When I started to explore what those things meant to me, I came to the conclusion that I was a little bit of both, and that it was fine to be the way I was. I didn't have to be trapped with this other [identity]. It wasn't even my idea. It was always other people's ideas about what I was supposed to be as a gay person."

Belovitch's testimony illustrates a major problem with ongoing legislation that seeks to add "gender identity" to existing bans on gay-conversion therapy. Trans activists who push for this legislation insist that gender-exploratory therapy is akin to conversion therapy. Gays and lesbians fear this will make it illegal for therapists to question whether a patient's trans identity is actually the result of internalized homophobia. The "gender-affirming care" model requires immediate affirmation.

After a year of sobriety, Belovitch "retransitioned." He discontinued hormones and cut his hair. One Sunday afternoon, during an AA meeting at Manhattan's Lesbian and Gay Community Center (now the

LGBT Community Center), he raised his hand and said, "I've decided that I would like you to call me Brian." The room exploded in applause. "They were banging on the floor with their chairs and screaming, like something out of a movie," he said.

What a difference a few decades can make, I thought when Belovitch told me this. I had recently attended an LGBT comedy festival in New York. When a butch lesbian comedian told the audience that she had recently started testosterone, the audience burst into applause. Progress, we see, is not always a straight line.

Belovitch's trans-identified friends reacted very differently than the gay people at the AA meeting: They shunned him. "[Once] you're trans, you can't not be trans," he told me. "It was very painful."

Belovitch said he marks the year 2000 as "the genesis of wokeness in the trans community." That year, he hung flyers in the LGBT Center to advertise a play he wrote called "Boys Don't Wear Lipstick." The title comes from a line in the play, when a mother catches her son dressed in drag for the first time. Obviously, Belovitch said, the title was meant to be ironic. "*Of course* boys can wear lipstick," he said. But trans visitors to the LGBT Center didn't like it. They said it promoted "anti-trans language" and tore his posters off the wall.

In May 2022, a video of a formerly trans-identified YouTuber who goes by the name Shape Shifter began circulating on Twitter. In the video, Shape talks about the backlash he has received since he stated publicly that he was detransitioning. "People think I'm an embarrassment to the trans community," he says in the video. "I don't know what I should be embarrassed of! I'm *embarrassed* that I tried to be a woman when I should've just been a gay feminine man and give a big 'fuck you' to society who doesn't accept my femininity! That was the problem. Society was the problem. It was social dysphoria, not gender dysphoria."

When I spoke with Shape, he said it was important that people know he grew up in a Muslim-majority country (he requested I omit the specifics in order to protect his family, who still live there). "Islam is very homophobic," he said. "I felt like I'd rather be a trans woman than a gay man because that was, like, the lowest and most disgusting thing you could be. That's how I was conditioned growing up."

As oppressive of gender-nonconforming men as his home country was, Shape ironically didn't consider transition until he began attending graduate school in the US.

"When I moved to the US, I was a proud gay man," he said, describing how it felt to be living in a country where he was free to be who he was. "I enjoyed being androgynous. But then I went to class and people were like, 'What are your pronouns?' because I was more feminine. And that's when I started doing more research and I found out [about] trans ideology."

He continued, "The minute I came across the ideology, I was like, 'Yay, thank God, I don't have to be a homosexual. I can get rid of this label.' I just wanted to blend in and not be targeted by society anymore. It's not that I really wanted to be a woman; it was a chance for me to be normal."

In October 2022, Reuters reported on a California study that found "a quarter of 869 vaginoplasty patients, with a mean age of 39, had a surgical complication so severe that they had to be hospitalized again. Among those patients, 44% needed additional surgery to address the complication, which included bleeding and bowel injuries."

Marci Bowers is a trans-identifying male surgeon and former president of WPATH who famously performed one of reality star Jazz Jennings's bottom surgeries (due to complications, Jennings has had to undergo multiple corrective surgeries). During a 2022 Duke University symposium, Bowers stated that every male whose puberty is blocked at Tanner Stage 2—the stage when the body begins to sexually mature—has never and possibly will never experience a proper orgasm. (This, of course, is on top of the fact that medical transition sterilizes them.)

Bowers revealed the experimental nature of gender-affirming care by wondering aloud to the audience what the solution to this could be. Options range from removing the blockers and letting "a little bit of puberty come back" to encouraging the child to masturbate so that they know what an orgasm feels like.

As Bowers made this latter suggestion, he acknowledged that some males might experience dysphoria around their penis, but went on to say, "All a penis is is just a large clitoris—it's all the same material—so, you know, use it for the pleasurable purposes that partially it was intended!"

To this, any thinking person might respond, "If a child getting over his dysphoria about his body is such a reasonable possibility, then why are we cutting off his penis?"

Unfortunately, none of the other panelists made a peep.

Bowers said that his work with female genital mutilation survivors, whose physical trauma has affected their ability to be intimate with their partners, is what "raised the red flag" for him about this particular issue in gender care.

To this I would say, "When the 'care' you provide to adolescents can be compared to female genital mutilation—that is, the excision of women's clitorises, performed in the name of Islam, to deny them sexual pleasure—you might want to rethink what you're doing." And leaving aside for a moment the total impropriety of an adult encouraging a prepubertal child to masturbate, I find it tragic that clinicians are taking away his possibility of having his own organic sexual awakening. Rather, he is a lab rat. His sexual life begins in a sterile clinic.

Paul, Ritchie, Shape, and Daniel each had a vaginoplasty—castration followed by the construction of a neovagina. The former three have continued to suffer severe post-surgical complications.

Daniel was in the hospital for twelve days after his surgery, a length of time that is pretty typical in his country. The results were "horrible," Daniel said. His doctor tried to sell him on it, saying that what he had constructed was identical to female genitalia, but Daniel could see with his own eyes what the area between his legs now looked like.

At follow-up appointments, Daniel tried to tell his doctor that he was dissatisfied. "Every time I went there to get it checked—one month after surgery, then three months, six months, a year, and two years—he only photographed it," said Daniel. When Daniel finally requested another surgery, the doctor said no. For five years, until he detransitioned and started taking testosterone again, Daniel could not achieve an orgasm.

When castrated men resume testosterone, their libido reawakens. This can be a good thing. However, for some, it is unpleasant, creating the sensation of a "phantom limb"—in this case, a phantom penis.

Tim had facial feminization surgery, which the doctor performed in a manner that went directly against Tim's wishes. When Tim confronted his doctor postsurgery, she told him she had vetoed his instructions because he wouldn't have looked as feminine. In the summer of 2022, Tim had reconstructive surgery on his nose. He said that it's not perfect, but it looks normal again, and his breathing, impaired by the first surgery, has improved.

Brian W. didn't undergo any surgeries. But, seven months into his detransition, he was still experiencing abnormally high levels of estrogen. When I asked him why, he said his former endocrinologist had told him that the higher the hormone dose, the more feminization that would result. Instead of the normal two, the doctor inserted seven estradiol and two progesterone pellets into his buttocks.

His current endocrinologist was shocked to learn this. "Insane" was the word he used to describe the practice.

"I REALIZE THERE was nothing wrong with me," Shape told me, describing how he feels today. "I don't need to become a woman; I still could be a feminine gay man. We're a part of natural variation among our own sex."

He added, "It's a hard realization to have, that all this was just internalized homophobia and being battered by society for my femininity."

Today, Shape is suing Boston's Fenway Health, the health organization that oversaw his transition. He is represented by Mitra Forouhar, an Iranian-American civil rights lawyer. The suit claims that Fenway Health "knowingly and willfully removed safety procedures, known as 'gatekeeping,' from its transgender healthcare practice," a decision unsupported by scientific evidence and one that was motivated by a desire to appease activists and acquire more patients. If this gatekeeping had remained in place, it says, Shape's "internalized homophobia" would have been rightly viewed as "a counter-indicator to transition," since, according to studies, internalized homophobia has been identified "as the leading cause of transition regret." As a result, "Shape was rapidly medicalized, and his sexual orientation and symptoms of internalized homophobia were treated with deliberate indifference." The suit claims that "Fenway's apathetic attitude toward Shape's sexual orientation and its associated distress violated his civil rights, and caused him irreversible, irreparable physical and mental injury. As a result of transitioning, Shape cannot express himself as a gay man and must live with dissonance between who he is and how he appears."

For some children and teenagers, gender dysphoria may be severe. Signs may even indicate that the dysphoria will persist, and that the minor will likely seek medical transition as an adult. But there is no clinical test to determine if a child's gender dysphoria will persist, and there is no way to determine what decisions that child will make about his body in the future when he is old enough to consent. The *only* ethical model of care, then, is to teach gender-nonconforming children—and people of every age, for that matter—that there is nothing wrong with breaking the rigid gender mold. That boys like Shape can be effeminate, and neither his unique interests nor his atypical desires mean he has to chemically and surgically modify his body to exist peacefully in society. And gender-nonconforming children, just like all children, should be protected from nefarious adults.

Today, we have a choice. We can either continue to follow the dictates of radical activists and their queer-theory-informed, antigay ideology, which not only mirrors Iran's but also constitutes a form of child abuse. Or we can recommit ourselves to furthering one of the promises of modern Western liberalism, which is for every child to grow up with his body healthy and whole, and for gay and lesbian individuals to live freely and openly, just as they are.

CHAPTER 22

On October 7, 2023, Drew and I were visiting my oldest sister and her family in Maryland. That morning, I struggled to take in the horrific images posted all over social media of the unfolding terrorist attack in Israel. As Erin made breakfast and my husband and I played with our rambunctious young nephews, it was eerie knowing that many miles away, on the same planet and under the same sky, unimaginable horrors were being visited upon families just like ours.

Later that morning, as videos of the ongoing slaughter circulated online, Columbia student activists got to work. "Oppression Breeds Resistance," they titled their open letter in response to Hamas's barbaric attack on innocent Israeli civilians.

"We cannot view the recent actions of Palestinian fighters in isolation," the students from Columbia's "Palestine Solidarity Groups" wrote. "The weight of responsibility for the war and casualties undeniably lies with the Israeli extremist government and other Western governments, including the US government, which fund and staunchly support Israeli aggression, apartheid and settler-colonization."

According to these enlightened student activists, the rape, murder, and immolation of Israeli civilians, the kidnapping of children and the elderly—including American citizens—was not terrorism. It was not barbarism. It was justified resistance. And the blame was on Israel alone.

Unsurprisingly to me, the open letter included a quote from Fanon's *The Wretched of the Earth*: "When we revolt it's not for a particular culture. We revolt simply because, for many reasons, we can no longer breathe."

On the same day, Najma Sharif, a Somali-American writer whose work has appeared in university and high school curricula tweeted, "what did y'all think decolonization meant? vibes? papers? essays? losers." A day later, she wrote, "everyone has read Fanon but no one has even read the first sentence in Wretched of the Earth. sad!"

The sentence in question, which is required reading for all Columbia students, reads, "National liberation, national renaissance, the restoration of nationhood to the people, commonwealth: whatever may be the headings used or the new formulas introduced, *decolonization is always a violent phenomenon*." (The emphasis is mine.)

On October 8, in *The Electronic Intifada*, Columbia professor Joseph Massad described images of the attacks as "stunning," "awesome," and "astonishing."

Russell Rickford, a history professor at Cornell, told students he found the attacks "exhilarating" and "energizing."

Ameil J. Joseph (he/him, according to his social media handle), an associate professor at McMaster University's School of Social Work, tweeted on the day of the Hamas attacks, "Postcolonial, anticolonial, and decolonial are not just words you heard in your EDI [Equity, Diversity, and Inclusion] workshop."

Meaning, it appears, that slaughtering, raping, and abducting civilians is also what these words mean.

Mohamed Abdou is the author of *Islam and Anarchism*, which Jasbir Puar, the Rutgers professor who once compared suicide bombing to "queerness," described as "a call to action" and "one of the fiercest books I've ever read." Abdou's personal website describes him as "a self-identifying Muslim anarchist and diasporic settler of color" and "an interdisciplinary scholar of Indigenous, Black, critical race, and Islamic studies, as well as antiracist feminist, gender, sexuality, women, decolonial and post-colonial studies."

Four days after the attack, he wrote on Facebook, "Yes, I'm with the *muqawamah* (the resistance) be it Hamas and Hezbollah and Islamic Jihad."

In January 2024, Columbia's Middle East Institute and its Department of Middle Eastern, South Asian, and African Studies hired Abdou as the Arcapita Visiting Professor of Modern Arab Studies. Abdou's Spring 2024 course was titled Decolonial-Queerness & Abolition. A month into his first semester at Columbia, he helped organize a protest that interrupted a Columbia panel featuring Hillary Clinton, where Clinton was called a "war criminal" who "will burn." On X, Abdou posted a video of the protest, writing that he was "proud of these students & deeply honoured to have been a part of organizing this."

He added, "May Allah safeguard & protect them."

In early April 2024, Columbia student protesters, led by Columbia University Apartheid Divest (which expanded after the October 7 attacks and now includes about one hundred student groups) and the anti-Zionist organization Within Our Lifetime occupied the south lawn in front of Butler Library, erecting an encampment they called "The People's University for Palestine." Soon, similar encampments popped up at universities across the US. Besides students and faculty, the protests reportedly involved outside agitators linked to shadowy leftist organizations funded by Qatar, Iran, and the US billionaire families Soros, Rockefeller, and Pritzker.

A few days into the Columbia demonstration, I visited campus to see it for myself. Just outside the university's gates, I spotted Professor Abdou, smoking a cigarette. Seeing an opportunity, I asked him if he wouldn't mind answering a question. He nodded.

"Could you tell me the difference between a Zionist and a Jew? Because I hear people chanting 'death to Zionists,' and I'm wondering how that's different from chanting 'death to Jews.'"

He puffed silently on his cigarette, staring past me, as if I had simply disappeared.

Once inside the campus (my alumni ID allows me access), I walked the perimeter of the encampment, reading the hand-painted signs hanging from clotheslines that stretched around the lawn. It was a warm, sunny spring day.

Free All Palestinian Prisoners. Ceasefire Now.

While You Read Gaza Bleeds.

There was one sign I was sure no one could refute: Admitted Students Enroll in Revolution.

Palestine flags and keffiyehs were everywhere. And trans flags, of course. By that time, the queer left-Islamic alliance was firmly established in the US. The group Queers for Palestine marched through New York City's streets, shouting for a global intifada.

Japan for Palestine, another sign read.

Hindus for Intifada.

Israel is a Terrorist State.

I couldn't help noticing how many of the "occupiers" were women. Nearly all of them were masked. In the encampment's northwest corner, ten or so women were spread out on the grass, painting signs and posters.

I continued around the encampment, filming what I saw on my iPhone. When one of the occupiers asked me to stop recording, I politely declined her request.

Just outside the entrance to Butler Library, I stopped to chat with four students who lingered near the encampment's manned entrance. They were clearly with the "resistance": white, blond, and accessorized with the appropriate regalia—bracelets and beanies and scarves.

The students insisted everything be off the record. One student in particular seemed paranoid. I imagined that her parents were probably investing a lot of money in her education. If she jeopardized her future job prospects by publicly aligning with Islamic jihadists, there would be hell to pay.

Later, from atop the Sundial in the center of the quad, a man spoke into a loudspeaker. The gathered crowd was large. He announced that

Columbia students had voted to divest from Israel. The crowd cheered. But, the man added, Students for Justice in Palestine had been silenced, and the university had ignored the referendum. "Shame!" replied the crowd.

"And now students at the encampment are suspended!" he added.

"SHAME!" they screamed.

Listening to the man speak, I recalled what I had learned about the 1968 protests. The university's punishment of six student protesters with probation outraged the student body, which helped activate the larger revolt that followed. Soon, students occupied campus buildings, including Hamilton Hall.

But this time, I knew, was different. Protesters weren't just motivated by their convictions. They were driven by a zealous desire to police the moral purity of their peers and publicly shame anyone who transgressed.

Disagreement is shouted at political opponents. "Shame!" is shouted at sinners.

Was this a university campus—or a Christian covenant community?

Days later, students would again occupy Hamilton Hall, busting the building's windows and doors and threatening and intimidating campus workers. From the upper levels, they would unfurl large banners: INTIFADA, FREE PALESTINE, and GLORY TO THE MARTYRS. The NYPD would later raid the campus, making over one hundred arrests, including a forty-something professional activist who appeared to be leading the charge.

Walking back toward the encampment's entrance, I stopped to talk to a woman who stood alone. She appeared to be in her late forties and had an accent I couldn't place. She didn't say her name, only that she was a human rights graduate professor. I told her I was an alum and that I had graduated from Columbia four years earlier.

"Does it look peaceful to you?" she asked me.

We both looked out over the encampment.

"Yes, for the most part," I said.

"What part doesn't look peaceful?"

I looked again. "Actually, it all looks pretty peaceful right now."

"See how peacefully students can protest when the police aren't involved?" she said.

Later, I learned that Israeli professor Shai Davidai, who hoped to lead a peaceful counterprotest, was denied entry to campus by Columbia's COO, Cas Holloway. Davidai reported on X that his Columbia ID had been deactivated. Then, a Columbia rabbi emailed Jewish students, telling them to stay home from campus because he feared it was now unsafe for Jews.

"Yes," I might have told the human rights professor, had I known about Davidai's banning and the rabbi's email. "Pro-Hamas students *can* protest peacefully—when Jews are kept off campus."

For Jews, Columbia was a "safe space" no longer. The university's inversion of morals had effectively transformed the victims into the aggressors.

Near the encampment, pro-Israel students had hung photos of the hostages that still remained in Gaza. I stopped to speak to one of them. She was an Israeli GS student, studying international relations. A couple weeks earlier, in class, she had become gripped by the fear that "today might be the day that someone decides to become violent." Since then, she'd mostly been attending her classes online. "I know what 'intifada' means," she said.

She mentioned the 364 civilians slaughtered by terrorists at the Nova Music Festival near Israel's kibbutz Re'im, where Hamas terrorists had descended upon the area in paragliders. Within days of the attacks, Black Lives Matter Chicago tweeted an image of a paraglider flying with a Palestinian flag. I STAND WITH PALESTINE was written below the image. BLM Chicago captioned the tweet, "That is all that is it!"

"So many Israeli students know someone who was there," the student said. Since October 7, she's "had a lot of meltdowns."

Back at the encampment's entrance, I spotted Jack (Judith) Halberstam, the Columbia professor who recommended that queer people embrace failure—like unemployment, stupidity, and self-harm—in her book *The Queer Art of Failure*.

I was not even a little surprised to see Halberstam there. It was all the same neo-Marxist struggle, after all.

Anti-West, anti-America, anti-Israel, anticapitalism, antinormativity. Anti- anti- anti-.

As I readied myself to leave, I watched the occupiers perform their afternoon prayers. Facing Mecca, they knelt on a blue tarp, touching their foreheads to the ground. In the center was a tall white student with a man-bun. Chants of "Allahu Akbar" sounded through a loudspeaker.

All around them stood their comrades. Students, professional activists, terrorists—who could tell? Their faces were entirely obscured by masks.

SINCE THEN, PROTESTS have continued to rage on and around Columbia's campus. In May 2025, about one hundred protesters stormed Butler Library and occupied the Lawrence A. Wien Reference Room. Wearing ski masks and keffiyehs, the potential terrorists shouted for an intifada, banged drums, and vandalized bookshelves.

COLUMBIA WILL BURN 4 THE MARTYRS, one of them wrote.

Two Columbia safety officers were injured in the melee. One had to be carried out on a gurney.

About eighty protesters were arrested. Sixty were Columbia students or faculty; the rest were from God knows where. Several had already been arrested for raiding other buildings on campus. The vast majority of them were women.

If I happen to catch a protest in action—if I get to see, up close, the young faces twisted in rage, their frail arms alternatively waving the black, red, and green flag of Palestine and the baby blue, pink, and white flag of the gender cult—I feel like I'm witnessing a religious revival. As if, at any moment, they'll all fall to their knees, lift their hands to the sky, and begin speaking in tongues.

Other times, I see it as nothing more than performance art, a staged reenactment of the protests of the '60s and '70s. A desperate need to be a part of something, to feel alive, to feel good and moral and righteous.

Sometimes, I just see spoiled teenagers rebelling against their parents.

Most often, though, I see the culmination of the "long march through the institutions" that began nearly six decades ago. On its surface it is the same movement, the same ideology, the same protests, reapplied to fit modern contexts.

At its core, though, is something that goes beyond mere rebellion. Heard in the protesters' cheers for the Hamas death cult is a boiling bloodlust against Jews and a furious desire to see America fall.

In an op-ed for *Columbia Daily Spectator*, published on November 14, 2023, CUAD described itself as "a continuation of the Vietnam anti-war movement," only more comprehensive and largely focused on anticolonialism. The column opened with a quote from Ghassan Kanafani, formerly a leading member of the Popular Front for the Liberation of Palestine: "The Palestinian cause is not a cause for Palestinians only, but a cause for every revolutionary, wherever [they are], as a cause of the exploited and oppressed masses in our era."

In 1972, the PFLP hired three members of the Japanese Red Army—a militant communist group designated a terrorist organization by both Japan and the US—to attack Israeli civilians. On May 30, the terrorists went on a shooting spree at Lod Airport (now Ben Gurion International Airport) near Tel Aviv, killing twenty-six people and injuring eighty more. Kanafani, who had been photographed with the three Japanese terrorists before their attack, was subsequently assassinated by Israel's intelligence agency, Mossad.

This revolutionary movement has been and will always be a violent phenomenon.

Today, I often have trouble understanding how highly educated people can willingly participate in a movement that so closely resembles China's Cultural Revolution. Is the influence of "mob mentality" really so strong that they can't see the parallels? Do they not know the history?

Maybe deep down they do notice something similar, but their religious zeal for critical social justice outweighs their ability to think and behave rationally. The hit of virtue and righteousness they get every time they renounce their privilege, their country, and their way of life is just too intoxicating to pass up.

Maybe this is even what we should expect from these students. Younger generations have always rebelled against their elders. About six years ago, the memetic phrase "Okay, boomer" took off on social media. In most cases it was delivered as a sarcastic response by a young progressive to an older person who disagreed with his or her radical views.

As a young person, I, too, had rebelled. But I had always been taught to respect my elders. And for good reason. My elders had the experience and the time on this earth to have a broader perspective. They were better at mapping cultural changes over time and comparing new developments with past phenomena. They understood more clearly the impact of these new developments—whether they are good or bad, progressive or regressive. They had the life experience to understand the phases of a human life—why these changes come about, how they begin, and how they end. They knew what life was like as a young person and as a mature person. They knew what it was like to age, and for one's ideas and perspectives to change over time and why. They knew what it was like to think and believe something so strongly and then years later come to see that they were wrong. They knew what it was like to have religion or to find it and then lose it.

Our elders are the ones with the "lived experience."

This has become a lost value in the West. And it's one of the reasons why a movement overwhelmingly led by young people who claim to be progressive is so backward. Old people and their values are of the past. And the past is irredeemably bad.

Today, the new Red Guard floods campuses and city streets, topples statues of "problematic" historical figures, sets fire to homes and businesses, assaults bystanders and peacekeepers, rips down posters of children kidnapped by Islamic terrorists, proclaims sympathy with jihadists, and carries placards that call for things like the abolition of police forces and the elimination of the world's only Jewish state.

In December 2023, at Columbia's School of Social Work, a student group called Columbia Social Workers 4 Palestine hosted a teach-in titled Significance of the October 7th Palestinian Counteroffensive. There, a female student declared, "On October 7th, the Palestinian liberation fighters...showed us through creativity, determination, and combined strength, the masses can accomplish great feats—a fact that we have seen in every struggle for liberation from Vietnam to Afghanistan."

The student concluded, "As Mao said, 'Dare to struggle, dare to win.'"

Welcome to America's Cultural Revolution.

CHAPTER 23

In March 2024, Donald Trump once again defied the odds by securing enough delegates to clinch the Republican nomination for president. In July, at an outdoor campaign stop in Butler, Pennsylvania, he turned his head just in time to avoid being assassinated on live television. A bullet, fired from a nearby rooftop by a twenty-year-old named Matthew Crooks, grazed Trump's right ear. Additional shots killed an audience member and critically injured two others. After ducking behind his lectern, Trump was ushered offstage, but not before pumping his fist in the air and crying "Fight!" Crooks was shot and killed by Secret Service's Counter Sniper Team. That September, a second man attempted to assassinate Trump in Florida.

As the election approached, media pundits and politicians said, just as they do every four years, that this was the most important election in US history. That if I didn't vote blue, I could kiss liberal democracy goodbye.

I had to admit they had a point. Trump's denial of the 2020 election results had caused a national crisis and eroded the American people's faith in our electoral process. That, to me, was inexcusable. And I feared that, if he lost, it would happen again.

But when Election Day finally rolled around, I did something I never thought I would do: I withheld my vote for president. Because the party I belonged to, the party I believed in, was no longer the party I once knew.

The progressive position, embraced by Democrats, used to be that there was no "right way" to be a boy or a girl. That boys can like dolls and girls can play football.

Not so today. Today, so-called progressives tell young boys that if they like pink; mermaids; and long, flowing dresses, they might be girls "on the inside," and they tell young girls that if they prefer short hair and hate makeup, they might really be boys.

Today, despite the overwhelming evidence of the harm it causes, the Democratic Party continues to advocate for medical treatments that block the natural development of gender-nonconforming young people. Medical treatments that leave them sterile and often sexually nonfunctional. Medical treatments that began as nothing more than an attempt to turn homosexual young people into straight adults.

This is not progressive. This is regressive, illiberal, and antigay.

And, just like Trump's election denial, it is inexcusable.

During her speech at a campaign event in Michigan shortly before the election, former First Lady Michelle Obama spoke directly to American men who were thinking about sitting this election out. "Are you, as men, prepared to look into the eyes of the women and children you love and tell them that you supported this assault on our safety?" she said, after detailing the consequences of Republican-led antiabortion laws.

Okay, I thought, *let's talk about women's and children's safety.*

Let's talk about the incarcerated males, who, because of Democratic policies, have been sent to women's prisons. In January 2024, NBC New York reported that a former female inmate at Riker's Island was now suing the state, alleging that the jail staff ignored her complaints about a trans-identified male who had groped her in the shower. The man, she says, ended up sexually assaulting her while she slept.

Don't believe her? Well, in April 2022, another man was sentenced to seven years in prison for rape. He, too, identified as a transwoman, and he, too, was placed in the women's jail on Riker's Island. He raped a female inmate in the shower.

Now let's talk about the males in women's sports who injure female athletes and take away their scholarships and opportunities. According to a 2024 United Nations report titled "Violence against women and girls in sport," injuries have included "knocked-out teeth, concussions resulting in neural impairment, broken legs and skull fractures." The report also states that "over 600 females in more than 400 competitions have lost more than 890 medals in 29 different sports."

Six hundred females.

And Democrats not only oppose legislation that protects women's sports; they're the ones who wrote the policies that allow males to compete against women to begin with.

Let's talk about the fact that, in many US states, if a woman sees a naked man in the women's locker room, where she and her young daughter might undress and shower after an aerobics class or a dip in the pool, she has no right to demand that that naked man leave. Because of Democratic policies, all that naked man has to say is, "I am a woman." And he has the legal right to stride right into that communal shower with that mother and her young daughter.

This is not progressive. It is regressive, illiberal, and antiwoman.

And it is inexcusable.

I've learned a lot since I started speaking out about these issues. One is how little the American people know about the medical harm being done to young people under the guise of "gender-affirming care," mainly due to a dereliction of duty by mainstream journalists. Another is how many American liberals agree with my opinions on these issues. Liberals who, like me, have only ever voted Democrat.

They, too, didn't want to see another Trump term. But, like me, they could not in good conscience cast a vote for a political party that stands behind policies that are causing irrevocable harm to gay people and women. They, too, see the Democratic Party as a mere shadow of its former self.

The day before the election, on the phone with a friend—another gay American who withheld his vote—I said that if Kamala Harris voiced her opposition to the antigay and antiwoman policies that proliferated during the Biden Administration, I would probably cast my vote for her. My friend answered, "Me too."

Yet Harris did no such thing. And all signs suggested that a Harris administration would be more of the same.

My friend and I knew we were far from alone. And we knew it was because of these very issues that the Democratic Party had bled support. It was because of these issues that so many liberal Americans now find themselves politically homeless.

And it is because of these issues that, against all odds, Donald Trump once again won the presidency.

CHAPTER 24

The Tuesday prior to Trump's second inauguration, I sat on stage in a middle school auditorium in downtown Manhattan, getting ready to speak on a school board panel about gender ideology in public schools. I was invited by Maud Maron, a Community Education Councilmember for District 2, the largest school district in Manhattan. Maron had become the target of trans activists the previous March, after she sponsored a successful resolution to review New York's 2019 Gender Guidelines, which had replaced the category of sex with "gender identity" in all areas, including school restrooms, locker rooms, and athletics. I would be joined by my friends, the journalist Lisa Selin Davis and the aforementioned Cori Cohn. Needless to say, I hadn't exactly enjoyed middle school, so to find myself in that setting, getting ready to discuss a fraught issue that was so personal to me, was nerve-racking. I couldn't wait for it to be over.

By that time, gender ideology in schools had been a hot-button issue for years. In 2022, Florida Governor Ron DeSantis had signed into law the Parental Rights in Education Act. The act prohibited classroom discussion about sexual orientation and gender identity in public schools from kindergarten through third grade and prohibited school personnel from withholding information about a student's sexual orientation or gender identity from his or her parents. In 2023, the Florida Board of

Education expanded the ban on class instruction through middle and high school, with the exception of health and reproductive courses.

LGBT organizations referred to the Florida legislation as the "Don't Say Gay" bill, which I found ironic, considering that the bill, while imperfect, actually had the potential to *protect* gay youth from irrevocable harm. In schools across the country, young people were being taught that one's gender expression was the ultimate determinant of one's sex, rather than his physical body.

"How we feel on the inside—our identity—always take priority over what is on the outside," said a New York City lesson plan for middle schoolers. As for someone who "feels neither completely like a man or completely like a woman"? Well, that person is "nonbinary." And as we all knew, even "nonbinary" people sometimes need puberty blockers, cross-sex hormones, and surgeries to excavate their true selves.

It was clear to me that activist groups had coined Florida's legislation the "Don't Say Gay" bill, rather than the "Don't Say Trans" or "Queer" bill, in order to make opposition to it more palatable for the average American. Gender cultists knew that public support of gay people was high. So why not ride the coattails of the gay movement by disguising their pseudoscientific doctrine as no more harmful to kids than the knowledge that most people will grow up to be straight while a minority will grow up to be gay or bisexual? Their strategy was galling. The gender dogma from which the Florida legislation would protect kids was significantly more dangerous. And if, in the long run, gay youth were to suffer because of the legislation—if they were further alienated or if they were outed by teachers to disapproving parents—it was mostly if not entirely the fault of the radical activists that made people think this legislation was necessary to begin with.

In the days leading up to the school board meeting, Maud texted Lisa, Cori, and I with details. She said that the audience might be hostile, adding that some parents had emailed the superintendent, demanding that the meeting be shut down for promoting "hate speech." This made me nervous, but Maud was unphased. For ten months at council meetings, trans activists and their allies had been shouting down council members, screaming obscenities, and, when anyone dared to speak favorably about the resolution, standing up, turning their backs to the council, and humming loudly in unison. (I implore readers to look up coverage of these past events online. Kara Dansky, author of *The Reckoning: How the Democrats and the Left Betrayed Women and Girls*, captured one very memorable video.) And all of this because a school committee council had voted to merely conduct a *review* of the existing guidelines.

Along with news of the emails from outraged parents, Maud also alerted us to a list of instructions trans activists had recently posted online for fellow protesters. The list, titled "This Week's Jazzy Tactics," advised comrades to enter the room "with pizzazz," "wear white and/or keffiyeh," and, "during transphobic testimony," "take care of ourselves and one another" with things like "headphones, fidgets, coloring books, bubbles, snacks, treats."

Oh, and "Macarena."

IN THE END, only about twenty people showed up for the board meeting, which was live-streamed on YouTube. I assumed this was because the activists knew they'd be confronted with logic and reason, and even the slightest bit of scrutiny causes their entire house of cards to tumble down.

When Maud opened the meeting around 6:45 p.m., she asked each of the panelists to share a little bit about themselves and why we agreed to come here.

Cori suggested that, before we begin, we should probably clarify what we mean by "gender ideology," since it's become such a loaded term. He proposed a definition. "I would say that gender ideology is the idea that we can self-identify our sex based on our internal insights instead of relying on material indicators of sex, like what gametes your body produces or what your genital configuration is. So, it's the idea that you can substitute gender identity for sex."

No one objected, so Cori continued with his story.

In the eighties, as a young kid, Cori was relentlessly bullied for being different. He prayed to be a girl, thinking that would solve a lot of his troubles. When he was fifteen, his parents took him to a psychologist, who suggested he was transexual. At eighteen, Cori socially transitioned and started cross-sex hormones, and at nineteen, he underwent vaginoplasty. The surgery left him sexually dysfunctional.

Around 2010, the radical trans movement really began to kick off. Whereas previously, a male had to medicalize with cross-sex hormones and undergo castration surgery to enter female spaces, now activists were demanding that any male, no matter his medical history or appearance, be able to claim a female identity. Even worse, policymakers and legislators were obliging them. This, Cori noticed, was seriously compromising women's rights and privileges.

After a lot of reflection, Cori eventually concluded that, if we think there's a need for sex-segregated spaces—and Cori believes there are *many* reasons why we need them, particularly for women and girls—then that separation must be based solely on sex. Further, by demanding that one take hormones, have surgery, and become infertile in order to access a space, the state is creating a mandate for people to surgically and medically modify themselves.

"That's not fair," he said. "So, the conclusion is that, one, these spaces have to be sex-segregated, and two, they have to be safe for all users. Boys who want to present in a feminine way, have long hair, take a feminine name—they have to be safe in male spaces. There cannot be any tolerance at all for any abuse of somebody based on their gender presentation. That has to be protected. But you cannot substitute gender identity for sex and at the same time have safe, single-sex spaces."

Cori then passed the mic to Lisa.

Lisa's kids attend District 2 schools. One of those kids is a masculine daughter. When her daughter was little, Lisa noticed people responding very oddly to her daughter's gender-nonconformity. They would ask what her pronouns were, and if she was a "trans boy." Lisa was mystified. Since when did it become unacceptable for girls to be tomboys? Why were people (*liberal* people) suggesting her daughter needed to identify as male in order to be herself?

In 2017, Lisa wrote an op-ed about this issue for the *New York Times*. Soon came the vitriol. People threatened to kidnap her daughter for not "affirming" her as trans. Before long, most of the news outlets to which Lisa had contributed for years deplatformed her.

Since then, not much has changed about Lisa's perspective, other than that she's collected a heck of a lot more information (she's currently writing a book about what she's learned). For her, the desistance literature was particularly enlightening. This consists of a series of studies on gender dysphoric young children, which all came to the same conclusion: If not socially transitioned, the bulk of the children desisted in their distress and grew up to be gay.

Lisa accepts that some people have a belief system she doesn't share, and she recognizes their right to live according to that belief system. But she objects to the idea that we all must accept the idea of gender identity as fact, and she worries about the imposition of this idea on gender-nonconforming children.

"Education can't be, 'There is one way to think about this and if you don't think this way, you're a bad person,'" said Lisa. "It has to be, 'There are a lot of ways to think about this, and let's try to create an environment in which multiple viewpoints and understandings can be heard."

In a normal world, a statement like that might draw at least a smattering of applause from an audience of supposedly liberal New Yorkers. But no one made a sound.

Then the mic came to me.

I started by speaking about my own gender-nonconformity in childhood—the lessons I was taught by my religious teachers about homosexuality and being relentlessly bullied by my peers. I told the audience about how I coped, which was to "defeminize" myself to become what a boy is "supposed to be." I spoke about my battles with anxiety, depression, drugs and alcohol, my eventual recovery, and my foray into activism.

"This was very grandiose of me," I said, "but I wanted to create a world where there's more space for gender-nonconforming boys and girls. Where little boys and little girls who are really different—yes, they might not be the norm, and the majority of young kids might act like your typical boys and girls—but there are going to be gender-nonconforming kids that are inherently that way. And rather than saying, 'There's something wrong with you,' we protect them from the bullies. We safeguard them. We tell them, 'Yes, you are different, and that's perfectly okay.'"

That vision, I found, was not very popular in the world of "LGBTQ" activism. Gender-nonconforming kids were not natural variations of their own sex. Instead, they were "trans" and therefore "born in the wrong bodies." Thus, in order for feminine boys to behave the way they wanted—in order for them to openly like pink and wear dresses and grow their hair long—they needed to identify *out* of their sex category, and then medically and surgically modify their bodies to fit properly into society.

Soon, like Lisa, I became really hungry for knowledge about this issue. After I learned that youth transition began not so long ago, with the medicalization of a small cohort of young people, nearly all of whom were homosexual, I became really concerned. And then I started meeting gay people who had been harmed by these treatment protocols.

Maud asked me if, at age twelve, I may have thought transition was an option if I had been exposed to the idea that I was perhaps born in the wrong body and actually a girl.

I said, "If the adults I trusted—the guidance counselors, teachers, whoever—had intervened and stopped the bullying and then told me, 'This is not a spiritual malady. This is not something evil about you. This is a medical defect that can be fixed.' My god, would I have thought, 'Hallelujah, I'm saved. Sign me up.' I would have finally fit in. I would have been allowed to express myself in the way that I wanted to—to be gender-nonconforming, so long as I identified as a girl. But that would mean that there would also be folks saying, 'There's a medical protocol that you follow.'"

So, there you have it. There's our "hate speech." Our "transphobic" screeds.

Pretty reasonable, right?

Apparently not. After that, things got spicy. Maud asked each of us to speculate about how we had gotten to a place where the only way to "protect kids"—something we all want—is to silence whoever disagrees with you.

Lisa took this one. She explained how our understanding of the concepts of "harm" and "safety" have changed over time. When antibullying measures were first developed in the '90s, they were a response to the extreme violence that gender-nonconforming kids endured. "How did we get from that to, 'If you don't use the pronoun I want, I'm in danger of suicide'?" Lisa said.

Which was a great segue to a very important point.

"The bottom line is," continued Lisa, "as Chase Strangio admitted to the Supreme Court,[5] the suicide statistics you're hearing are not true. There are not increased suicides among unaffirmed trans youth. There is nothing in the history of this research that suggests that we need to only treat people in a specific way or they are in imminent risk of harm."

A woman sitting near the back of the audience interjected. "Why would you not treat someone the way they want to be treated?!" she yelled. "It doesn't make sense!"

"Well, we can talk about compelled speech," said Lisa. "We did try to explain that there is a belief system around gender identity that we do not share. And I respect your right to believe in it, but I don't. The curriculum requires us to bow to a belief system we don't share, and it includes lessons that we have concerns about, as former gender-nonconforming children and as a parent of a gender-nonconforming child."

"What curriculum are you referring to?" yelled an audience member.

"We're gonna take questions," Maud reminded the audience. In the meantime, she asked them not to shout out questions.

A woman in the audience became irate. "This was publicized as a parent-led discussion, and this is not..."

Maud put her foot down, saying she would close the meeting down if people didn't follow the rules.

---

5 During the *United States v. Skrmetti* oral arguments in December 2024.

The woman continued yelling. "This was falsely advertised!"

"I've raised four kids, and I know how to shut down temper tantrums," said Maud. "You guys have five more seconds to stop interrupting me and then the meeting's over."

"Heads down! Heads down!" a man in the audience shouted. He put his head in his arms and leaned against the chair in front of him. This, apparently, is one of the "jazzy tactics" the activists use to signal their collective disapproval of whatever is being said. This time, though, none of the other audience members put their heads down.

By now, my heart was about to pound out of my chest. I just don't fare all that well when adults are yelling at each other. Not to mention that Cori, Lisa, and I had just shared some really vulnerable stuff with a bunch of strangers, so to be met so quickly with hostility was disorienting.

Soon after that, the question-and-answer portion officially began. The first person to speak was a female who had masculinized with testosterone. I'll call her Alex. Alex introduced herself as a trans person, a Trevor Project representative, a crisis counselor, and "someone whose life was saved by my community." She said she was saddened that we would come there and "smear" kids "who were so vulnerable and so sad." She accused Lisa of misquoting Chase Strangio (Lisa did not misquote Strangio), then said, "There are so many people who are dead. Who are dead!"

Finally, Alex got to her question. She asked Cori to define what a woman is.

"Can we talk about female, or do you want woman?" Cori said.

"You were like, 'There needs to be women's spaces,'" said Alex.

"I think I said 'sex-segregated,'" Cori responded. "What do I mean by sex-segregated? It's your biological plan. So, if your body was developed to produce eggs, you're female."

Alex proceeded to interject with an activist talking point so clichéd, any of us could have predicted it.

"So, it's just if you have eggs," Alex gibed. "So, people who are infertile..."

"No," Cori said. Clearly, he, too, was expecting this exact response. "If your body's development plan is to produce eggs, you're female. If your body's development plan is to produce sperm, you're male."

Alex called this "hypothetical."

"It's not hypothetical," said Cori. "It's observable. If you believe in science, then you know that there's instruments that can be used to determine which body plan…" He paused, frustrated that he needed to explain the birds and the bees to an adult. Or maybe I was just projecting. "Even in the extremely odd case where the chromosomes are XY, that female development pattern is still female. So, we have these really weird corner cases…"

"Those people are intersex, they're not *really weird*," sniped Alex.

"I'm gonna ignore you for a minute," said Cori, "because that's really rude to twist…"

"Well, you said 'really weird.'"

"I didn't say individuals were weird."

"Can you have a seat?" Maud asked Alex.

"I thought this was a dialogue," Alex said.

So Cori dialogued. "It's sort of dirty to say that a difference of sexual development is unusual or weird, and then for somebody to say you're saying *the people* are weird. No, it's an unusual condition. So you are a woman if you are an adult and your body follows the female development, and you're a man, like I am, like some other people in the audience are. Some people are male but look more feminine, some people are female but look more masculine. But you're a man if you're an adult human male, and you're a woman if you're an adult human female. There's nothing wrong with that, there's nothing shameful about that. And if you're like me, and you've done something unusual with your body so that you've modified your sex traits, your sex characteristics, you may have some of the outward appearances of the opposite sex, but that doesn't make me not a man, and it wouldn't make somebody like Buck Angel[6] not a woman."

---

6 A public figure who is a very masculinized transman (trans-identified female). He typically passes as a man.

Alex returned to her seat.

Maud asked Lisa if she wanted to add anything to that. "Sure," she said, adding how distracting it is to have to argue that a woman is an adult human female. She then spoke briefly about two very rare DSD conditions, which, when it came to sex-segregated spaces, would probably be the edge cases we need to consider.

"How does this show up in the curriculum?" came a question from the audience.

Lisa said, "On the first day of fourth grade, my daughter was asked to create an identity web and put whether she was cisgender, transgender, or nonbinary on it. So, there are lessons about gender identity, and they are, again, taught as fact. You can look up the New York City DoE regulations, they say exactly what you have to do. There's a lot of compelled speech. I don't know how that works with the First Amendment..."

"It doesn't," said Maud.

A man sitting in the front row spoke up. He introduced himself as a District 2 parent and a father of two daughters, "one trans and one not." He asked how he could prevent his trans kid from experiencing gender dysphoria when sex-segregated spaces are a constant reminder that he is not the sex he wants to be.

Cori thanked the man for coming and for sharing his story with us. He said he could imagine that, over the years, a lot of "good-hearted people" had given him "the worst possible advice at the worst possible time." He told the father that a lot of doctors and therapists are not telling parents the real risks of these treatments. The surgeries aren't great, and if his child was on puberty blockers, there's a good chance he won't be able to have a normal sex life. Earlier, Cori recounted for the audience an op-ed he had written for the *Washington Post* in 2022, in which he admitted that, as a result of his vaginoplasty at nineteen, he has never been able to orgasm with a partner.

"That's crushing, actually," said Cori. "Because in order to partner with people, a healthy sex life is really important."

"I have made post-op girls cum, just for the record," Alex, the Trevor Project representative, shouted. "It's not..."

"We're gonna let them answer, please," said Maud.

Cori continued. He advised the father to think about his child in the future, and that he will have to live for many years with the decisions that his parents made for him.

"I promise you they will come for answers," said Cori. "They'll say, 'What was I really like? Was there anything else that I could have done, were there any other treatments?' And you'll be able to say, 'No, the doctors didn't give me any other options,' because institutionally talk therapies and [cognitive-behavioral therapy] have been recategorized as conversion therapy."

At some point, as Cori spoke, Alex stood up and walked to the front row. She had the father stand up so that she could give him a hug in front of everyone.

Next up: a mother of a nonbinary child with chronic health conditions. The mother is a volunteer facilitator for PFLAG. She called Cori arrogant for projecting his own experience onto everyone else's. She said we're facing "a tsunami of anti-LGBTQ policy coming our way." She asked him if he supports Trump's proposal of eliminating X gender makers for adults who identify as nonbinary.

"You're so articulate, I appreciate the question," Cori said. "PFLAG no longer stands for Parents and Friends of Lesbians and Gays, right?"

The woman said no, it's just the acronym.

Cori proceeded to answer her question. "If there's a marker that's supposed to list your sex, it should be male or female, and there's no need at all for your gender marker to reflect your gender identity."

Next came a question for me. A woman sitting in the back asked why I think there's *not* a space for gender-nonconforming kids right now. She said she's not understanding the debate.

I reiterated that I object to the reductive way that gender expression is talked about in schools, which I fear will lead gender-nonconforming children to think they might've been born in the wrong body simply because they behave more like the opposite sex. If, as a child, I had been asked which sex I "feel" like, I certainly would have said I "felt" like a girl. While I can acknowledge there are some people whose gender dysphoria will persist into adulthood, and that those adults might make decisions to modify their bodies in order to appear more like the opposite sex, I believe that every kid has a right to grow up with their bodies intact and healthy.

Lisa spoke next. She thanked the woman for her question and said she had one of her own. "Why are so many people here so hostile to incorporating our ideas?" She added that most of the questions have assumed that gender identity is a fact, while we see it as a kind of religious belief. She doesn't believe that everyone has a separate gendered soul that can be "excavated and revealed."

"It's fine if you believe that," she said. "What we are asking for people to consider is that some people don't, and it doesn't make them bigots."

Lisa then mentioned a book often seen in schools, *I Am Jazz*, in which the protagonist says he has a girl's brain in a boy's body because he likes pink and mermaids, and that makes him transgender.

"Therefore, what many children learn, if they're a boy who likes pink and mermaids, is that they're in the wrong body," said Lisa. "And it needs to be okay for us to raise our concerns about that."

After that came a question from a woman wearing a mask, who identified herself as a "cis queer woman" with some kind of LGBTQ certificate from NYU. She said she's gender-nonconforming because she has short hair and sometimes wears pants. She told Lisa that, "Actually, yes, you do have a gender identity."

When it appeared she was just going to keep rambling, Maud asked if she had a question.

"Maud!" shouted the irate woman. "Can you actually show some respect for the people asking questions?!"

Maud gave the masked woman a few more chances. She continued to ramble but never got to a question. Finally, she passed the mic to a very tall man wearing a blue cardigan. It was the same man who had ordered everyone to put their heads down.

The man stood up. Along with the blue cardigan, he wore a dress. His question was for Cori. "I'm a trans mom, I'm a transwoman," he said. "I've got two kids, and I'm at the airport, and I've got 'F' on my passport. And I think, in the universe that you're creating, that would not fly—excuse the pun. Then what happens? Like, what would happen to me and my family?"

"Well, depending on how you were presenting yourself..." Cori began to answer.

"I'm in a dress. I'm wearing a fucking dress."

Maud asked him not to curse, since it was a school committee meeting.

"Oh, I can't say 'fuck?' Fucking fuck fuck fuck," he said.

Cori went on. "I use men's spaces, and it's okay. It's a little uncomfortable. But you know what? Men just wanna pee."

"What does that mean?" the man said.

"It means, if you use the men's room, they're not interested in what you're doing, they're just there to pee."

"Are you calling her a man?" said Alex.

"I'm saying that, if you use the facility that accords to your sex, you don't have to worry about the men that are in there mistreating you, because they're just there to pee."

"I think you are suggesting that I have to go to the men's room," the man said.

Cori replied, "You should use the sex space that's accorded for your sex."

Shortly thereafter, the man in the blue cardigan gathered his things and stomped out of the room. The mother of the nonbinary child with chronic health conditions followed him.

Finally, we made it to the last question. A person in the audience asked what kinds of policies we would propose to replace the existing ones.

Cori answered, "Sex should be treated as sex, and what we consider 'gender' should be protected as gender expression. Boys should be able to wear female-coded clothes, females should be able to wear masculine clothes, they should be able to adopt nicknames, they should be safe in school and not targeted for violence or bullying because of their gender expression. If all of the energy that went into gender identity instead went into just how we express ourselves, I think that would be the best way to help these kids."

I concurred. I said that there are males and females and rare cases of DSDs, and that people can express themselves however they want. I said that the way gender is currently being talked about in schools might actually be priming gender-nonconforming children to *become* gender dysphoric as they grow up. If a young boy says he "feels like a girl," and all of the adults in his life affirm him as one, then, as his body matures, reality will betray what everyone has been telling him. He'll become dysphoric, and medicalizing will seem like the most viable option.

After me, Lisa made a plug for viewpoint diversity when it comes to creating policy. She said we need to hear people who have been helped by existing policies, but we also need to hear from people who have been harmed.

"We cannot make good policy if we do not acknowledge the cost," she said.

And with that, the meeting was adjourned.

LATER THAT NIGHT, Maud realized she left behind some of the recording equipment. She emailed the school principal about it and thanked him for allowing us to use the space for our meeting. He responded by saying that his mother, who once represented the KKK when she worked for the ACLU, taught him that "suppressing hate speech is counterproductive, making martyrs of bigots." He hadn't watched the program, but he thinks he would have vehemently disagreed with a lot of it.

Maud responded, "You would likely learn a lot from, be impressed by, and find yourself agreeing with the panelists last night. Defending the 1st [Amendment] and viewpoint diversity, as your mom did, is at its most robust when you do more than just begrudgingly allow speech but when you actually listen to other points of views. And here those points of view included multiple [District 2] parents."

She pasted a link to the live stream and thanked him again.

To the principle's credit, he followed up with Maud after he watched the video. He thanked her for suggesting he watch it and was glad he did. He said he still disagreed with a lot of what was said, particularly the underlying assumption that schools are pushing a particular ideology. He wondered whether the "fear mongering and scapegoating of trans people during the election made people pay attention and think there is a crisis."

Isn't that always the way?

These people are bigots.

OK, they're not necessarily bigots, but they're overreacting. This stuff isn't happening. Besides, it's probably all because of Trump.

Eventually, down the road:

OK, this stuff is happening.

And finally:

It's good that it's happening... Bigot!

If I had been harboring any doubts after the event, it was now very clear how deeply gender ideology had embedded itself within our schools and communities. As a result, we were no longer speaking the same language. Maud, Lisa, Cori, and I acknowledge the material reality of sex. We're run-of-the-mill liberals who believe in things like free speech and viewpoint diversity. But not these folks.

In his final email to Maud, the principal did mention that he doesn't see a lot of kids identifying as trans or nonbinary in his school. And that very well might be true, since his school serves a lot of low-income and immigrant students—not a primary demographic for metastasizing gender ideology. I only hope that stays true.

But what everyone must realize is that this *is* occurring in schools. *Widely* occurring. Right now, in the most advanced nation in the world, kids are being taught that sex isn't real. They're being taught that they can *choose* their sex, and that that choice rests upon the most regressive ideas of what it means to be a boy and what it means to be a girl. Girls are being taught to simply accept the presence of boys in their sports and private spaces. They're being told that it's *their problem* and that they *might be in trouble* if they object to a boy who claims to be a girl coming into their locker room.

Right now, in America.

Perhaps that's okay for some people. But I'm worried about the consequences of an entire generation being taught a pseudoscience. And I don't think it's wise for kids to be told to disregard their personal boundaries.

THE PAST FIVE years have been a special kind of hell for Americans who think that all forms of racism suck and that sex is real. Especially for liberal, Democrat-voting Americans. And that's why I can't help but feel that everyone responsible for this nightmare deserve exactly what they got on November 5, 2024. If you refuse to stand up to the extremists that have hijacked your party, then you should expect even your most stalwart supporters to defect.

A red wave wouldn't have sufficed. It needed to be a tsunami.

Am I worried what the next four years will bring? Absolutely. Just as in 2017, I worry about Trump's erratic and authoritarian nature as well as his divisiveness. But I'm just as worried about the unhinged response from the left. I fear what kind of mayhem it will decide is the "equal and opposite reaction" to the president's action.

As I write this, Trump has been in office again for four months. During that time, he has signed a slew of executive orders, many of them concerning DEI and gender ideology. I have welcomed these orders, in particular his January 28 order that called for an end to so-called gender-affirming care, which the Trump team crassly—but rightly—termed the "chemical and surgical mutilation" of children. On federal websites, including the Stonewall National Monument's website, the nonsensical "LGBTQ+" acronym disappeared, only to be replaced by "LGB." Universities have suffered massive cuts in federal funding, and noncitizen campus agitators now face deportation. Among the demands the Trump administration placed on Columbia, if it hoped to retain its full funding, was for the university to wrest control of its department of Middle East, South Asian and African studies from the faculty and place it under "academic receivership" for at least five years.

Thanks to the Democrats' fealty to ideologically captured NGOs like the ACLU, GLAAD, and HRC, Trump was able to score easy political wins with his executive orders that pertain to gender ideology. Believe it or not, an overwhelming majority of Americans oppose things like men in women's sports and "sex changes" for kids.

Does it look like the right-wing approach to correcting course is going to be sensitive and measured? Of course not. But again, the left had its chance to take the lead.

The gender cult's response to Trump's actions has been predictably rabid. As Democratic politicians stand on the floor of the House and Senate, zealously denouncing the reality of the sex binary as if it were genocide, hundreds gather in protest outside of pediatric gender clinics. They wave long flagpoles displaying Lebanon flags, Palestinian flags, and the creepy pink and blue flags that look like they belong in a child's nursery, screaming "protect trans kids," i.e., the right to maim and sterilize vulnerable children. Just as Foucault once said that children can consent to sex with adults, so do these queer activists insist that young boys can consent to being made into eunuchs.

After the Stonewall website incident, MSNBC host Rachel Maddow stated on her show, "Hundreds of people showed up today to protest the Trump administration's removal of all mention of trans people from the Stonewall Memorial site…which, after all, commemorates a riot by trans people. It's like telling Cooperstown they're not allowed to mention baseball anymore."

On Substack, Andrew Sullivan penned an apt description of Maddow's ahistorical statement. "The correct term for this is historic negationism," he wrote. "Stalin would approve. The gay men and lesbians Maddow just wiped from history? Not so much."

Occasionally I find myself contemplating an idea I never could have imagined I would one day consider: *Maybe Trump's not so bad.*

Then, Trump will tweet something like, "He who saves his Country does not violate any Law"—an authoritarian statement if there ever was one—and I'm brought back to reality.

As for Trump's actions against universities, the jury is still out. Reform is necessary, but unfortunately it appears that those who suffer the most from funding cuts will be health researchers. I'm not crazy about the idea of the feds determining what is or isn't acceptable to teach at a university. And if the administration can deport students—including legal permanent residents—whose "beliefs, statements or associations" are "counter to foreign policy interests," as it argues in the case of Columbia graduate Mahmoud Khalil, then who else among us might this or any future administration deem improperly supportive of his country?

If you allow the government to violate your enemies' First and Fifth Amendment rights, so, too, will it be able to violate yours.

Besides empowering people to think critically and for themselves, I don't know what the solution is. What I do know is that I resent the free pass that anti-Western professors have been given at universities like Columbia. I resent the formation of entire academic departments whose goal is to engineer social change rather than to educate students. I resent our immigration system's lack of proper safeguarding. I resent those who cried "Free Mahmoud" but failed to demand the same for US citizen Edan Alexander, who was finally released by Hamas on May 12, 2025—nineteen months after he was taken hostage. I resent the illiberal cult of Islamist sympathizers marching unabated through our institutions, a cult that continues to occupy campus buildings, distribute terrorist propaganda, and call for "Death to America" and the eradication of the world's only Jewish state. Perhaps most of all, I resent those who want to gaslight me into believing that all of this is normal. That bands of terrorist sympathizers marching through our city streets, chanting "We will honor all our martyrs" is just another day in the land of the free.

How will our country survive if its youngest generations are being indoctrinated to hate it? How will it survive if we're taught to hate ourselves?

Every day I fear what the future holds. I fear that if an October 7–like event were to occur in the US, a sizeable minority of Americans would frame that, too, as a justified form of "resistance." I fear those who mistakenly think that Christian nationalism is any better than Islamism. And I fear the authoritarian extremes that Trump will go to "make America great again."

But as much as I worry, after years of screaming into the void, it's vindicating to watch the left finally reckon with what it has wrought.

Call me selfish; I don't care.

As a "cis white gay," I've heard it all before.

ACKNOWLEDGMENTS

I'm going to keep this short and sweet, since the list of people I could thank is endless.

Thank you to my agent, Lisa Bankoff, for taking a chance on me, and my editor, Adam Bellow, for believing in me.

For your guidance and support, thank you Meghan Daum, Andrew Sullivan, Pamela Paresky, Lisa Selin Davis, Leor Sapir, Cori Cohn, Paul Garcia-Ryan, Grace Lidinsky-Smith, Wesley Yang, Julie Bindel, and J.K. Rowling.

Thank you to everyone who has taken the time to read my work, especially those who have reached out to tell me I'm not alone.

Thank you to Jessica Secrest (and Ruth!), Jenny Dowling, Bernadette Roe, and Shawn Sprecker, for your friendship, love, and encouragement.

Thank you to my family, for always being there.

And thank you, Drew, for everything.

This project was made possible by grant funding from the Foundation Against Intolerance and Racism (FAIR) in the Arts.